Family Letter

Greetings!

This year, your child, like many students across the country, will be taking a standardized achievement test called the *Iowa Tests of Basic Skills® (ITBS)*. We will be administering this test for several reasons.

- It gives us a snapshot of what your child has learned (achieved). It is one of many ways we assess the skills and knowledge of students because no one test or assessment tool can give an accurate, ongoing picture of your child's development.

- We use ITBS to help us determine where to strengthen our curriculum to better meet the needs of the students. It also helps us see if we are meeting the learning goals we set previously.

In order to give students the best opportunity to show what they know on this standardized achievement test, we will be using SRA/McGraw-Hill's test preparation program, *Scoring High on the Iowa Tests of Basic Skills*. It is designed specifically for the *Iowa Tests of Basic Skills*. Why will we be spending time preparing for this test?

- What happens to your heartbeat when you hear the word *test*? When students hear that word, their anxiety level can rise. However, when they know what to expect, their confidence soars—they are less nervous.

- Test-taking skills can be learned. When preparing, we focus on such skills as reading and listening carefully to directions; budgeting time; answering the easy questions first so more time can be spent on the harder ones; eliminating answer choices that are obviously wrong, and more. These are life skills that students will take with them and use again and again.

- Preparing for the test assures that students won't be surprised by the format of the test. They won't be worried about the type of questions they will see, or how hard the questions will be. They'll know how to fill in answers appropriately. These, and other skills learned ahead of time, will free students to focus on the content of the test and thus give a much more accurate picture of what they know.

How can you help?

- Talk with your child about the purpose of the test. Be positive about the experience.

- Talk to us here at school if you have any questions. Remember, we are a team with the **same** goals in mind—the improvement of your child's educational experience.

- Assure your child that the results of the test are private and won't be used on his or her report card. Remind your child that the test does not measure how smart he or she is, nor does it predict how successful he or she will be in the future.

- Encourage reading at home, and spend time together talking about what you read.

- Be sure your child has plenty of rest on a regular basis, and eats nourishing foods. That's important every day—not just on the day of the test.

Additional information will be provided about the specific subject areas and dates of the tests. Until then, please feel free to contact me if you have any questions about your child's performance or about standardized testing.

Sincerely,

_____

Your child's teacher

Scoring High

Iowa Tests of Basic Skills®
A Test Prep Program for ITBS®

Book 8 — Now with Science

Columbus, OH

The McGraw·Hill Companies

SRAonline.com

Copyright © 2007 by SRA/McGraw-Hill.

All rights reserved. Except as permitted under the United States Copyright Act, no part of this publication may be reproduced or distributed in any form or by any means, or stored in a database or retrieval system, without the prior written permission of the publisher, unless otherwise indicated.

Send all inquiries to:
SRA/McGraw-Hill
4400 Easton Commons
Columbus, Ohio 43219

Printed in the United States of America.

ISBN 0-07-604387-8

3 4 5 6 7 8 9 QDB 11

The **McGraw·Hill** Companies

On Your Way to Scoring High
On the Iowa Tests of Basic Skills®

	Page
Family Letter	v
Introduction: Scoring High on ITBS	vii
Scope and Sequence Charts	viii
Orientation Lesson	xii

Unit 1	**Vocabulary**	**1**
Lesson 1a		2
Lesson 1b		4
Test Yourself		6

Unit 2	**Reading Comprehension**	**8**
Lesson 2a		9
Lesson 2b		13
Test Yourself		17

Unit 3	**Spelling**	**23**
Lesson 3a		24
Lesson 3b		26
Test Yourself		28

Unit 4	**Capitalization and Punctuation**	**30**
Lesson 4a		31
Lesson 4b		33
Lesson 5a		35
Lesson 5b		37
Test Yourself		39

Unit 5	**Usage and Expression**	**41**
Lesson 6a		42
Lesson 6b		44
Lesson 7a		46
Lesson 7b		48
Test Yourself		50

Unit 6	**Math Concepts and Estimation**	**54**
Lesson 8a		55
Lesson 8b		58
Lesson 9a		61
Lesson 9b		63
Test Yourself		65

Unit 7	**Math Problem Solving and Data Interpretation**	**69**

Lesson 10a 70

Lesson 10b 72

Lesson 11a 74

Lesson 11b 76

Test Yourself 77

Unit 8	**Math Computation**	**79**

Lesson 12a 80

Lesson 12b 82

Lesson 13a 84

Lesson 13b 86

Test Yourself 88

Unit 9	**Maps, Diagrams, and Reference Materials**	**90**

Lesson 14a 91

Lesson 14b 93

Lesson 15a 95

Lesson 15b 97

Lesson 16a 99

Lesson 16b 102

Test Yourself 104

Unit 10	**Science**	**113**

Lesson 17a 114

Lesson 17b 120

Test Yourself 126

Unit 11	**Test Practice**	**137**

Test 1 Vocabulary 142

Test 2 Reading Comprehension 144

Test 3 Spelling 150

Test 4 Capitalization 152

Test 5 Punctuation 154

Test 6 Part 1 Usage 156

Test 6 Part 2 Expression 158

Test 7 Part 1 Math Concepts 161

Test 7 Part 2 Math Estimation 164

Test 8 Part 1 Math Problem Solving 166

Test 8 Part 2 Data Interpretation 168

Test 9 Math Computation 169

Test 10 Maps and Diagrams 171

Test 11 Reference Materials................... 174

Scoring High on the Iowa Tests of Basic Skills
A program that teaches achievement test behaviors

Scoring High on the Iowa Tests of Basic Skills is designed to prepare students for these tests. The program provides instruction and practice in reading, spelling, language, mathematics, study, and science skills. *Scoring High* also familiarizes students with the kinds of test formats and directions that appear on the tests and teaches test-taking strategies that promote success.

Students who are used to a comfortable learning environment are often unaccustomed to the structured setting in which achievement tests are given. Even good students who are used to working independently may have difficulty maintaining a silent, sustained effort or following directions that are read to a large group. *Scoring High*, with its emphasis on group instruction, teaches these test-taking skills systematically.

Using *Scoring High* to help prepare students for the Iowa Tests of Basic Skills will increase the probability of your students doing their best. Students' self-confidence will be at a maximum, and their proficiency in the skills tested will be higher as a result of the newly learned test-taking strategies and increased familiarity with test formats.

Scoring High can be used effectively along with your regular reading, language, science, and mathematics curriculums. By applying subject-area skills in the context of the test-taking situation, students will not only strengthen their skills, but will accumulate a reserve of test-taking strategies.

Eight Student Books for Grades 1–8

To choose the most appropriate book for each student, match the level of the Iowa Tests of Basic Skills that the student will take to the corresponding Scoring High book.

Grade Levels	Test Levels
Book 1	Level 7
Book 2	Level 8
Book 3	Level 9
Book 4	Level 10
Book 5	Level 11
Book 6	Level 12
Book 7	Level 13
Book 8	Level 14

Sequential Skill Development

Each student book is organized into units reflecting the subject areas covered on the corresponding levels of the Iowa Tests of Basic Skills. This book covers reading, spelling, language, mathematics, study, and science skills. Each lesson within a unit focuses on one or two of the subject-area skills and the test-taking strategies that complement the skills. The last lesson in each unit is designed to give students experience in taking an achievement test in that subject area.

The Test Practice section at the end of each book also provides practice in taking achievement tests and will increase students' confidence in their test-taking skills.

Features of the Student Lessons

Each student lesson in subject-area skills contains:

- A Sample(s) section including directions and one or more teacher-directed sample questions
- A Tips section providing test-taking strategies
- A Practice section

Each Test Yourself lesson at the end of a unit is designed like an achievement test in the unit's subject area.

How the Teacher's Edition Works

Since a program that teaches test-taking skills as well as subject-area skills may be new to your students, the Teacher's Edition makes a special effort to provide detailed lesson plans. Each lesson lists subject-area and test-taking skills. In addition, teaching suggestions are provided for handling each part of the lesson—Sample(s), Tips, and Practice. The text for the subject-area and Test Yourself lessons is designed to help students become familiar with following oral directions and with the terminology used on the tests.

Before you begin Lesson 1, you should use the Orientation Lesson on pages xii–xv to acquaint students with the program organization and the procedure for using the student book.

Scope and Sequence: Test-taking Skills

	UNIT										
	1	2	3	4	5	6	7	8	9	10	11
Analyzing answer choices				✓		✓					✓
Comparing or evaluating answer choices						✓	✓		✓	✓	✓
Computing carefully							✓	✓			✓
Considering every answer choice	✓									✓	✓
Converting items to a workable format							✓	✓			✓
Eliminating answer choices			✓								✓
Estimating an answer							✓				✓
Finding the answer without computing						✓	✓				✓
Following printed directions	✓	✓			✓	✓	✓		✓		✓
Identifying and using key words, numbers, and pictures		✓				✓					✓
Indicating that the correct answer is not given							✓	✓			✓
Indicating that an item has no mistakes			✓	✓	✓						✓
Managing time effectively	✓	✓	✓	✓	✓	✓	✓	✓	✓	✓	✓
Marking the right answer as soon as it is found									✓		✓
Noting the lettering of answer choices	✓										✓
Performing the correct operation							✓	✓			✓
Prioritizing items	✓										✓
Reasoning from facts and evidence			✓								✓
Recalling error types				✓	✓						✓
Recalling prior knowledge									✓		✓
Recalling word meanings	✓										✓
Referring to a graphic						✓					✓
Referring to a passage to answer questions		✓								✓	✓
Referring to a reference source									✓		✓
Rereading or restating a question						✓			✓	✓	✓
Skimming a passage		✓									✓
Skimming questions or answer choices				✓	✓						✓
Skimming a reference source									✓		✓
Skipping difficult items and returning to them later		✓			✓			✓			✓
Subvocalizing answer choices					✓						✓
Taking the best guess when unsure of the answer	✓		✓		✓		✓	✓	✓		✓
Transferring numbers accurately							✓	✓			✓
Understanding unusual item formats				✓	✓						✓
Using charts, diagrams, and graphs								✓			✓
Using context to find an answer					✓	✓					✓
Working methodically	✓	✓	✓	✓	✓	✓	✓	✓	✓	✓	✓

Scope and Sequence: Reading

	\multicolumn{11}{c}{UNIT}
	1	2	3	4	5	6	7	8	9	10	11
Identifying synonyms	✓										✓
Analyzing characters		✓									✓
Comparing and contrasting		✓									✓
Deriving word meanings		✓									✓
Drawing conclusions		✓									✓
Identifying feelings		✓									
Making inferences		✓									✓
Making predictions											✓
Recognizing an author's technique		✓									✓
Recognizing an author's purpose		✓									✓
Recognizing details		✓									✓
Recognizing genre or text source		✓									✓
Recognizing setting		✓									
Understanding literary devices		✓									✓
Understanding the main idea		✓									✓
Understanding reasons		✓									✓
Understanding sequence		✓									

Scope and Sequence: Language Skills

	\multicolumn{11}{c}{UNIT}
	1	2	3	4	5	6	7	8	9	10	11
Identifying spelling errors			✓								✓
Choosing the best paragraph for a given purpose					✓						✓
Choosing the best word to complete a sentence					✓						✓
Identifying capitalization errors				✓							✓
Identifying the best closing sentence for a paragraph					✓						✓
Identifying the best location for a sentence in a paragraph					✓						✓
Identifying the best opening sentence for a paragraph					✓						✓
Identifying the sentence that does not fit in a paragraph					✓						✓
Identifying correctly formed sentences					✓						✓
Identifying mistakes in usage					✓						✓
Identifying punctuation errors				✓							✓

Scoring High on the Iowa Tests of Basic Skills

Scope and Sequence: Mathematics Skills

	\multicolumn{11}{c}{UNIT}
	1	2	3	4	5	6	7	8	9	10	11
Adding, subtracting, multiplying, and dividing whole numbers, fractions, and decimals								✓			✓
Comparing and ordering whole numbers, decimals, fractions, and integers						✓					✓
Estimating and rounding						✓					✓
Estimating measurement											
Finding area						✓					✓
Finding perimeter						✓					
Finding squares and square roots						✓					
Identifying the best measurement unit						✓					
Identifying problem-solving strategies						✓					✓
Interpreting tables, diagrams, and graphs							✓				✓
Naming numerals						✓					
Recognizing alternate forms of a number						✓					✓
Recognizing equivalent fractions and decimals						✓					✓
Recognizing fractional parts						✓					✓
Recognizing transformations						✓					
Sequencing numbers or shapes						✓					
Solving equations or expressions						✓					✓
Solving measurement problems						✓					✓
Solving word problems							✓				✓
Understanding average (mean)						✓					✓
Understanding characteristics of related numbers						✓					
Understanding congruence						✓					
Understanding decimal operations						✓					✓
Understanding lines and angles						✓					✓
Understanding number sentences						✓					✓
Understanding order of operations											✓
Understanding probability						✓					
Understanding ratio and proportion						✓					✓
Understanding scientific notation						✓					
Understanding variability						✓					✓
Using a coordinate grid						✓					

Scoring High on the Iowa Tests of Basic Skills

Scope and Sequence: Study Skills

	UNIT										
	1	2	3	4	5	6	7	8	9	10	11
Differentiating among reference sources									✓		
Understanding a diagram									✓		
Understanding a map									✓		✓
Understanding the Dewey decimal system									✓		
Using a chart									✓		✓
Using a dictionary									✓		✓
Using an index									✓		✓
Using key words									✓		✓
Using the *Reader's Guide to Periodical Literature*									✓		✓

Scope and Sequence: Science Skills

	UNIT										
	1	2	3	4	5	6	7	8	9	10	11
Differentiating plants and animals											✓
Recalling characteristics of Earth and bodies in space										✓	✓
Recalling characteristics and functions of the human body										✓	✓
Recognizing characteristics of a habitat											✓
Recognizing chemical changes										✓	✓
Recognizing forms, sources, and principles of energy										✓	✓
Recognizing importance of environmentally sound practices											✓
Recognizing states, properties, and composition of matter										✓	✓
Understanding characteristics of bodies of water										✓	
Understanding diseases and their sources										✓	
Understanding electricity and circuits										✓	✓
Understanding form and function										✓	
Understanding gravity, inertia, and friction										✓	✓
Understanding the history and language of science										✓	✓
Understanding life cycles and reproduction										✓	✓
Understanding plant and animal behaviors and characteristics										✓	✓
Understanding properties of light										✓	✓
Understanding scientific instruments, measurement, and processes										✓	✓
Understanding sound										✓	✓
Understanding the water cycle										✓	✓
Understanding weather, climate, and seasons										✓	✓
Using illustrations, charts, and graphs										✓	✓

Orientation Lesson

Focus
Understanding the purpose and structure of *Scoring High on the Iowa Tests of Basic Skills*

Note: Before you begin Lesson 1, use this introductory lesson to acquaint the students with the program orientation and procedures for using this book.

Say Taking a test is something that you do many times during each school year. What kind of tests have you taken? *(math tests, reading tests, spelling tests, daily quizzes, etc.)* Have you ever taken an achievement test that covers many subjects? An achievement test shows how well you are doing in these subjects compared to other students in your grade. How are achievement tests different from the regular tests you take in class? *(many students take them on the same day; special pencils, books, and answer sheets are used; etc.)* Some students get nervous when they take achievement tests. Has this ever happened to you?

Encourage the students to discuss their feelings about test taking. Point out that almost everyone feels anxious or worried when facing a test-taking situation.

Display the cover of Scoring High on the Iowa Tests of Basic Skills.

Say Here is a new book that you'll be using for the next several weeks. The Book is called *Scoring High on the Iowa Tests of Basic Skills.*

Distribute the books to the students.

Say This book will help you improve your reading, language, mathematics, study, and science skills. It will also help you gain the confidence and skills you need to do well on achievement tests. What does the title say you will be doing when you finish this book? *(scoring high)* Scoring high on achievement tests is what this program is all about. If you learn the skills taught in this book, you will be ready to do your best on the *Iowa Tests of Basic Skills.*

Share this information with the students if you know when they will be taking the *Iowa Tests of Basic Skills*. Then make sure the students understand that the goal of their *Scoring High* books is to improve their test-taking skills.

xii   Scoring High on the Iowa Tests of Basic Skills

Tell the students to turn to the table of contents at the front of their books.

Say This page is a progress chart. It shows the contents of the book. How many units are there? *(11)* Let's read the names of the units together. In these units you will learn reading, spelling, language, mathematics, study skills, science, and test-taking skills. The last lesson in each unit is called Test Yourself. It reviews what you have learned in the unit. In unit 11, the Test Practice section, you will have a chance to use all the skills you have learned on tests that are somewhat like real achievement tests. This page will also help you keep track of the lessons you have completed. Do you see the box beside each lesson number? When you finish a lesson, you will write your score in the box to show your progress.

Make sure the students understand the information presented on this page. Ask questions such as, "On what page does Lesson 9b start?" *(48)* "What is Lesson 2a called?" *(Reading Comprehension)* "What do you think Lesson 10a is about?" *(solving mathematics problems)*

Book 8

On Your Way to Scoring High
On the Iowa Tests of Basic Skills®

Name _____

Unit 1	Vocabulary	
My Score	Lesson	Page
☐	1a Vocabulary	1
☐	1b Vocabulary	2
☐	Test Yourself	3

Unit 2	Reading Comprehension	
My Score	Lesson	Page
☐	2a Reading Comprehension	5
☐	2b Reading Comprehension	9
☐	Test Yourself	13

Unit 3	Spelling	
My Score	Lesson	Page
☐	3a Spelling	19
☐	3b Spelling	20
☐	Test Yourself	21

Unit 4	Capitalization and Punctuation	
My Score	Lesson	Page
☐	4a Capitalization	23
☐	4b Capitalization	24
☐	5a Punctuation	25
☐	5b Punctuation	26
☐	Test Yourself	27

Unit 5	Word Usage and Expression	
My Score	Lesson	Page
☐	6a Usage	29
☐	6b Usage	31
☐	7a Expression	33
☐	7b Expression	35
☐	Test Yourself	37

Unit 6	Math Concepts and Estimation	
My Score	Lesson	Page
☐	8a Math Concepts	41
☐	8b Math Concepts	44
☐	9a Math Estimation	47
☐	9b Math Estimation	48
☐	Test Yourself	49

Unit 7	Math Problem Solving and Data Interpretation		Unit 10	Science	
My Score	Lesson	Page	My Score	Lesson	Page
☐	10a Math Problem Solving	53	☐	17a Science Skills	86
☐	10b Math Problem Solving	54	☐	17b Science Skills	92
☐	11a Data Interpretation	55	☐	Test Yourself	98
☐	11b Data Interpretation	56			
☐	Test Yourself	57			

Unit 8	Math Computation		Unit 11	Test Practice	
My Score	Lesson	Page	Name and Answer Sheet............ 109		
☐	12a Adding and Subtracting	59	My Score	Lesson	Page
☐	12b Adding and Subtracting	60	☐	1 Vocabulary	113
☐	13a Multiplying and Dividing	61	☐	2 Reading Comprehension	115
☐	13b Multiplying and Dividing	62	☐	3 Spelling	121
☐	Test Yourself	63	☐	4 Capitalization	123
			☐	5 Punctuation	124
Unit 9	Maps, Diagrams, and Reference Materials		☐	6 Part 1 Usage	125
My Score	Lesson	Page	☐	6 Part 2 Expression	126
☐	14a Maps and Diagrams	65	☐	7 Part 1 Math Concepts	129
☐	14b Maps and Diagrams	67	☐	7 Part 2 Math Estimation	132
☐	15a Reference Materials	69	☐	8 Part 1 Math Problem Solving	133
☐	15b Reference Materials	71	☐	8 Part 2 Data Interpretation	135
☐	16a Reference Materials	73	☐	9 Math Computation	136
☐	16b Reference Materials	76	☐	10 Maps and Diagrams	137
☐	Test Yourself	78	☐	11 Reference Materials	140
			☐	12 Science	144

Say Now let's look at two of the lessons. Turn to Lesson 1a on page 1. Where is the lesson number and title? *(at the top of the page, beside the unit number)* What is the title of the lesson? *(Vocabulary)*

Familiarize the students with the lesson layout and sequence of instruction. Have them locate the directions and sample items. Explain that you will work through the Samples section together. Then have the students find the STOP sign in the lower right-hand corner of the page. Explain that when they come to the STOP sign at the bottom of a page, they should not continue on to the next page. They may check their work on the present lesson.

Have the students locate the Tips sign below the Samples section.

Say What does the sign point out to you? *(the tips)* Each lesson has tips that suggest new ways to work through the items. Tests can be tricky. The tips will tell you what to watch out for. They will help you find the best answer quickly.

Have the students locate the Practice section below the tips. Explain that they will do the practice items by themselves. Tell the students they will have an opportunity to discuss any problems they had when they complete the Practice section.

Ask the students to turn to the Test Yourself lesson on page 3 of their books. Tell the students the Test Yourself lessons may seem like real tests, but they are not. The Test Yourself lessons are designed to give them opportunities to apply the skills and tips they have learned in timed, trial-run situations. Then have the students find the GO sign in the lower right-hand corner of the page. Explain that when they come to the GO sign at the bottom of a page, they should turn to the next page and continue working.

Explain that you will go over the answers together after the students complete each lesson. Then they will figure out their scores and record the number of correct answers in the boxes on the progress chart. Be sure to point out that the students' scores are only for them to see how well they are doing.

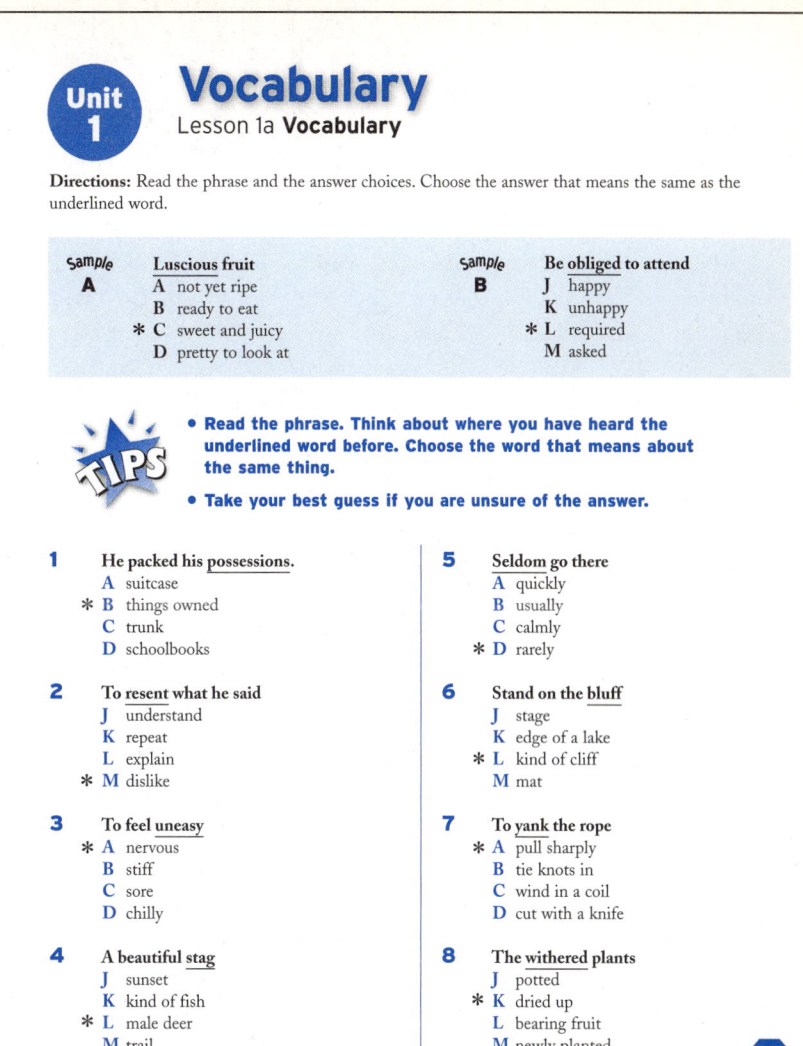

Say Each lesson will teach you new skills and tips. What will you have learned when you finish this book? *(vocabulary, reading, spelling, language arts, mathematics, study skills, science, and test-taking skills; how to do my best on an achievement test)* When you know you can do your best, how do you think you will feel on test day? You may be a little nervous, but you should also feel confident that you are ready to do your best.

Scoring High on the Iowa Tests of Basic Skills

Unit 1

Background

This unit contains three lessons that deal with vocabulary skills. Students are asked to identify words with similar meanings.

• **In Lesson 1a,** students identify words that have the same meaning as target words in phrases. Students are encouraged to follow printed directions. They note the lettering of answer choices, recall word meanings, consider every answer choice, and take their best guess when they are unsure of the answer.

• **In Lesson 1b,** students identify words that have the same meaning as target words in phrases. In addition to reviewing the test-taking skills introduced in Lesson 1a, students learn the importance of prioritizing items.

• **In the Test Yourself lesson,** the vocabulary skills and test-taking skills introduced and used in Lessons 1a and 1b are reinforced and presented in a format that gives students the experience of taking an achievement test. Techniques for managing their time effectively when they are taking a standardized test are reinforced.

Instructional Objectives

Lesson 1a **Vocabulary** Lesson 1b **Vocabulary**	Given a phrase with a target word, students identify which of four answer choices means the same as the target word.
Test Yourself	Given questions similar to those in Lessons 1a and 1b, students utilize vocabulary skills and test-taking strategies on achievement test formats.

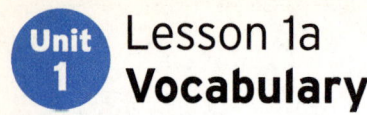

Lesson 1a
Vocabulary

Focus
Reading Skill
• identifying synonyms

Test-taking Skills
• following printed directions
• noting lettering of answer choices
• recalling word meanings
• considering every answer choice
• taking the best guess when unsure of the answer

Samples A and B

Say Turn to Lesson 1a on page 1. The page number is at the bottom of the page on the right.

Check to see that the students have found the right page.

Say In this lesson, you will find words that have the same or nearly the same meaning as another word used in a phrase. Read the directions at the top of the page to yourself while I read them aloud to you.

Read the directions to the students.

Say Let's do Sample A. Listen carefully. Read the phrase with the underlined word. Think about what the word means as it is used in the phrase. Now, look at the four answer choices below the phrase. Which of the four answers means about the same as the underlined word? *(pause)* The answer is C, *sweet and juicy*, which is what *luscious* means. Fill in the circle for answer C in the answer rows at the bottom of the page. Be sure your answer circle is completely filled in with a dark mark and that you have marked the correct answer circle.

Check to see that the students have marked the correct circle.

Say Now do Sample B by yourself. Read the phrase and fill in the circle for the word that means the same as the underlined word. *(pause)* Which answer choice is correct? *(answer L)* Yes, *obliged* means *required* in this phrase. Make sure that circle L for Sample B is completely filled in. Press your pencil firmly so your mark comes out dark.

Check to see that the students have marked the correct circle.

 TIPS

Say Now let's look at the tips.

Read the tips aloud to the students.

Say Be sure to read the phrase and look at each answer choice carefully. Think about where you might have heard or read the underlined word before. Choose the answer that means about the same as the underlined word. If you are not sure which answer is correct, take your best guess. It is better to guess than to leave an answer blank.

Vocabulary
Lesson 1a Vocabulary

Directions: Read the phrase and the answer choices. Choose the answer that means the same as the underlined word.

Sample A Luscious fruit
A not yet ripe
B ready to eat
* C sweet and juicy
D pretty to look at

Sample B Be obliged to attend
J happy
K unhappy
* L required
M asked

 TIPS
• Read the phrase. Think about where you have heard the underlined word before. Choose the word that means about the same thing.
• Take your best guess if you are unsure of the answer.

1 He packed his possessions.
A suitcase
* B things owned
C trunk
D schoolbooks

2 To resent what he said
J understand
K repeat
L explain
* M dislike

3 To feel uneasy
* A nervous
B stiff
C sore
D chilly

4 A beautiful stag
J sunset
K kind of fish
* L male deer
M trail

5 Seldom go there
A quickly
B usually
C calmly
* D rarely

6 Stand on the bluff
J stage
K edge of a lake
* L kind of cliff
M mat

7 To yank the rope
* A pull sharply
B tie knots in
C wind in a coil
D cut with a knife

8 The withered plants
J potted
* K dried up
L bearing fruit
M newly planted

STOP

Answer rows   A ⒶⒷ●Ⓓ   1 Ⓐ●ⒸⒹ   3 ●ⒷⒸⒹ   5 ⒶⒷⒸ●   7 ●ⒷⒸⒹ
               B ⒿⓀ●Ⓜ   2 ⒿⓀⓁ●   4 ⒿⓀ●Ⓜ   6 ⒿⓀ●Ⓜ   8 Ⓙ●ⓁⓂ

Practice

Say We are ready for the Practice items. Remember, the letters for the answer choices change from question to question. For odd-numbered questions, they are A-B-C-D. For even-numbered questions, they are J-K-L-M. You must pay careful attention to the letters for the answer choices and the circles in the answer rows at the bottom of the page. It's a good idea to double-check to be sure that you have filled in the circle for the answer choice you think is correct. Check both the item number and the answer letter. If you make a mistake when you fill in the answer circle, your answer will be counted wrong, even if you knew what the correct answer was.

Work until you come to the STOP sign at the bottom of the page. Fill in your answer circles with dark marks and completely erase any marks for answers that you change. Do you have any questions? Start working now.

Allow time for the students to do Numbers 1 through 8.

Say: It's time to stop. You have finished Lesson 1a.

Review the answers with the students. Ask them whether they remembered to look at all the answer choices and take the best guess if they were unsure of the correct answer. Did they have any difficulty marking the circles in the answer rows? If any questions caused particular difficulty, work through each of the answer choices. You may want to discuss with the students where they heard or read a word before.

Have the students indicate completion of the lesson by entering their score for this activity on the progress chart at the beginning of the book.

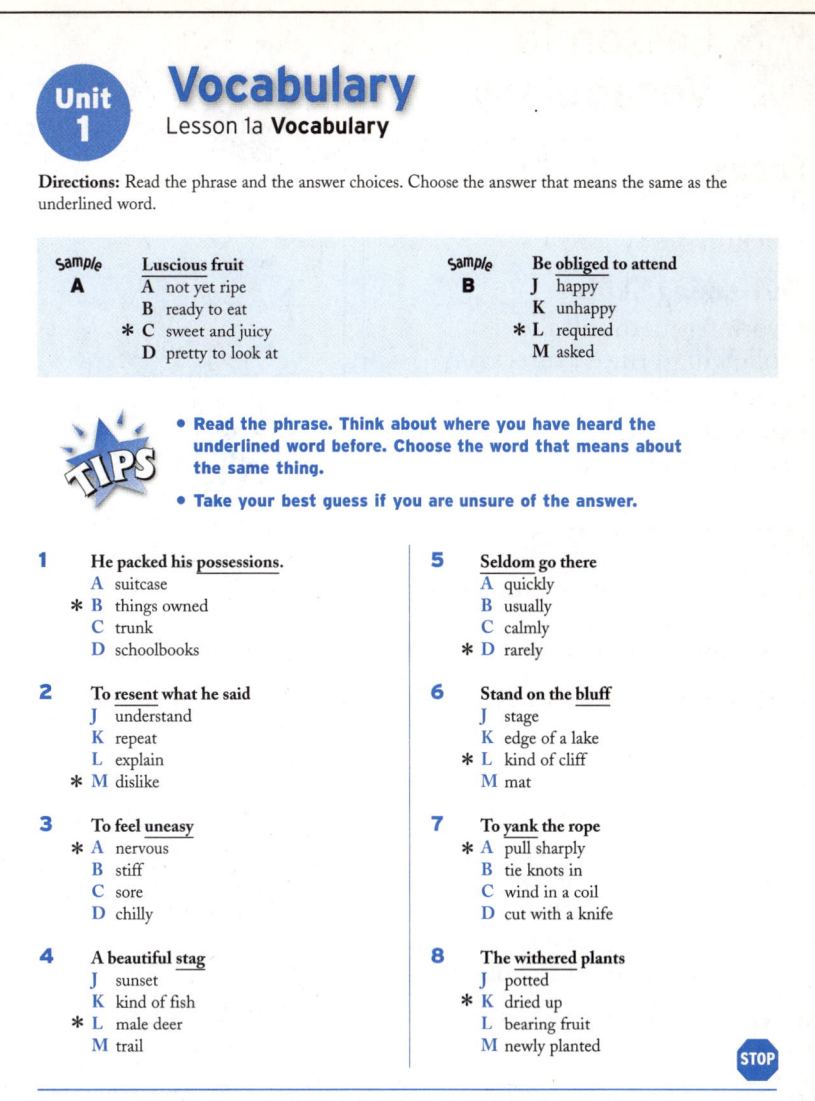

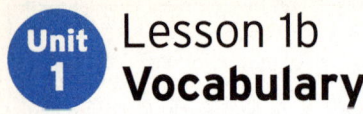

Lesson 1b
Vocabulary

Focus

Reading Skill
- identifying synonyms

Test-taking Skills
- working methodically
- following printed directions
- noting lettering of answer choices
- considering every answer choice
- prioritizing items

Samples A and B

Say Turn to Lesson 1b on page 2. The page number is at the bottom of the page on the left.

Check to see that the students have found the right page.

Say In this lesson, you will find more words that have the same or nearly the same meaning as another word used in a phrase. Read the directions at the top of the page to yourself while I read them aloud to you.

Allow time for the students to read the directions.

Say Read the phrase with the underlined word for Sample A. Think about what the word means as it is used in the phrase. Now, look at the four answer choices below the phrase. Which of the four answers means about the same as the underlined word? *(pause)* The answer is C, *mixture of metals*. An *alloy* is a *mixture of metals*. Fill in the circle for answer C in the answer rows at the bottom of the page. Be sure your answer circle is completely filled in with a dark mark and that you have marked the correct answer circle.

Check to see that the students have marked the correct circle.

Say Now do Sample B by yourself. Read the phrase and fill in the circle for the answer that means the same as the underlined word. *(pause)* Which answer choice is correct? *(answer M)* Yes, *attainable* and *reachable* mean about the same thing. Make sure that circle M for

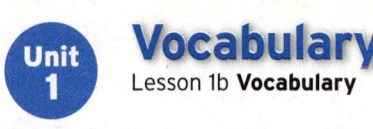

Vocabulary
Lesson 1b **Vocabulary**

Directions: Read the phrase and the answer choices. Choose the answer that means the same as the underlined word.

Sample A	A strong <u>alloy</u>	Sample B	An <u>attainable</u> goal
	A flavor		J required
	B lock		K challenging
*	C mixture of metals		L impossible
	D kind of spice	*	M reachable

- Skim the items. Do the easiest items first. Then come back and do the harder items.

1. <u>Thaw</u> the food
   - A cook in a microwave
   - *B unfreeze
   - C cut into pieces
   - D serve

2. A <u>blunt</u> knife
   - *J dull
   - K hunting
   - L plastic
   - M long

3. The <u>despised</u> enemy
   - A attacking
   - B defeated
   - *C hated
   - D nearby

4. <u>Propose</u> the plan
   - J analyze
   - *K suggest
   - L approve
   - M reject

5. On <u>alternate</u> days
   - A cloudy
   - B not busy
   - C breezy
   - *D every other

6. To <u>tend</u> animals
   - *J take care of
   - K ride
   - L take pictures of
   - M track

7. A <u>barricade</u> on the road
   - A parade
   - *B blockade
   - C bag of trash
   - D empty box

8. A <u>textile</u> mill
   - J steel
   - K lumber
   - L grain
   - *M cloth

2 Answer rows   A ⓐⒷ●Ⓓ 1 ⓐ●ⒸⒹ 3 ⓐⒷ●Ⓓ 5 ⒶⒷⒸ● 7 ⓐ●ⒸⒹ
              B ⒿⓀⓁ● 2 ●ⓀⓁⓂ 4 Ⓙ●ⓁⓂ 6 ●ⓀⓁⓂ 8 ⒿⓀⓁ●

Sample B is completely filled in. Press your pencil firmly so your mark comes out dark.

Check to see that the students have marked the correct circle.

★ TIPS

Say Let's review the tip.

Read the tip aloud to the students.

Say A good strategy to use for vocabulary items is to skim the items and do the easiest items first. When you have finished the easy items, you can come back and do the others.

Practice

Say We are ready for the Practice items. Remember, the letters for the answer choices change from question to question. For odd-numbered questions, they are A-B-C-D. For even-numbered questions, they are J-K-L-M. You must pay careful attention to the letters for the answer choices and the circles in the answer rows at the bottom of the page. It's a good idea to double-check to be sure that you have filled in the circle for the answer choice you think is correct. Check both the item number and the answer letter. If you make a mistake when you fill in the answer circle, your answer will be counted wrong, even if you knew what the correct answer was.

Work until you come to the STOP sign at the bottom of the page. Fill in your answer circles with dark marks and completely erase any marks for answers that you change. Do you have any questions? Start working now.

Allow time for the students to do Numbers 1 through 8.

Say It's time to stop. You have finished Lesson 1b.

Review the answers with the students. Ask them whether they tried doing the easiest items first and if any questions caused particular difficulty. Work through each of the answer choices with the students.

Have the students indicate completion of the lesson by entering their score for this activity on the progress chart at the beginning of the book.

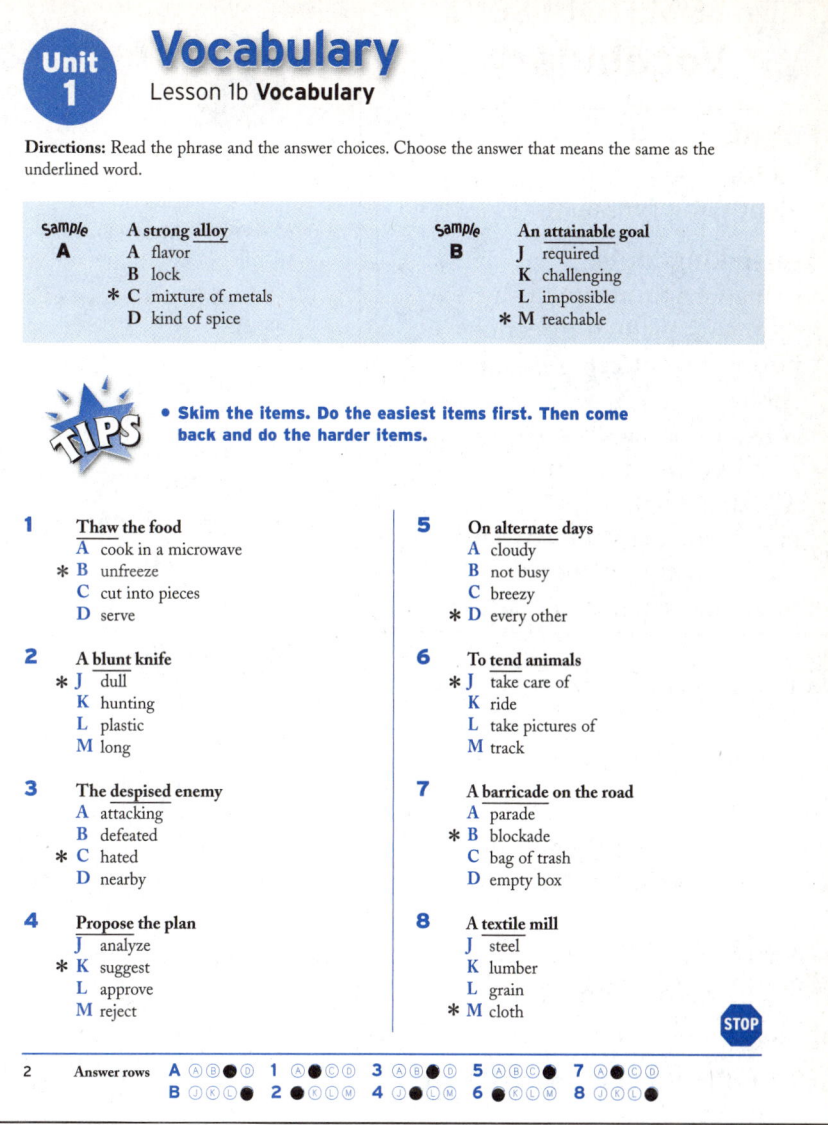

Unit 1 Test Yourself: Vocabulary

Focus

Reading Skill
- identifying synonyms

Test-taking Skills
- managing time effectively
- following printed directions
- noting the lettering of answer choices
- considering every answer choice
- recalling word meanings
- working methodically
- taking the best guess when unsure of the answer
- prioritizing items

This lesson simulates an actual test-taking experience. Therefore, it is recommended that the directions be read verbatim and that the suggested procedures and time allowances be followed.

Directions

Administration Time: approximately 20 minutes

Say Turn to the Test Yourself lesson on page 3.

Check to be sure the students have found the right page. Point out to the students that this Test Yourself lesson is timed like a real test, but that they will score it themselves to see how well they are doing. Explain that it is important to work quickly and to answer as many questions as possible.

Say This lesson will check how well you understand word meanings. Remember to make sure that the circles for your answer choices are completely filled in. Press your pencil firmly so that your marks come out dark. Completely erase any marks for answers that you change. Do not write anything except your answer choices in your books.

Look at Sample A. Read the phrase and fill in the circle for the word that means the same as the underlined word. Mark your answer in the row for Sample A at the bottom of the page.

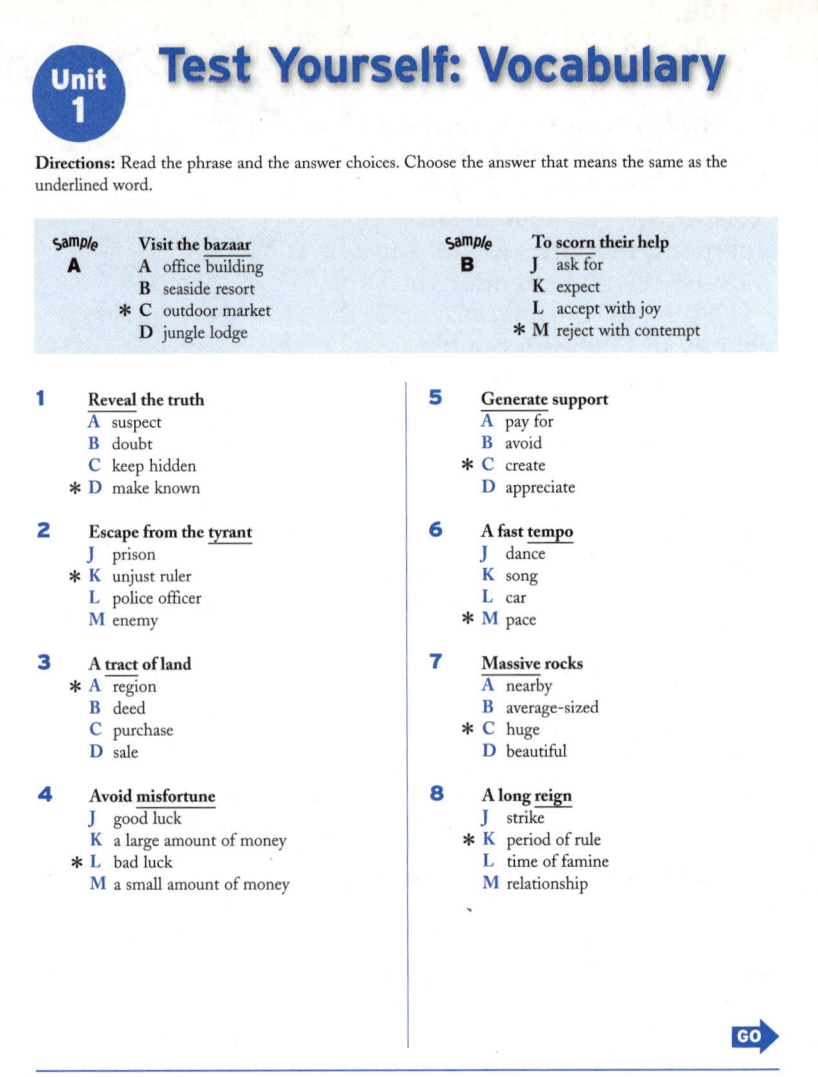

Allow time for the students to read the item and to mark their answers.

Say You should have filled in answer circle C because a *bazaar* is a kind of *outdoor market*. If you did not fill in answer C, erase your answer and fill in answer C now.

Check to see that the students have filled in the correct answer circle.

Say Do Sample B now. Read the phrase and fill in the circle for the word or words that means the same as the underlined word. Mark the circle for the answer you think is correct for Sample B in the answer rows at the bottom of the page.

Allow time for the students to read the item and to mark their answers.

6 Unit 1 Test Yourself Vocabulary

Say You should have filled in answer circle M because *scorn* means to *reject with contempt*. If you did not fill in answer M, erase your answer and fill in answer M now.

Check to see that the students have filled in the correct answer circle.

Say Now you will answer more questions. Fill in the spaces for your answers in the rows at the bottom of the page. When you come to the GO sign at the bottom of the page, turn to the next page and continue working. Work until you come to the STOP sign at the bottom of page 4. When you have finished, you can check your answers to this test. Then wait for the rest of the group to finish. Any questions?

Answer any questions that the students have.

Say Start working now. You have 15 minutes.

Allow 15 minutes.

Say It's time to stop. You have completed the Test Yourself lesson. Check to see that you have completely filled in your answer circles with dark marks. Make sure that any marks for answers that you changed have been completely erased. Now you may close your books.

Have the students indicate completion of the lesson by entering their score for this activity on the progress chart at the beginning of the book.

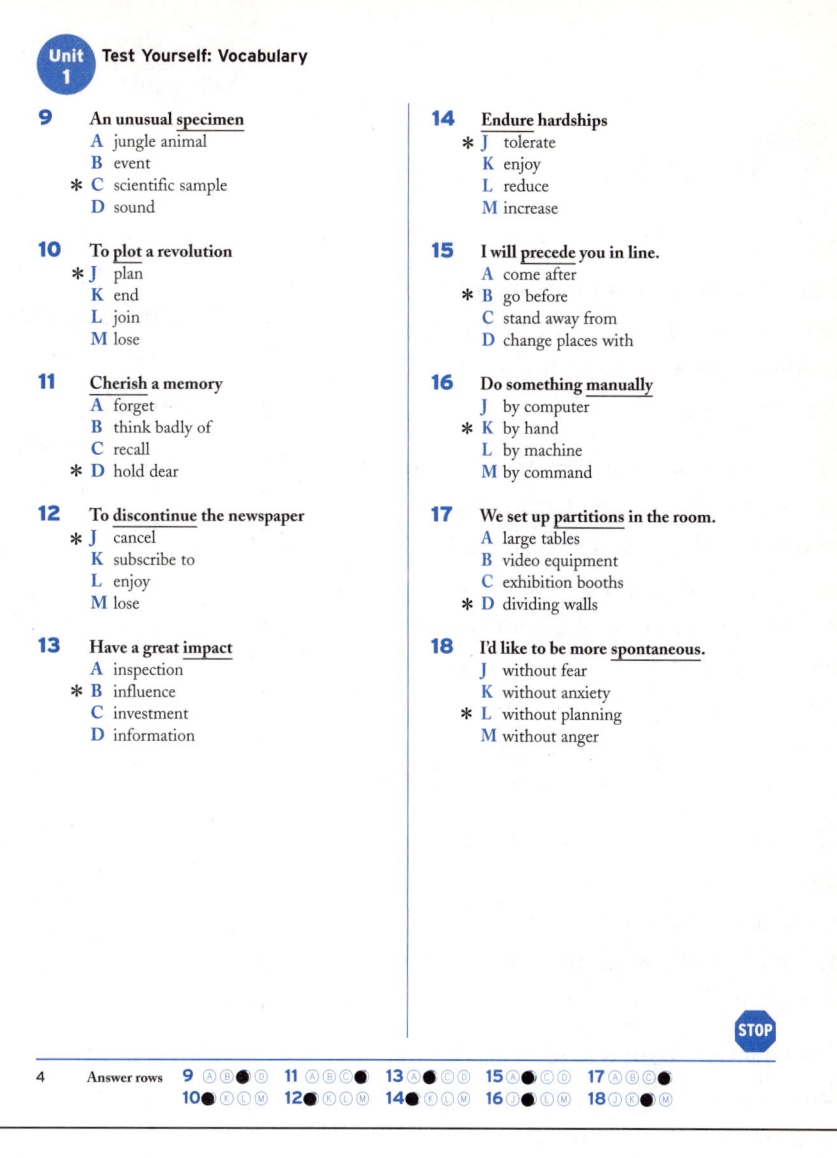

Unit 1 Test Yourself Vocabulary 7

Unit 2

Background

This unit contains three lessons that deal with reading comprehension skills. Students answer questions about stories that they read.

• **In Lesson 2a,** students read a passage and answer questions based on the content of the passage. Students are encouraged to skim a passage and refer to the passage to answer questions. They use key words to find the answer, work methodically, and reason from facts and evidence. They are reminded to skip difficult items and return to them later.

• **In Lesson 2b,** students read a passage and answer questions based on the content of the passage. Students review the test-taking skills that were introduced in Lesson 2a.

• **In the Test Yourself lesson,** the reading skills and test-taking skills introduced and used in Lessons 2a and 2b are reinforced and presented in a format that gives students the experience of taking an achievement test. Techniques for managing time effectively when they are taking a standardized test are reinforced.

Instructional Objectives

Lesson 2a **Reading Comprehension** Lesson 2b **Reading Comprehension**	Given a written passage and a literal or inferential question based on the passage, students identify which of four answer choices is correct.
Test Yourself	Given questions similar to those in Lessons 2a and 2b, students utilize reading skills and test-taking strategies on achievement test formats.

Unit 2 Lesson 2a
Reading Comprehension

Focus

Reading Skills
- drawing conclusions
- recognizing an author's technique
- deriving word meanings
- understanding reasons
- recognizing details
- making inferences
- understanding the main idea
- analyzing characters
- understanding literary devices
- recognizing setting

Test-taking Skills
- skimming a passage
- referring to a passage to answer questions
- using key words to find the answer
- working methodically
- reasoning from facts and evidence
- skipping difficult items and returning to them later

Unit 2 Reading Comprehension
Lesson 2a Reading Comprehension

Directions: Read the passage and the answer choices. Choose the best answer.

Sample A
When Maxine said she wanted a dog, she never expected to get one. Now that Maxine had one, she wasn't sure she wanted one. Maxine loved Mollie, a golden retriever, but taking care of her consumed a lot of her time. She would rather be with her friends than walking a dog.

Maxine has discovered that
- A a dog is more fun than she thought.
- B friends are better than a dog.
- *C a dog is more work than she thought.
- D a dog is better than friends.

- Skim the passage. Read each question and look for key words. Refer back to the passage to find the answer.
- If a question is too difficult, skip it and go on to the next one.

In this passage, a gardener expresses her opinion about a common vegetable.

If you want my opinion, zucchini is an alien life-form. It remains dormant through the winter, but when summer comes, it takes over everyone's garden. And for some reason, most of the extra zucchini ends up in our house.

The encyclopedia entry says that *cucurbita pepo*, the zucchini, is a summer squash, a group that also includes yellow, crookneck, and scallop squashes. The name *zucchini* is Italian for "little squash," but as any gardener will attest, a zucchini can grow to huge proportions if not picked early.

A gardening book I read suggests that people like zucchini because it is easy to grow and produces a huge quantity of fruit. Once the fruit appears at the base of a flower, it matures rapidly. Ideally, a zucchini should be picked when it is small, perhaps six inches long. If a zucchini remains on a plant too long, it will slow down the growth of additional fruit.

Friends often give us their extra zucchini. I'm not sure if that's a curse or a blessing.

1. The author's tone in this passage is
   - A a combination of fact and fiction.
   - B a combination of dislike and fiction.
   - C informational and questioning.
   - *D humorous and factual.

2. What does "dormant" mean?
   - *J Inactive
   - K Small in size
   - L Alien
   - M Producing many fruit

3. What causes zucchini plants to produce fewer fruit?
   - A Picking too many fruit
   - *B Letting fruit grow too large
   - C Picking fruit when they are small
   - D Letting the flowers grow too long

Answer rows A ⓐⓑ●ⓓ   1 ⓐⓑⓒ●   2 ●ⓚⓛⓜ   3 ⓐ●ⓒⓓ

5

Sample A

Say Turn to Lesson 2a on page 5. In this lesson, you will answer questions about passages that you read. Begin by reading the directions at the top of the page to yourself while I read them out loud.

Read the directions to the students.

Say Now we'll do Sample A. Skim the passage to yourself. *(pause)* Now, read the question next to the passage. To find the correct answer, look back at the passage. What is the correct answer? *(answer C)* Even though the story doesn't say so, Maxine probably discovered that *a dog is more work than she thought.* Fill in answer circle C for Sample A in the answer rows at the bottom of the page. Make sure the circle is completely filled in. Press your pencil firmly so that your mark comes out dark.

Check to see that the students have marked the correct answer circle.

★TIPS

Say Now let's look at the tips. Who will read them?

Have a volunteer read the tips aloud.

Say The best way to answer reading comprehension questions is to skim the passage quickly and then read the questions. Refer back to the passage to answer the questions, but don't reread the story for each question. Key words in the question will tell you where in the passage to look for the correct answer. If you can find the same key words in the passage, you can usually find the correct answer nearby. And remember, if an item seems difficult, skip it and move on to another item. This will keep you from wasting time on an achievement test.

Practice

Say Now we are ready for Practice. You will read more passages and answer questions about them in the same way that we did the Sample. Work as quickly as you can. Skim the passage and then read the questions. Use the meaning of the passage to find the answers. Key words in the question will help you find the part of the passage that contains the answer. Fill in your answers in the circles at the bottom of the page. When you see a GO sign, continue working. Work until you come to the STOP sign at the bottom of page 8. Remember to make sure that your answer circles are filled in with dark marks. Completely erase any marks for answers that you change. Do you have any questions? Start working now.

Allow time for the students to read the stories and to answer the questions.

 Lesson 2a **Reading Comprehension**

One of America's greatest explorers is also one of its least known. This passage tells about this man.

If you ever wanted to write a book about little-known Americans who have made significant contributions to the country, your subjects would include people such as Grace Hopper, a computer scientist; Charles Drew, the inventor of the blood bank; and Luis Alvarez, one of the creators of the guidance system that allows planes to land in difficult weather. Your book would also include an obscure character, John Charles Frémont, who in his time was larger than life.

Born in Savannah, Georgia, in 1813, Frémont was known as "the Pathfinder" because of his explorations of the American West. He was appointed to the Army Topographic Corps and joined an expedition to map the region between the upper Mississippi and Missouri Rivers. In 1842, he was given his own expedition to survey the Oregon Trail. His success led to a second expedition, which explored much of the West that was still uncharted territory. His hardships and deprivations made news around the country.

To understand how difficult exploration was for Frémont and his men, consider this: There was not a single road through the Rocky or Sierra Mountains. With limited supplies of food and clothing, Frémont's expedition was often traveling in winter at elevations above 10,000 feet. They had no accurate maps, yet they successfully traversed an area about one-third the size of the whole United States.

Although many people doubted Frémont's discoveries, his findings were, in fact, correct. He verified the existence of the Salt Lake in Utah and described a Great Basin between the Rockies and the Sierra Mountains. He found the best pass through the mountains. He proved false the idea that a great river flowed due west from the Rockies to the Pacific Ocean.

At the conclusion of his second expedition, Frémont moved to California, a land he had come to love. He was one of the moving forces behind the attempt to gain independence for California from Spain, which finally occurred in 1848. Frémont contributed in many ways to the development of California and was one of its first senators to the U.S. Congress. When gold was discovered in California, Frémont was among the many who became rich overnight. As history has proven, this was the high point of his life.

Because of his popularity among the public and his strong stand against slavery, Frémont was chosen to run for President by the newly formed Republican party. He was defeated by James Buchanan and returned to California. When the Civil War broke out, he fought for the Union, holding the rank of major general. He was not an effective general, which, combined with his strong opinions, caused him to leave the army.

After the war, Frémont's fortunes continued to slide. He mismanaged his land holdings and made poor investments, losing most of his fortune. He was appointed as governor of the Arizona Territory from 1878 to 1883, after which he again returned to California. He died in 1890 while on a visit to New York City.

Throughout his life, John Charles Frémont was a controversial figure. He constantly sought the support of political figures for personal advancement. During his expeditions, he often ignored direct orders. His men were extremely loyal to him, even though he put them in constant danger and many died. In the army, Frémont was found guilty of disobedience and unacceptable conduct, but he received a Presidential pardon. Despite these controversies, no one can dispute the fact that Frémont's courage and determination opened up the West and hastened America's rise to greatness.

6

Lesson 2a **Reading Comprehension**

4 What was the purpose of the Army Topographic Corps?
 J To seek independence for California
 K To build roads through the Rockies
*L To explore and make maps
 M To build towns in the West

5 In the first paragraph, what does the word "obscure" mean?
*A Little-known
 B Famous
 C Successful
 D Highly regarded

6 What does it mean to say Frémont was a "moving force" behind the attempt to gain independence for California?
 J He moved to California because it would soon be independent.
 K He was one of the people who wanted independence, but he did not want to fight for it.
 L He was one of the people who was not sure about independence.
*M He was one of the people who worked hard for independence.

7 When Frémont first arrived in California,
*A it was a Spanish possession.
 B it had recently gained independence.
 C it was an American state.
 D gold had just been discovered.

8 What is this passage mainly about?
 J The exploration of the American West
 K What it takes to run for President
*L A little-known American hero
 M How politics can cause the fall of a hero

9 Why were Frémont's men loyal even though he put them in danger?
*A He probably respected them, and they knew the importance of their job.
 B He was probably mean, and they feared him.
 C They were just as interested in getting rich as he was.
 D They didn't mind traveling through the mountains in the winter.

10 Why would the President have granted Frémont a pardon?
 J Frémont was working under secret orders from another country.
 K There was little evidence to prove Frémont was a troublemaker.
 L Frémont promised to help California become independent.
*M Despite his problems, Frémont had accomplished a great deal.

11 Why does the author believe that the discovery of gold in California was the high point of Frémont's life?
 A He had more money then than he ever would again.
*B From that point onward, most of what he tried ended in failure.
 C Being rich is more important than running for President.
 D He accomplished nothing before and nothing afterward.

Say It's time to stop. You have finished Lesson 2a.

Review the answers with the students. Ask them whether they remembered to look back at the passage to find the answers to the questions. If any questions caused particular difficulty, work through the story, questions, and answer choices. Ask the students which key words helped them find the answers and discuss any strategies they used.

Have the students indicate completion of the lesson by entering their score for this activity on the progress chart at the beginning of the book.

 Lesson 2a **Reading Comprehension**

It is my favorite time,
The earliest light in the greatest city.
I walk down almost soundless streets,
Their crowds and cars still for now.
The few I meet are much like me,
Seekers of a peace that comes
But once a day.
As I walk, the quiet fades sound by sound
Until my favorite time is once again
A day away.

12 What time of day is the author writing about?
 ∗ J Morning
   K Afternoon
   L Evening
   M Midnight

13 What does it mean to say "the quiet fades sound by sound"?
   A It is becoming more and more quiet.
   B The sun is moving higher in the sky.
   C The author's friends are arriving.
 ∗ D The city is gradually coming alive.

14 Is the writer disappointed when her favorite time is over?
   J No, because it is to be enjoyed only once, not many times.
   K Yes, because it might never come again.
 ∗ L No, because it will come again the next day.
   M Yes, because other people will ruin it.

15 Where is the setting for this poem?
   A A small town
 ∗ B A large city
   C A city park
   D The country

8 Answer rows 12   13   14   15

---

12 Lesson 2a **Reading Comprehension**

Unit 2 Lesson 2b Reading Comprehension

Focus

Reading Skills
- drawing conclusions
- recognizing an author's purpose
- deriving word meanings
- understanding sequence
- making inferences
- understanding reasons
- understanding literary devices
- identifying feelings
- recognizing an author's technique
- understanding the main idea

Test-taking Skills
- reasoning from facts and evidence
- working methodically
- skimming a passage
- referring to a passage to answer questions

Sample A

Say Turn to Lesson 2b on page 9. In this lesson, you will answer questions about passages that you read. Begin by reading the directions at the top of the page to yourself while I read them out loud.

Read the directions to the students.

Say Now we'll do Sample A. Skim the passage to yourself. *(pause)* Now, read the question next to the passage. To find the correct answer, look back at the passage. What is the correct answer? *(answer C)* You can conclude from the paragraph that *radio was invented before many other forms of entertainment.* Fill in answer circle C for Sample A in the answer rows at the bottom of the page. Make sure the circle is completely filled in. Press your pencil firmly so that your mark comes out dark.

Check to see that the students have marked the correct answer circle.

Unit 2 Reading Comprehension
Lesson 2b Reading Comprehension

Directions: Read the passage and the answer choices. Choose the best answer.

Sample A

People today have all sorts of entertainment possibilities. Television, movies, videos, computer games, and the computer are just a few of the things we can do. For most of the twentieth century, however, the radio was the only form of entertainment for most Americans.

What can you conclude from this paragraph?
A Radio is better than other forms of entertainment.
B The twentieth century was a long time ago.
* C Radio was invented before many other forms of entertainment.
D People are smarter today because we have more entertainment.

TIPS • Sometimes the answer is not stated directly in the story. You have to draw a conclusion or make an inference.

This passage talks about some unexpected dangers in an unlikely place.

Pets think blooming, lush gardens are especially for them. This can cause problems. Here are a few tips to make your yard safe for your pet.
  Use garden and lawn-care products safely. Products that kill bugs can be harmful to pets. Keep these out of reach of your pets.
  React quickly to accidents. If you see your dog rolling around in an area you just sprayed, give your dog a bath immediately. If you notice your dog acting strangely, call your veterinarian.
  Use nontoxic garden treatments to control weeds and pests. These new products are made with natural ingredients. They will create a healthier, happier place for your pet to play in.
  Animals are curious creatures. Accidents are bound to happen. It is best to be prepared. If you plan ahead, you and your furry friend can enjoy a safe and healthy life together.

1 What was the author's main purpose for writing this story?
A To describe ways to get rid of pests
B To tell a story about a pet who loves a garden
* C To explain how to make a yard safe for pets
D To show how to plant a healthy garden

2 Something that is toxic is
J sharp.
K mild.
L natural.
* M poisonous.

3 What should you do right after your pet has rolled in a sprayed area?
A Call a veterinarian.
* B Give your pet a bath.
C Go to a veterinary hospital.
D Read the label on the product.

★**TIPS**

Say Now let's look at the tip. Who will read it?

Have a volunteer read the tip aloud.

Say Sometimes you can answer a question from information that is in the story, but other times you have to "read between the lines." This means you use the information in the story and your experience to draw a conclusion or to make an inference.

Explain the tip further, if necessary. Have the students identify the information in the story that leads to the correct answer.

Unit 2 Lesson 2b **Reading Comprehension** 13

Practice

Say Now we are ready for Practice. You will read more passages and answer questions about them in the same way that we did the Sample. Work as quickly as you can. Skim the passage and then read the questions. Use the meaning of the passage to find the answers. Fill in your answers in the circles at the bottom of the page. When you see a GO sign, continue working. Work until you come to the STOP sign at the bottom of page 12. Remember to make sure that your answer circles are filled in with dark marks. Completely erase any marks for answers that you change. Do you have any questions? Start working now.

Allow time for the students to read the stories and to answer the questions.

 Lesson 2b **Reading Comprehension**

Gus is going for a raft ride in rough water, but he is a little concerned about one of the other rafters.

1   For most of the people standing around the raft rental office, today was a day that promised adventure. They buckled up their life jackets, smeared sunscreen lotion across their faces and shoulders, and buzzed with tales of previous rafting trips and past glories.

2   Gus was more apprehensive than excited, but not because he was worried about himself. He had shot the rapids several times before, but this time his grandfather was determined to join him. Surely such a trip would be too much for a man his age. Gus had even asked the owner of the rafting resort if someone who was sixty-five years old should raft down the river. The owner would not commit one way or the other, saying it depended more on physical fitness than age. So there stood twelve members of Gus's extended family, including cousins, aunts, uncles, and grandfather, ready to climb aboard one of two rafts and begin the trip downriver.

3   The anxious rafters shoved off the rocky shore and immediately started navigating toward a narrow opening in a stone wall called Needle Nose Gate. Gus's raft made it swiftly through the gate, taking in substantial water but nothing that couldn't be bailed out with a scoop. Gus turned to see how Grandfather's raft would do. He waited…and watched…and yet…no raft came. Then Gus caught a glimpse of something…a hat…then a shoe…then an oar…then, finally, an empty raft.

4   Kicking himself into rescue mode, Gus jumped overboard, pulled the empty raft ashore, and clambered upriver above Needle Nose Gate. There on the shore stood the soaked inhabitants of the abandoned raft—all except for Grandfather. Gus's eyes scanned the surface of the bubbling waters and saw Grandfather, who was desperately trying to stand but was caught in a powerful swirling eddy.

5   "Grandfather, can you hear me?" Gus hollered through his shaking cupped hands. Grandfather raised a hand, acknowledging that he could. "Okay. Listen to me. Forget about standing, and let yourself float with your feet pointed downstream. I'll meet you on the other side of the gate!"

6   Safely on shore a few minutes later, Grandfather's face was wrapped with a permanent grin. "Never had so much fun in my life," he said while wringing out his hat. "Now, let's get this show back on the road!"

10

Unit 2 Lesson 2b **Reading Comprehension**

4 What was unusual about this rafting trip?
  J Gus would be shooting the rapids.
  K Gus was in charge of two rafts instead of one.
  L Gus was taking his family rafting for the first time.
  ∗ M Gus's grandfather had decided to go along.

5 Why wouldn't the owner of the rafting company admit there was an age limit for rafting?
  A He thought rafting was a good experience for all ages.
  ∗ B He believed physical fitness was more important than age.
  C He was trying to make more money from Gus's group.
  D He wanted to be able to go rafting himself when he got older.

6 In paragraph 2, what does "shot the rapids" mean?
  J Gus had grown bored with rafting down the river.
  K Gus had not been rafting for a very long time.
  ∗ L Gus had been river rafting in fast water before.
  M Gus had enjoyed rafting, but in smooth, calm water.

7 In what sense did Gus kick himself into rescue mode?
  A He was angry and blamed himself for the accident.
  ∗ B He did not waste any time helping the others.
  C He accidentally kicked himself when he jumped out of the raft.
  D He knew exactly what had happened as he left his raft.

8 How did Gus feel when he was shouting instructions to Grandfather?
  J Furious
  K Thrilled
  L Amused
  ∗ M Worried

9 Whose thoughts are expressed at the end of the story?
  A The raft resort owner's
  B Gus's
  ∗ C Grandfather's
  D The family members'

10 In the last paragraph, what is the effect of the description of Grandfather's grin as permanent?
  J It indicates that Grandfather looked like he always did.
  ∗ K It shows that Grandfather is thrilled with what happened.
  L It suggests that Grandfather has no idea he almost drowned.
  M It hints that Grandfather fell overboard on purpose.

11 The use of ellipses in paragraph 3 helps the reader understand that
  A the raft Grandfather was on turned completely upside down.
  ∗ B the clues about what has happened come bit by bit.
  C the people and items fell out of the boat one at a time.
  D the rafts move so quickly it is hard to tell what is happening.

Say It's time to stop. You have finished Lesson 2b.

Review the answers with the students. Ask them whether they remembered to look back at the passage to find the answers to the questions. If any questions caused particular difficulty, work through the story, questions, and answer choices.

Have the students indicate completion of the lesson by entering their score for this activity on the progress chart at the beginning of the book.

 Lesson 2b **Reading Comprehension**

Family traditions are often humorous, and this one is no exception.

1 As I sat alone in my bedroom—bed freshly made and books neatly stacked on the shelf—I praised myself for enduring another year of the Smith Family Campout.

2 It's not that I don't become absolutely giddy from the time the invitation comes until the moment our station wagon rolls into Wright's Happy Camping and RV Park. It's not that I don't look forward to seeing all forty-two aunts, uncles, first cousins, second cousins, grandparents, and great-grandparents. In fact, the Smith Family Campout is one of the highlights of my year.

3 The same routine takes place every year. Our family arrives first because we make the reservations for the group. With six in our family, the wagon is packed so tightly that Dad can't see out the back window. This always makes the four-hour drive interesting. Every time Dad makes a turn, we have to yell "Clear!" Last year we almost hit a cement truck.

4 After settling in, exploring all the sites, and choosing the best spot to pitch our tents, the kids go for a hike. We walk about two miles to the spring, drink the freezing water out of our hands, and return to mayhem. The campsites are covered with Smiths and people who married into the Smith family. We creep in, trying to act like we've been there for a while to dodge colorful kisses and pinches on the cheek. This tactic never works.

5 After that, it's a blur. With activities like hot-dog roasts, seeing who can find rocks shaped like the fifty states, and the talent show, the week disappears as quickly as it came. By Saturday, however, everyone begins to miss having a shower and bathroom and no one is polite any more because we've gotten so used to each other.

6 When we arrive home, I go to my own room. I shut the door and remember what stillness sounds like. Then I start planning for next year's Smith Family Campout.

---

12 In paragraph 6, what does the narrator mean when she says she remembers "what stillness sounds like"?
   J She listens to the crickets outside her window.
   K She prefers spending time alone in her room to camping with the family.
 * L She enjoys the quiet after a busy week of camping with her family.
   M She makes an effort to spend time alone during the campout.

13 In paragraph 2, what does "giddy" mean?
   A Curious
 * B Excited
   C Nervous
   D Exhausted

14 What is the meaning of the last paragraph?
 * J Though the narrator is glad when the campout is over, she always looks forward to the next one.
   K Unless she has time by herself, the narrator's family drives her crazy.
   L The narrator expresses relief at not having to share a room with other family members.
   M The narrator tries to keep in mind positive aspects of the campout to improve her attitude.

12 Answer rows

---

16   Lesson 2b **Reading Comprehension**

Unit 2 Test Yourself: Reading Comprehension

Focus

Reading Skills
- recognizing details
- deriving word meanings
- drawing conclusions
- making inferences
- understanding reasons
- comparing and contrasting
- recognizing genre or text source
- understanding the main idea
- recognizing an author's technique
- understanding literary devices
- identifying feelings
- analyzing characters

Test-taking Skills
- managing time effectively
- following printed directions
- skimming a passage
- referring to a passage to answer questions
- using key words to find the answer
- working methodically
- reasoning from facts and evidence
- skipping difficult items and returning to them later

This lesson simulates an actual test-taking experience. Therefore, it is recommended that the directions be read verbatim and the suggested procedures and time allowances be followed.

Directions

Administration Time: approximately 40 minutes

Say Turn to the Test Yourself lesson on page 13.

Check to be sure the students have found the right page. Point out to the students that this Test Yourself lesson is timed like a real test, but that they will score it themselves to see how well they are doing. Explain that it is important to work quickly and to answer as many questions as possible.

Unit 2 Test Yourself: Reading Comprehension

Directions: Read the passage and the answer choices. Choose the best answer.

Sample A
In 1993, a device we use every day celebrated its 100th birthday. Invented by Whitcomb L. Judson, the Hookless Fastener was a pair of metal chains that were interlocked by a slider. Surprisingly, the zipper was invented for boots and shoes, not clothing. It was not until 1910 that Judson put his zipper on pants and skirts.

The zipper was first used for
A hats.
B skirts.
C shirts.
* D boots.

The early inhabitants of North America continue to fascinate scientists and the public alike.

Tens of thousands of years ago, several groups of nomads from Asia appear to have crossed a land bridge into North America. They wandered through almost all of North and South America and established many different cultures. One of the most remarkable was the ancient Maya.

The Maya occupied the region that is now southern Mexico, Belize, Guatemala, and Honduras. Scientists believe they moved down the Pacific coast in stages, reaching southern Mexico by about 5000 B.C. At first, they lived in simple communities that depended on fishing and gathering fruits, vegetables, and grains. They gradually moved inland, and by 2000 B.C. or earlier, they learned how to grow crops rather than just depend on gathering food. They cultivated a variety of foods, including beans, squash, tomatoes, peppers, and different fruit. Their chief food, however, was maize, a type of corn which was so important that their word for maize—wa—was also their word for food.

As the Maya became more successful at agriculture, they were able to trade with other cultures in the area. The wealth they acquired became concentrated in a few families, and the Maya made a transition from communities in which people were more or less equal to an oligarchy with a small, strong ruling class.

While this social change was taking place, an architectural change was also occurring. Communities that were previously built without much thought became planned and eventually grew into cities. These cities featured huge ceremonial centers and stelae—stone columns—that people marvel at even today.

The Maya developed a sophisticated written language based on hieroglyphics, studied astronomy, and created a unique calendar. They also kept historic records that have helped scientists today understand the Mayan culture.

Around the year A.D. 1000, the Mayan culture entered a period of decline. Groups within the Mayan culture began fighting with one another, and outside cultures warred with them. During the sixteenth century, the Maya made contact with Spanish explorers with terrible results. They contracted European diseases for which they had no immunity, and many Maya died. Eventually, the Spanish conquered them and the Mayan culture broke up into small groups.

GO →

Answer rows A Ⓐ Ⓑ Ⓒ ●

Say This lesson will check how well you understand what you read. Remember to make sure that the circles for your answer choices are completely filled in. Press your pencil firmly so that your marks come out dark. Completely erase any marks for answers that you change. Do not write anything except your answer choices in your books.

Look at Sample A. Read the passage and answer the question about it. The answer rows are at the bottom of the page.

Allow time for the students to fill in their answers.

Say The correct answer is D. The story says that the zipper was first used for *boots*. If you chose another answer, erase yours and fill in answer D now.

Check to see that the students have correctly filled in their answer circles with a dark mark.

Say Now you will do more items like Sample A. Read each passage and answer the questions that follow it. When you come to the GO sign at the bottom of a page, continue working. Work until you come to the STOP sign at the bottom of page 18. Fill in your answers in the rows at the bottom of the page. Make sure you fill in the circles completely with dark marks. Completely erase any marks for answers you change. You will have 35 minutes. You may begin.

Allow 35 minutes.

 Test Yourself: Reading Comprehension

1. What is a "culture" in this passage?
   A A group living in the Americas
   B A group made up of people from Mexico
   C A group that enjoys music and art
   *D A group that has a similar way of life

2. The ancient Maya were
   *J related to other Native Americans.
   K not related to other Native Americans.
   L related to the early Spanish explorers.
   M among the best boat builders.

3. What kind of written language did the Maya use?
   A One based on an alphabet, like the English language
   B One based on sign language, like other Native Americans
   *C One based on hieroglyphics, like the Egyptians
   D One based on the Spanish language introduced in the sixteenth century

4. What allowed the ancient Maya to move away from the coastline?
   J Building planned cities
   *K Learning how to grow crops
   L Creating a calendar
   M Fighting with other cultures

5. What makes a culture an oligarchy?
   A A king or queen who holds all power
   B Equality among all people
   *C A small but powerful ruling class
   D Great wealth

6. What is the "land bridge" that is mentioned in the first paragraph?
   *J Dry land that connected Asia and North America
   K A bridge built by the nomads
   L Something that the Maya built after reaching Mexico
   M A structure made by people before the nomads began their travels

7. Stelae are most like
   A mountains.
   B restaurants.
   C office buildings.
   *D monuments.

8. What did the Maya probably trade with other cultures?
   J Fish they caught
   K Calendars they made
   *L Food they grew
   M Historic records they created

GO

14 Answer rows   1 Ⓐ Ⓑ Ⓒ ●   3 Ⓐ Ⓑ ● Ⓓ   5 Ⓐ Ⓑ ● Ⓓ   7 Ⓐ Ⓑ Ⓒ ●
                 2 ● Ⓚ Ⓛ Ⓜ   4 Ⓙ ● Ⓛ Ⓜ   6 ● Ⓚ Ⓛ Ⓜ   8 Ⓙ Ⓚ ● Ⓜ

18   Test Yourself **Reading Comprehension**

Test Yourself: Reading Comprehension

A zoo is a wonderful place to visit, but most people don't know much about the history of zoos. This passage presents an interesting look at this popular attraction.

Almost every major city in the world shares one attraction, a zoo. From the Philadelphia Zoological Garden, America's oldest zoo, to the one in Sydney, Australia, which most people reach by ferry, zoos are loved by tourists and residents alike.

Humans have kept animals for their enjoyment and entertainment from prehistoric times. The ancient Egyptians, Greeks, and Romans kept small zoos, but the origin of the zoo as we know it today took place during the Renaissance in sixteenth-century Europe. These zoos were termed "menageries" because they were an attempt to bring together at least one of each type of animal. By the eighteenth century, there were major zoos in Vienna, Austria; Paris, France; Madrid, Spain; and London, England.

Over the past several hundred years, zoos have changed considerably. At first, they were no better than prisons for animals, with small cages and barely acceptable food. In the last fifty or so years, however, zoos have provided animals with larger and more natural habitats, better food, and opportunities for recreation and socialization. Zoos also moved from being purely entertainment to serving as research and education centers. These changes have improved life for the animals in the zoos, have helped us preserve animals in the wild, and have made visiting a zoo more enjoyable for both children and adults.

The idea that a zoo should be a menagerie is also changing. In some places, the zoo has focused on animals from a particular habitat, such as the Arizona-Sonora Desert Museum in Tucson or Ghost Ranch in northern New Mexico. In others, the emphasis is providing an "up close and personal" experience by allowing visitors to drive through large areas where the animals range freely in an open habitat.

Almost all zoos are owned by nonprofit organizations or municipalities such as cities or counties. They are supported by admission fees, the sale of food or merchandise in the zoo, taxes, and gifts from charitable foundations. In the United States, Canada, and most European nations, zoos belong to a professional association that conducts regular inspections to see that the animals are receiving appropriate treatment.

Many people are surprised to learn that the majority of the employees in a zoo are responsible for overseeing administration, maintaining grounds, taking tickets, selling food and merchandise, and handling other routine functions. The two "glamour" jobs are curator and zookeeper, and there are relatively few of these positions available in any zoo. A curator is responsible for acquiring animals, designing exhibits, supervising animal care, and performing related tasks. A zookeeper is the person visitors see bathing the elephants, feeding the lions, or making sure the rhinoceros has a stout rubbing post. In addition to these two positions, most zoos have at least one veterinarian, some technicians, and perhaps an animal researcher or two.

A modern zoo requires as much administration as a small city. Visitors see only a small part of what is involved in running a zoo. A great deal of effort must be expended to maintain the health and well-being of the animals, protect keepers who work with the animals, and create an environment that is stimulating for the animals and entertaining for visitors. All this effort seems to be paying off, however, for zoos are popular attractions year-round, and it is a rare person indeed who doesn't enjoy spending a day at a zoo.

Unit 2 Test Yourself: Reading Comprehension

9 A menagerie would have
  A many examples of the same animal.
  *B examples of many different animals.
  C animals in a natural setting.
  D animals in cramped cages.

10 What is a major difference between modern zoos and those of a hundred years ago?
  *J Animals are treated better today.
  K Animals are treated worse today.
  L Cages were larger a hundred years ago.
  M Most zoos are in large cities today.

11 In the third paragraph, what does the word "socialization" mean?
  A To exercise
  B To eat natural foods
  *C To spend time together in natural groups
  D To learn more about keepers and people who visit a zoo

12 What is a "glamour" job?
  J One that requires the worker to be attractive
  *K One that seems like fun and everyone is familiar with
  L One that involves a lot of behind-the-scenes work
  M One that pays well

13 Who ensures that zoos do a good job caring for their animals?
  A A curator
  B A zookeeper
  C A charitable organization
  *D A professional association

14 Where would a passage like this be most likely to appear?
  *J In a popular magazine
  K On the front page of a newspaper
  L In a science book
  M On an advertisement for a city zoo

15 According to this passage,
  A zoos were developed only in the last century.
  *B people have been fascinated by animals for thousands of years.
  C Philadelphia is the home of the first zoo in the world.
  D the best zoos were built during the Renaissance.

16 Other than animals, who else benefits when zoos provide animals with better living conditions?
  J Zoo administrators
  K Zoo curators
  *L Visitors to a zoo
  M Owners of a zoo

17 What is this passage mostly about?
  A Managing zoos
  B The history of zoos
  C Animals
  *D Zoos

16 Answer rows 9 Ⓐ●ⒸⒹ   11 ⒶⒷ●Ⓓ   13 ⒶⒷⒸ●   15 Ⓐ●ⒸⒹ   17 ⒶⒷⒸ●
                10 ●ⓀⓁⓂ 12 Ⓙ●ⓁⓂ   14 ●ⓀⓁⓂ   16 ⒿⓀ●Ⓜ

Unit 2 Test Yourself: Reading Comprehension

In this essay, a young man today tries to describe what it must have been like for his grandmother to come to America many years ago.

1   The year was 1914. In a few months, Archduke Francis Ferdinand, the heir to the Austrian throne, would be assassinated in Sarajevo. Woodrow Wilson was President of the United States; a recent invention, the flying machine, was all the rage; and moving pictures were silent.

2   None of this, however, mattered to Mariana Potalivo, a fifteen-year-old girl standing in a train station in a small Italian town. She and her brother, Nicholas, were taking the first step on a journey that would end almost halfway around the world in America. Mariana was frightened of what lay ahead, but she was also excited. Besides, she had no choice. She had been promised in marriage to someone she had never even met, a young man from a nearby village who had already made the journey to America and who had found a most precious treasure, a job.

3   The small town of Compobasso was a very poor farming community in a poor country. Had she stayed in Compobasso, Mariana would have married a local boy, raised a family in the same house as his parents, and most likely never have traveled farther than Pescara, a city on the Adriatic coast. Her husband would have tried his best to scrabble out a living from the rocky soil, and her children would have done the same, as her family had done for over a thousand years.

4   The train ride across Italy to Naples was difficult. Although Francisco, her husband-to-be, had paid for Mariana's ticket on the ship, her parents had spent almost every cent they had on passage for her brother. Nicholas was only nine years old, but he was supposed to serve as her protector on the journey. The family had barely enough money left for two third-class train tickets to Naples. The two children sat on a hard bench for almost two days with dozens of other people, many of whom carried all their earthly possessions and who were making the same journey as Mariana and Nicholas. In addition, the third-class cars held farmers bringing their goods to market.

5   The children carried very few possessions themselves, some clothes, a photograph or two, and letters that would introduce them to people in America. Most of what they brought was food: cheese, dried fruit, bread, and sausage. They had no idea if anything would be available to eat on the train or the ship, and even if it was, they had only a few pennies to pay for it. Hour after hour they sat on the bench, swaying with the train, barely speaking, trying not to think of the family and friends they were leaving, perhaps forever. Both Mariana and Nicholas knew that going to America would open up a whole new life for them, but they were sad to be leaving the only life they had ever known.

6   When the train reached Naples early in the morning, they were tired and sore from the trip. They had no time to complain, however, because their ship would be leaving that afternoon. The children began the long walk from the railroad station to the dock, following the hundreds of other people doing exactly the same thing.

7   At the dock, Mariana and Nicholas stared at the ship. It was the hugest thing they had ever seen. They slowly made their way up the gangplank and handed the steward their tickets. As they did, they realized once the ship left the dock, they would never set foot in Italy again, never sit in the town square on a warm summer evening and sing the old songs, never see their family again.

Say It's time to stop. You have completed the Test Yourself lesson.

Check to see that the students have correctly filled in their answer circles. At this point, go over the answers with the students. Did they have enough time to complete the lesson? Did they remember to skim the passage and to look for key words in the questions? Did they take their best guess when they were unsure of the answer?

Work through any questions that caused difficulty. It may be helpful to discuss the strategies that students used to answer the comprehension items. You may also want to have the students identify the specific part of a passage that helped them find the right answer.

Have the students indicate completion of the lesson by entering their score for this activity on the progress chart at the beginning of the book.

Unit 2 Test Yourself: Reading Comprehension

18 In paragraph 4, what is the meaning of the word "passage"?
   J The trip to Naples
   K A brief story
   L The food the children carried
 * M The trip across the ocean

19 Why does the writer begin with a description of world affairs in 1914?
   A World events would play an important part in the story.
 * B They help the reader understand the time period in which the story is set.
   C They caused Mariana and her brother to leave their village.
   D The children were interested in what was happening.

20 How does the writer feel about his grandmother?
 * J He admires her for undertaking such a difficult journey.
   K He feels she gave up too much by leaving her village.
   L He wishes she had been more aware of world affairs.
   M He wishes she had stayed in her village in Italy.

21 In paragraph 3, what is the Adriatic?
   A A small town
   B A region of Italy
 * C A body of water
   D A large city on the coast

22 How did Mariana feel about marrying someone she had never met?
   J Unhappy and angry about having to leave her village
   K Happy to have the opportunity to take a trip on a boat
   L Disappointed because her brother had to go with her
 * M Willing to accept it because it was a tradition

23 In paragraph 2, why is a job called a "precious treasure"?
   A The job paid very well.
 * B Not many people in the village had jobs.
   C The job was in America.
   D Jobs were easier to find in Italy than in America.

24 Around 1914, it appears as if
 * J many other people were leaving Italy for America.
   K only a few people were leaving Italy for America.
   L the trip from Italy to America was easy and inexpensive.
   M farming in Italy was a good way to earn a living.

18 Answer rows 18 Ⓙ Ⓚ Ⓛ ●   20 ● Ⓚ Ⓛ Ⓜ   22 Ⓙ Ⓚ Ⓛ ●   24 ● Ⓚ Ⓛ Ⓜ
                 19 Ⓐ ● Ⓒ Ⓓ   21 Ⓐ Ⓑ ● Ⓓ   23 Ⓐ ● Ⓒ Ⓓ

Background

This unit contains three lessons that deal with spelling skills. Students are asked to identify a misspelled word in isolation.

• **In Lesson 3a,** students identify an incorrectly spelled word. Students work methodically, skim answer choices, take their best guess when they are unsure of the answer, and indicate that an item has no mistakes.

• **In Lesson 3b,** students identify an incorrectly spelled word. In addition to reviewing the test-taking skills introduced in Lesson 3a, students learn about eliminating answer choices.

• **In the Test Yourself lesson,** the spelling skills and test-taking skills introduced and used in Lessons 3a and 3b are reinforced and presented in a format that gives students the experience of taking an achievement test. Techniques for managing time effectively when taking a standardized test are reinforced.

Instructional Objectives

Lesson 3a **Spelling** Lesson 3b **Spelling**	Given four words, students identify which of the four is misspelled or indicates that there are no mistakes.
Test Yourself	Given questions similar to those in Lessons 3a and 3b, students utilize spelling skills and test-taking strategies on achievement test formats.

Lesson 3a
Spelling

Focus

Spelling Skill
- identifying spelling errors

Test-taking Skills
- working methodically
- skimming answer choices
- taking the best guess when unsure of the answer
- indicating that an item has no mistakes

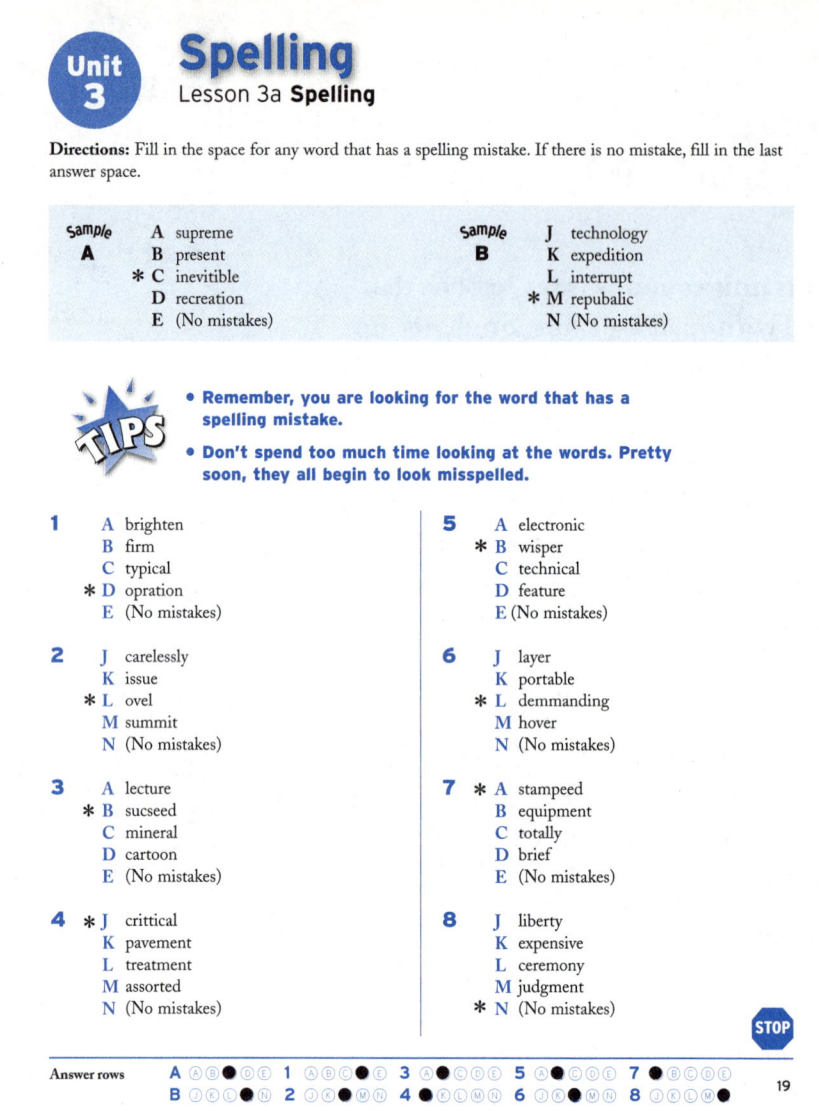

Samples A and B

Say Turn to Lesson 3a on page 19. In this lesson you will find misspelled words. Read the directions at the top of the page to yourself while I read them out loud.

Read the directions out loud to the students.

Say Let's look at Sample A. Look at the answer choices. Find the word that has a spelling mistake. If none of the words has a mistake, choose the last answer, *No mistakes*. Which answer did you choose? *(answer C, i-n-e-v-i-t-i-b-l-e)* Mark circle C for Sample A in the answer rows at the bottom of the page. Make sure the circle is completely filled in. Press your pencil firmly so that your mark comes out dark.

Check to see that the students have filled in the correct answer circle. Review the correct spelling of the word *inevitable*.

Say Do Sample B yourself. Find the word that has a spelling mistake. If none of the words has a mistake, choose the last answer. *(pause)* Which answer should you choose? *(answer M)* You should have marked answer M because r-e-p-u-b-a-l-i-c is an incorrect spelling. What should you do now? *(Mark the circle for answer M in the answer rows.)* Make sure the circle is completely filled in with a dark mark.

Check to see that the students have filled in the correct answer circle. Review the correct spelling of the word *republic*.

★TIPS

Say Now let's look at the tips.

Have a volunteer read the tips aloud.

Say Don't forget, you are looking for the word that is spelled wrong. Try to avoid spending too much time looking at the answer choices. This will waste time, and after a while, all the words may begin to look misspelled. If you can't figure out which word has a mistake, take your best guess.

Practice

Say Now we are ready for Practice. Do Numbers 1 through 8 in the same way that we did the samples. Work as quickly as you can, and if you aren't sure which word has a mistake, take your best guess. Don't forget, if all the words are spelled correctly, choose the last answer, No mistakes. Work until you come to the STOP sign at the bottom of the page. Remember to make sure that your answer circles are completely filled in with dark marks. Completely erase any marks for answers that you change. Any questions? Start working now.

Allow time for the students to mark their answers.

Say It's time to stop. You have finished Lesson 3a.

Review the answers with the students. If any items caused particular difficulty, work through each of the answer choices.

Have the students indicate completion of the lesson by entering their score for this activity on the progress chart at the beginning of the book.

Spelling
Lesson 3a **Spelling**

Directions: Fill in the space for any word that has a spelling mistake. If there is no mistake, fill in the last answer space.

Sample A			Sample B		
	A	supreme		J	technology
	B	present		K	expedition
∗	C	inevitible		L	interrupt
	D	recreation	∗	M	repubalic
	E	(No mistakes)		N	(No mistakes)

- Remember, you are looking for the word that has a spelling mistake.
- Don't spend too much time looking at the words. Pretty soon, they all begin to look misspelled.

1			5		
	A	brighten		A	electronic
	B	firm	∗	B	wisper
	C	typical		C	technical
∗	D	opration		D	feature
	E	(No mistakes)		E	(No mistakes)

2			6		
	J	carelessly		J	layer
	K	issue		K	portable
∗	L	ovel	∗	L	demmanding
	M	summit		M	hover
	N	(No mistakes)		N	(No mistakes)

3			7		
	A	lecture	∗	A	stampeed
∗	B	sucseed		B	equipment
	C	mineral		C	totally
	D	cartoon		D	brief
	E	(No mistakes)		E	(No mistakes)

4			8		
∗	J	crittical		J	liberty
	K	pavement		K	expensive
	L	treatment		L	ceremony
	M	assorted		M	judgment
	N	(No mistakes)	∗	N	(No mistakes)

Answer rows

Unit 3 Lesson 3a **Spelling**

Lesson 3b
Spelling

Focus

Spelling Skill
- identifying spelling errors

Test-taking Skills
- eliminating answer choices
- working methodically
- indicating that an item has no mistakes

Samples A and B

Say Turn to Lesson 3b on page 20. In this lesson, you will find misspelled words. Read the directions at the top of the page to yourself while I read them out loud.

Read the directions out loud to the students.

Say Find Sample A at the top of the page. Look at the answer choices. Find the word that has a spelling mistake. If none of the words has a mistake, choose the last answer. Which answer did you choose? *(answer D, s-t-u-m-b-l-e-i-n-g)* Mark circle D for Sample A in the answer rows at the bottom of the page. Make sure the circle is completely filled in. Press your pencil firmly so that your mark comes out dark.

Check to see that the students have filled in the correct answer circle. Review the correct spelling of the word *stumbling*.

Say Do Sample B yourself. Find the word that has a spelling mistake. If none of the words has a mistake, choose the last answer. *(pause)* Which answer should you choose? *(answer M, l-i-t-t-l-e-s-t)* What should you do now? *(Mark circle M.)* Yes, mark circle M for Sample B in the answer rows at the bottom of the page. Make sure the circle is completely filled in. Press your pencil firmly so that your mark comes out dark.

Check to see that the students have filled in the correct answer circle. Review the correct spelling of the word *littlest*.

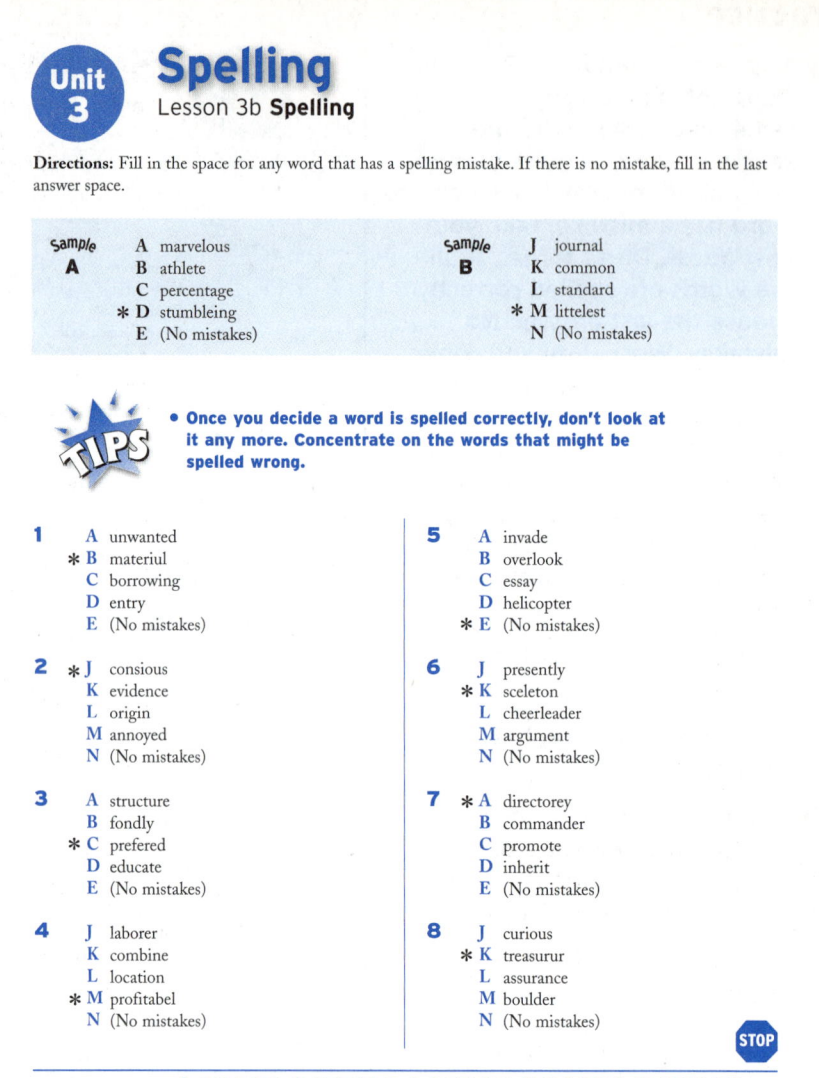

 TIPS

Say Now let's look at the tip.

Have a volunteer read the tip aloud.

Say Sometimes you will be sure a word is spelled correctly. When this happens, don't waste time looking at this word again. Focus on the other answer choices. This will save you time and will help you find the word with a spelling mistake.

26 Lesson 3b **Spelling**

Practice

Say Now we are ready for Practice. Do Numbers 1 through 8 in the same way that we did the samples. Work as quickly as you can and don't waste time looking at words you are sure are spelled correctly. Work until you come to the STOP sign at the bottom of the page. Remember to make sure that your answer circles are completely filled in with dark marks. Completely erase any marks for answers that you change. Any questions? Start working now.

Allow time for the students to mark their answers.

Say It's time to stop. You have finished Lesson 3b.

Review the answers with the students. If any items caused particular difficulty, work through each of the answer choices. Do an informal item analysis to determine which items were most difficult. Discuss with the students the words that gave them the most difficulty, including the misspelled words and the distractors that are spelled correctly and that the students identify as wrong.

Have the students indicate completion of the lesson by entering their score for this activity on the progress chart at the beginning of the book.

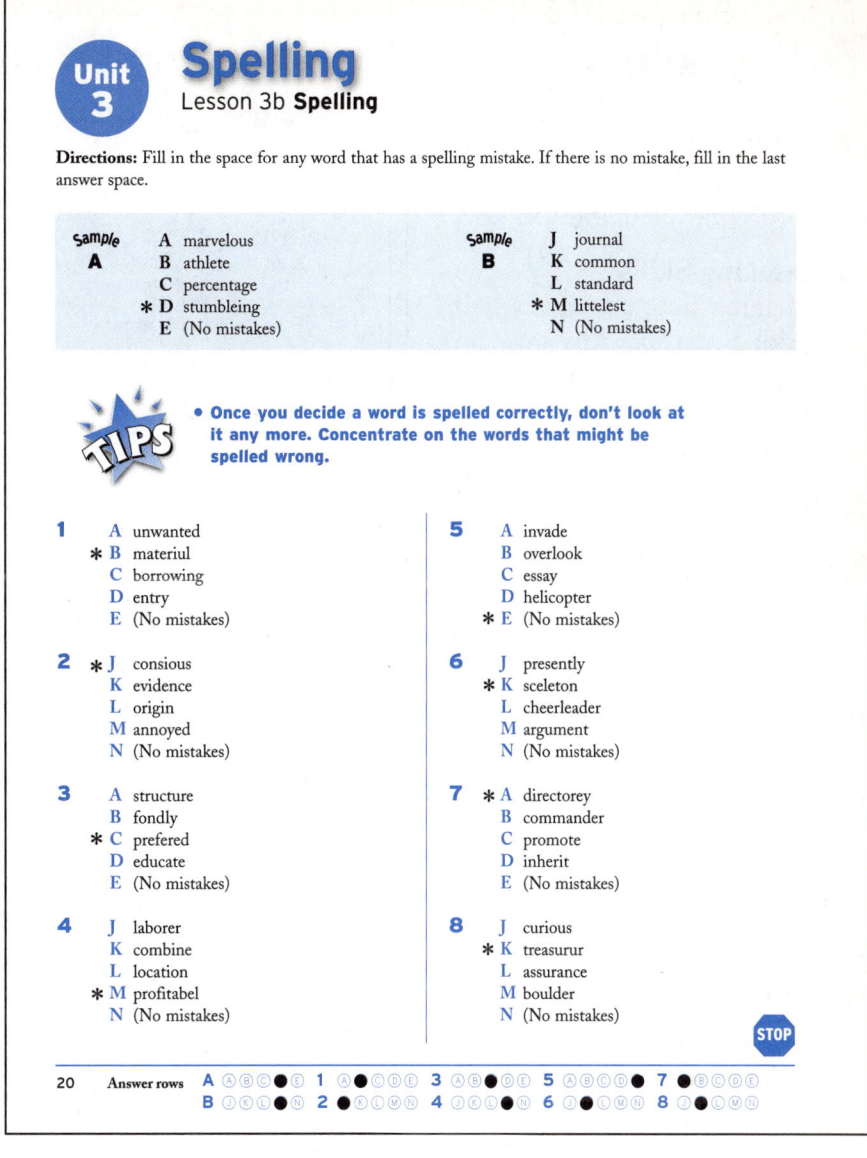

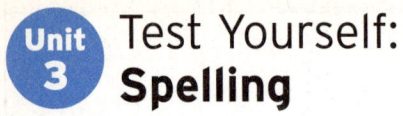

Unit 3 Test Yourself: Spelling

Focus

Spelling Skill
• identifying spelling errors

Test-taking Skills
• managing time effectively
• working methodically
• skimming answer choices
• taking the best guess when unsure of the answer
• indicating that an item has no mistakes
• eliminating answer choices

This lesson simulates an actual test-taking experience. Therefore, it is recommended that the directions be read verbatim and that the suggested procedures and time allowances be followed.

Directions

Administration Time: approximately 20 minutes

Say Turn to the Test Yourself lesson on page 21.

Point out to the students that this Test Yourself lesson is timed like a real test, but that they will score it themselves to see how well they are doing. Remind the students to work quickly and to mark the answer as soon as they are sure which word is misspelled.

Say This lesson will check how well you can find words with spelling errors. Remember to make sure that the circles for your answer choices are completely filled in. Press your pencil firmly so that your marks come out dark. Completely erase any answers that you change. Do not write anything except your answer choices in your books.

Look at the answer choices for Sample A. Find the answer choice that has a spelling error. If there is no error, choose the last answer choice. Mark the circle for your answer.

Allow time for the students to mark their answers.

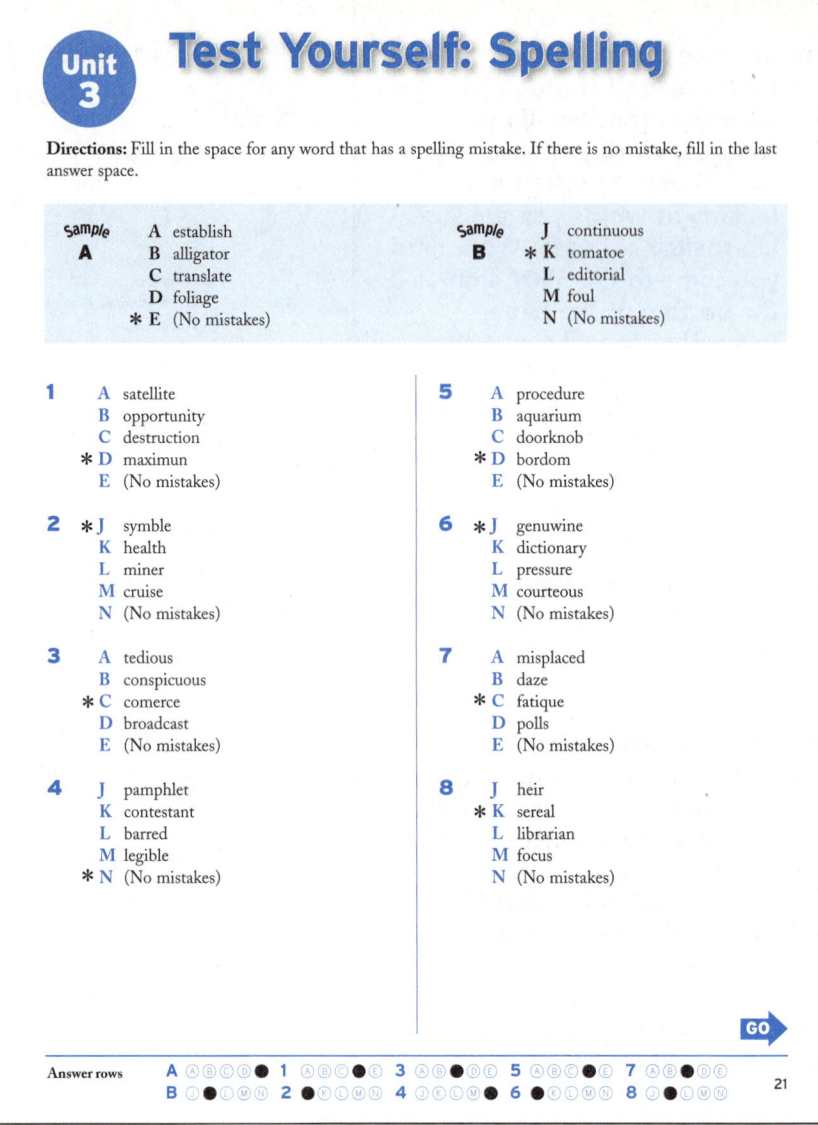

Say You should have filled in the circle for answer E because none of the words has a spelling error. If you chose another answer, erase yours and fill in circle E now.

Check to see that the students have correctly marked their answer circles for Sample A.

Say Do Sample B yourself. Mark the circle for the answer choice that has a spelling mistake. If there is no error, choose the last answer choice. Mark the circle for your answer.

Allow time for the students to fill in their answers.

Say The circle for answer K should have been marked because it is the incorrect spelling of *t-o-m-a-t-o*. If you chose another answer, erase yours and fill in circle K now.

Check to see that the students have correctly marked their answer circles for Sample B.

28 Unit 3 Test Yourself Spelling

Say Now you will do Numbers 1 through 18 in the same way that we did the samples. When you come to the GO sign at the bottom of the page, turn the page and continue working. Work until you come to the STOP sign at the bottom of page 22. When you have finished, you can check your answers to this lesson. Then wait for the rest of the group to finish. Any questions? You will have 15 minutes. Begin working now.

Allow 15 minutes.

Say It's time to stop. You have completed the Test Yourself lesson. Check to see that you have completely filled in your answer circles with dark marks. Make sure that any marks for answers that you changed have been completely erased.

Go over the lesson with the students. Ask them whether they had enough time to finish the lesson. Ask for volunteers to identify the spelling errors in each item.

Work through any questions that caused difficulty. Discuss any rules the students used to determine whether or not a word is spelled correctly. If necessary, provide additional practice questions similar to the ones in this unit.

Have the students indicate completion of the lesson by entering their score for this activity on the progress chart at the beginning of the book.

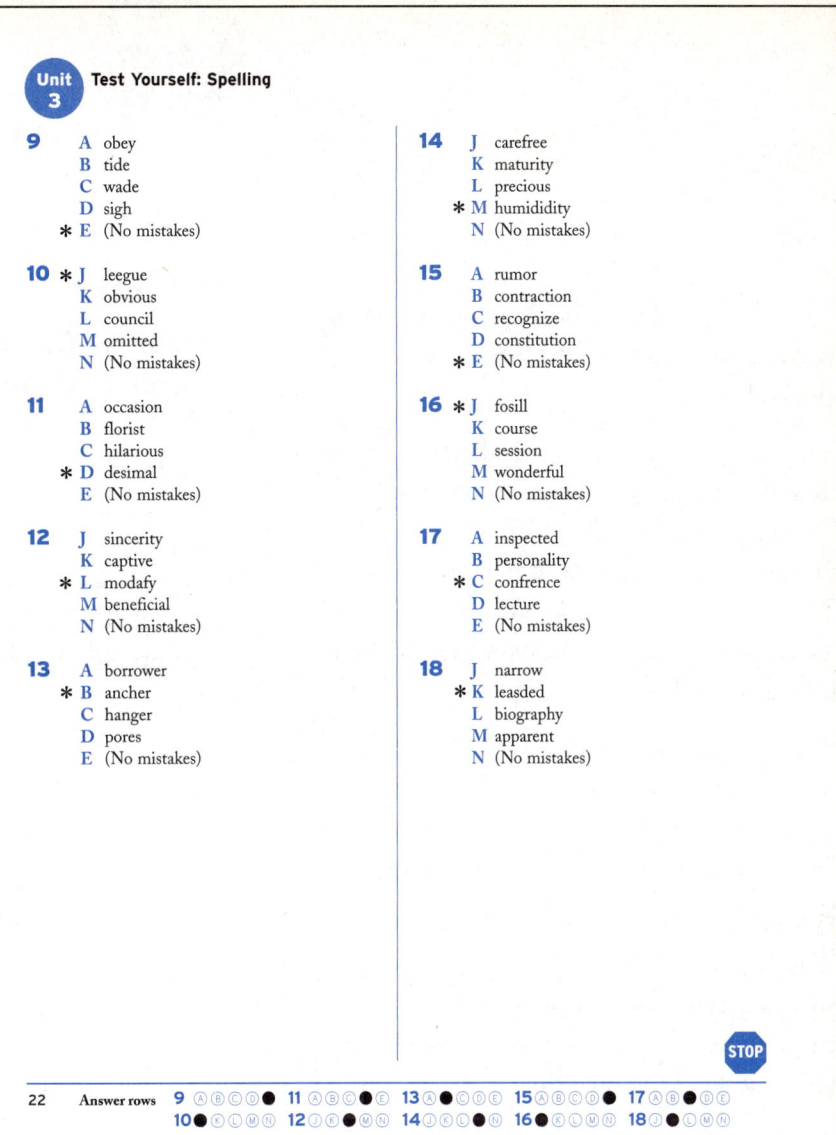

Background

This unit contains five lessons that deal with capitalization and punctuation skills.

• **In Lessons 4a and 4b,** students identify mistakes in capitalization in written text. Students work methodically and practice understanding unusual item formats. They also recall error types, analyze answer choices, and indicate that an item has no mistakes.

• **In Lessons 5a and 5b,** students identify mistakes in punctuation in written text. In addition to reviewing the test-taking skills introduced in the two previous lessons, students learn the importance of skimming answer choices.

• **In the Test Yourself lesson,** the capitalization and punctuation skills and test-taking skills introduced in Lessons 4a through 5b are reinforced and presented in a format that gives students the experience of taking an achievement test. Techniques for managing time effectively when taking a standardized test are reinforced.

Instructional Objectives

Lesson 4a **Capitalization** Lesson 4b **Capitalization**	Given text that is divided into three parts, students identify which part has a capitalization mistake or indicates that there is no mistake.
Lesson 5a **Punctuation** Lesson 5b **Punctuation**	Given text that is divided into three parts, students identify which part has a punctuation mistake or indicates that there is no mistake.
Test Yourself	Given questions similar to those in Lessons 4a through 5b, students utilize capitalization, punctuation, and test-taking strategies on achievement test formats.

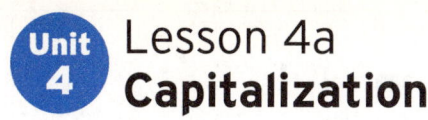

Unit 4 — Lesson 4a Capitalization

Focus

Language Skill
- identifying capitalization errors

Test-taking Skills
- working methodically
- understanding unusual item formats
- recalling error types
- indicating that an item has no mistakes

Samples A and B

Say Turn to Lesson 4a on page 23. In this lesson, you will look for capitalization in sentences. Read the directions at the top of the page to yourself while I read them out loud.

Read the directions out loud to the students.

Say Let's begin with Sample A. It is a sentence divided into three parts. You are to find the part that has a mistake in capitalization. If there is no mistake, choose the last answer, *No mistakes*. Read the answer choices to yourself. Does one of them have a mistake in capitalization? *(yes, answer A)* Answer A has a mistake because *Senator* should begin with a capital letter. Fill in circle A for Sample A in the answer rows at the bottom of the page. Check to make sure your answer circle is completely filled in with a dark mark.

Check to see that the students have filled in the correct answer circle.

Say Do Sample B yourself. Mark the circle for the answer choice that has a capitalization mistake. If there is no error, choose the last answer choice. Mark the circle for your answer.

Allow time for the students to fill in their answers.

Say You should have filled in the circle for answer L. The word *circle* should not be capitalized. If you chose another answer, erase yours and fill in circle L now.

Capitalization and Punctuation

Lesson 4a Capitalization

Directions: Fill in the space for the answer that has a mistake in capitalization. Fill in the last answer space if there is no mistake.

 ✱ A   When senator Garvey came to
 B   our town, she spent several hours
 C   meeting with students in the library.
 D   (No mistakes)

 J   Planes going from the United
 K   States to Japan fly in a great
 ✱ L   Circle across the Pacific Ocean.
 M   (No mistakes)

- Remember, you are looking for the answer that has a mistake in capitalization.
- The first word in a sentence and proper nouns should be capitalized. Look carefully for these words.

1
 A   Many customs found in the U.S.,
 B   Canada, Latin America, and Australia
 ✱ C   came from the european continent.
 D   (No mistakes)

2
 J   The California gold rush was
 K   triggered by one man in 1848.
 ✱ L   his name was James Marshall.
 M   (No mistakes)

3
 A   As part of a city awareness program,
 B   the students from Jackson High School
 ✱ C   collected trash in pioneer square.
 D   (No mistakes)

4 ✱ J   Our town holds a giant Barbeque
 K   in Hasselhoff Park every June.
 L   It's become a summer tradition.
 M   (No mistakes)

5
 A   The seven-day week comes from
 ✱ B   the jewish custom of observing
 C   a day of rest every seven days.
 D   (No mistakes)

6
 J   The United States Army ran a
 K   popular advertising campaign with
 L   the phrase "Be all that you can be."
 ✱ M   (No mistakes)

7
 A   In 1826, Thomas Telford
 B   built a suspension bridge over
 ✱ C   the Menai straits in Wales.
 D   (No mistakes)

8
 J   If you look at my skin,
 K   you won't have to ask why
 ✱ L   my family calls me freckles.
 M   (No mistakes)

Answer rows A ●BCD   1 AB●D   3 AB●D   5 A●CD   7 AB●D
             B JKL●   2 JK●M   4 ●KLM   6 JKL●   8 JK●M

Check to see that the students have filled in the correct answer circle.

★**TIPS**

Say Now let's look at the tips.

Have a volunteer read the tips aloud.

Say The best way to find capitalization mistakes is to look at the answer choices word by word. Be sure the first word in a sentence and important words in a sentence are capitalized. And don't forget, sometimes the mistake will be a word that begins with a capital letter when it should not.

Discuss with the students the different kinds of words that should begin with a capital letter.

Unit 4 Lesson 4a Capitalization   31

Practice

Say Now you will do the Practice items. Remember to look carefully at all the answer choices for a capitalization mistake. Make sure you fill in the circles in the answer rows with dark marks. Do not write anything except your answer choices in your books. Completely erase any marks for answers that you change. Work until you come to the STOP sign at the bottom of the page. Any questions? Start working now.

Allow time for the students to fill in their answers.

Say It's time to stop. You have finished Lesson 4a.

Review the answers with the students. It will be helpful to discuss the errors in the items and the capitalization rules with which the errors are associated. If any questions caused particular difficulty, work through each of the answer choices.

Have the students indicate completion of the lesson by entering their score for this activity on the progress chart at the beginning of the book.

 Unit 4 Capitalization and Punctuation

Lesson 4a **Capitalization**

Directions: Fill in the space for the answer that has a mistake in capitalization. Fill in the last answer space if there is no mistake.

Sample A
* A When senator Garvey came to
  B our town, she spent several hours
  C meeting with students in the library.
  D (No mistakes)

Sample B
  J Planes going from the United
  K States to Japan fly in a great
* L Circle across the Pacific Ocean.
  M (No mistakes)

- Remember, you are looking for the answer that has a mistake in capitalization.
- The first word in a sentence and proper nouns should be capitalized. Look carefully for these words.

1. A Many customs found in the U.S.,
    B Canada, Latin America, and Australia
  * C came from the european continent.
    D (No mistakes)

2. J The California gold rush was
    K triggered by one man in 1848.
  * L his name was James Marshall.
    M (No mistakes)

3. A As part of a city awareness program,
    B the students from Jackson High School
  * C collected trash in pioneer square.
    D (No mistakes)

4. * J Our town holds a giant Barbeque
    K in Hasselhoff Park every June.
    L It's become a summer tradition.
    M (No mistakes)

5. A The seven-day week comes from
  * B the jewish custom of observing
    C a day of rest every seven days.
    D (No mistakes)

6. J The United States Army ran a
    K popular advertising campaign with
    L the phrase "Be all that you can be."
  * M (No mistakes)

7. A In 1826, Thomas Telford
    B built a suspension bridge over
  * C the Menai straits in Wales.
    D (No mistakes)

8. J If you look at my skin,
    K you won't have to ask why
  * L my family calls me freckles.
    M (No mistakes)

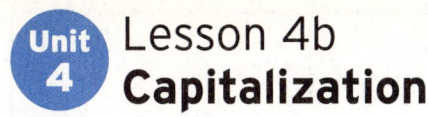

Lesson 4b
Capitalization

Focus

Language Skill
- identifying capitalization errors

Test-taking Skills
- working methodically
- understanding unusual item formats
- analyzing answer choices
- indicating that an item has no mistakes

Samples A and B

Say Turn to Lesson 4b on page 24. This is another lesson about capitalization. Read the directions at the top of the page to yourself while I read them out loud.

Read the directions out loud to the students.

Say Let's do Sample A. It is one sentence divided into three parts. You are to find the part that has a mistake in capitalization. If there is no mistake, choose the last answer, *No mistakes*. Does one of the answer choices have a mistake in capitalization? *(yes, answer A)* Answer A has a mistake. The word *Life* should begin with a capital letter because it is part of the title of a book. Fill in circle A for Sample A in the answer rows at the bottom of the page. Check to make sure your answer circle is completely filled in with a dark mark.

Check to see that the students have filled in the correct answer circle.

Say Do Sample B yourself. Mark the circle for the answer choice that has a capitalization mistake. If there is no error, choose the last answer choice. Mark the circle for your answer. *(pause)* You should have filled in the circle for answer K because the organization name *American Civil Liberties Union* should be capitalized. If you chose another answer, erase yours and fill in circle K now.

Capitalization and Punctuation

Lesson 4b **Capitalization**

Directions: Fill in the space for the answer that has a mistake in capitalization. Fill in the last answer space if there is no mistake.

| Sample A | * A In the biography *Appetite for life*,
B readers discover that Julia Child had
C no idea she would become a chef.
D (No mistakes) | Sample B | J With about 300,000 members,
* K the american civil liberties union is
L headquartered in New York City.
M (No mistakes) |

 • Read each answer word by word. Look for the names of important people, places, and things.

1 A Shikibu Murasaki, also called
  * B lady Murasaki, is a well-known
    C writer of early Japanese literature.
    D (No mistakes)

2 J Felice and her friends would be
   K leaving their city lives behind for a
  * L hike in the Mountains near Denver.
    M (No mistakes)

3 * A The Civil war, which lasted from
   B 1861 to 1865, took more American
   C lives than any other war in history.
   D (No mistakes)

4 J With homes located between the
  * K north and the south, people in
    L Delaware were divided during the war.
    M (No mistakes)

5 * A The league of nations was
   B formed to maintain peace
   C amoung nations of the world.
   D (No mistakes)

6 J Badminton was brought to England
   K by British officials who, while living
   L in India, had grown fond of the game.
  * M (No mistakes)

7 * A The upper west side consists mostly
   B of apartment houses, hotels, and
   C long blocks of brick row homes.
   D (No mistakes)

8 * J Ford Motor company, organized by
   K Henry Ford in 1903, is one of the
   L largest manufacturers of automobiles.
   M (No mistakes)

24 Answer rows

Check to see that the students have filled in the correct answer circle.

Say Now let's look at the tip.

Have a volunteer read the tip aloud.

Say In order to find a capitalization mistake, you should look at the answer choices word by word. Be sure the first word in a sentence is capitalized and that the proper nouns inside the sentence begin with capital letters.

Practice

Say Now you will do the Practice items. Remember to look carefully at each word for a capitalization mistake. Make sure you fill in the circles in the answer rows with dark marks. Do not write anything except your answer choices in your books. Completely erase any marks for answers that you change. Work until you come to the STOP sign at the bottom of the page. Any questions? Start working now.

Allow time for the students to fill in their answers.

Say It's time to stop. You have finished Lesson 4b.

Review the answers with the students. It will be helpful to discuss the errors in the items and the rules for capitalization. If any questions caused particular difficulty, work through each of the answer choices.

Have the students indicate completion of the lesson by entering their score for this activity on the progress chart at the beginning of the book.

 Unit 4 Capitalization and Punctuation

Lesson 4b **Capitalization**

Directions: Fill in the space for the answer that has a mistake in capitalization. Fill in the last answer space if there is no mistake.

 Sample A
* A   In the biography *Appetite for life*,
  B   readers discover that Julia Child had
  C   no idea she would become a chef.
  D   (No mistakes)

 Sample B
  J   With about 300,000 members,
* K   the american civil liberties union is
  L   headquartered in New York City.
  M   (No mistakes)

 TIPS • Read each answer word by word. Look for the names of important people, places, and things.

1   A   Shikibu Murasaki, also called
  * B   lady Murasaki, is a well-known
    C   writer of early Japanese literature.
    D   (No mistakes)

2   J   Felice and her friends would be
    K   leaving their city lives behind for a
  * L   hike in the Mountains near Denver.
    M   (No mistakes)

3 * A   The Civil war, which lasted from
    B   1861 to 1865, took more American
    C   lives than any other war in history.
    D   (No mistakes)

4   J   With homes located between the
  * K   north and the south, people in
    L   Delaware were divided during the war.
    M   (No mistakes)

5 * A   The league of nations was
    B   formed to maintain peace
    C   amoung nations of the world.
    D   (No mistakes)

6   J   Badminton was brought to England
    K   by British officials who, while living
    L   in India, had grown fond of the game.
  * M   (No mistakes)

7 * A   The upper west side consists mostly
    B   of apartment houses, hotels, and
    C   long blocks of brick row homes.
    D   (No mistakes)

8 * J   Ford Motor company, organized by
    K   Henry Ford in 1903, is one of the
    L   largest manufacturers of automobiles.
    M   (No mistakes)

 STOP

24   Answer rows   A ●ⒷⒸⒹ 1 Ⓐ●ⒸⒹ 3 ●ⒷⒸⒹ 5 ●ⒷⒸⒹ 7 ●ⒷⒸⒹ
                  B ⒿⓀ●Ⓜ 2 ⒿⓀ●Ⓜ 4 Ⓙ●ⓁⓂ 6 ⒿⓀⓁ● 8 ●ⓀⓁⓂ

Lesson 4b **Capitalization**

Lesson 5a
Punctuation

Focus

Language Skill
- identifying punctuation errors

Test-taking Skills
- working methodically
- understanding unusual item formats
- using context to find an answer
- analyzing answer choices
- indicating that an item has no mistakes

Samples A and B

Say Turn to Lesson 5a on page 25. In this lesson, you will look for punctuation mistakes. Read the directions at the top of the page to yourself while I read them out loud.

Read the directions out loud to the students.

Say Let's begin with Sample A. It is two sentences divided into three parts. You are to find the part that has a mistake in punctuation. If there is no mistake, choose the last answer. Read the answer choices to yourself. Does one of them have a mistake in punctuation? *(yes, the second one)* The second answer has a mistake because there should be an apostrophe in the word *he'd*. Fill in circle B for Sample A in the answer rows at the bottom of the page. Check to make sure your answer circle is completely filled in with a dark mark.

Check to see that the students have filled in the correct answer circle.

Say Now do Sample B yourself. Read the answer choices and look for a mistake in punctuation. Choose the last answer if the punctuation is correct. *(pause)* Which answer did you choose? *(answer K)* A period is needed after the word *month* because it is the end of a sentence. Fill in circle K for Sample B in the answer rows at the bottom of the page. Check to make sure that answer circle K is completely filled in with a dark mark.

Capitalization and Punctuation

Lesson 5a **Punctuation**

Directions: Fill in the space for the answer that has a mistake in punctuation. Fill in the last answer space if there is no mistake.

| Sample A | A
* B
C
D | Zenobia told her friend Stephen
that hed better be prepared to play
his best tennis that afternoon.
(No mistakes) | Sample B | J
* K
L
M | Our final project took me more
than a month Melanie finished
her project in about six weeks.
(No mistakes) |

- Read each answer choice word by word. Look for places in each answer that need punctuation.
- Pay attention to the meaning of the answers. This will help you decide where punctuation is needed.

1 * A Books magazines and papers
B are piled on my father's desk. I
C don't know how he finds anything.
D (No mistakes)

2 J It is amazing how builders can
K construct a huge skyscraper in the
L very center of a crowded city.
* M (No mistakes)

3 * A Nylon a tough elastic substance
B can be formed into many shapes but is
C used primarily for fibers and fabrics.
D (No mistakes)

4 J Ninety crew members were on the
* K Nina the Pinta and the Santa Maria
L during the first voyage of Columbus.
M (No mistakes)

5 A When she was twelve years old,
* B Vera my next door neighbor moved
C to Paris to live with her grandparents.
D (No mistakes)

6 J At the web site, we learned that the
* K company had three goals expanding,
L educating, and exploring the mind.
M (No mistakes)

Answer rows A ⓐ●ⓒⓓ 1 ●ⓑⓒⓓ 3 ●ⓑⓒⓓ 5 ⓐ●ⓒⓓ
B ⓙ●ⓛⓜ 2 ⓙⓚⓛ● 4 ⓙ●ⓛⓜ 6 ⓙ●ⓛⓜ

25

Check to see that the students have filled in the correct answer circle.

★**TIPS**

Say Now let's look at the tips.

Have a volunteer read the tips aloud.

Say One of the most important things you can do to find punctuation mistakes is to read each answer choice word by word. Think about what the answer choice means and use this meaning to find the answer.

Discuss with the students the errors in the sample items and how it would be easy to miss them if you didn't read each answer carefully and use their meaning to decide where punctuation was needed.

Unit 4 Lesson 5a **Punctuation** 35

Practice

Say Now you will do some Practice items. Remember to look at the answer choices word by word. Use the meaning of the sentence to find the answer. Make sure you fill in the circles in the answer rows with dark marks. Do not write anything except your answer choices in your books. Completely erase any marks for answers that you change. Work until you come to the STOP sign at the bottom of the page. Any questions? Start working now.

Allow time for the students to fill in their answers.

Say It's time to stop. You have finished Lesson 5a.

Review the answers with the students. It will be helpful to discuss the punctuation errors in the items. If any questions caused particular difficulty, work through each of the answer choices.

Have the students indicate completion of the lesson by entering their score for this activity on the progress chart at the beginning of the book.

 Unit 4 **Capitalization and Punctuation**
Lesson 5a **Punctuation**

Directions: Fill in the space for the answer that has a mistake in punctuation. Fill in the last answer space if there is no mistake.

 Sample A
   A   Zenobia told her friend Stephen
∗ B   that hed better be prepared to play
   C   his best tennis that afternoon.
   D   (No mistakes)

 Sample B
   J   Our final project took me more
∗ K   than a month Melanie finished
   L   her project in about six weeks.
   M   (No mistakes)

 TIPS
- Read each answer choice word by word. Look for places in each answer that need punctuation.
- Pay attention to the meaning of the answers. This will help you decide where punctuation is needed.

1 ∗ A   Books magazines and papers
   B   are piled on my father's desk. I
   C   don't know how he finds anything.
   D   (No mistakes)

2   J   It is amazing how builders can
   K   construct a huge skyscraper in the
   L   very center of a crowded city.
∗ M   (No mistakes)

3 ∗ A   Nylon a tough elastic substance
   B   can be formed into many shapes but is
   C   used primarily for fibers and fabrics.
   D   (No mistakes)

4   J   Ninety crew members were on the
∗ K   Nina the Pinta and the Santa Maria
   L   during the first voyage of Columbus.
   M   (No mistakes)

5   A   When she was twelve years old,
∗ B   Vera my next door neighbor moved
   C   to Paris to live with her grandparents.
   D   (No mistakes)

6   J   At the web site, we learned that the
∗ K   company had three goals expanding,
   L   educating, and exploring the mind.
   M   (No mistakes)

Answer rows A ● B C D   1 A ● C D   3 ● B C D   5 A ● C D
                        B J ● L M   2 J K L ●   4 J ● L M   6 J ● L M

25

Lesson 5b
Punctuation

Focus

Language Skill
- identifying punctuation errors

Test-taking Skills
- working methodically
- skimming answer choices
- understanding unusual item formats
- indicating that an item has no mistakes
- working methodically

Samples A and B

Say Turn to Lesson 5b on page 26. In this lesson you will look for punctuation mistakes in sentences. Read the directions at the top of the page to yourself while I read them out loud.

Read the directions out loud to the students.

Say Find Sample A at the top of the page. Read the answer choices and look for a mistake in punctuation. Choose the last answer if the punctuation is correct. *(pause)* Which answer did you choose? *(answer A)* There should be a comma after the word *me*. Fill in circle A for Sample A in the answer rows at the bottom of the page. Check to make sure that answer circle A is completely filled in with a dark mark.

Check to see that the students have filled in the correct answer circle.

Say Now do Sample B yourself. Fill in the space for the answer that has a mistake in punctuation. Choose the last answer if the punctuation is correct. *(pause)* Answer J has a mistake because the question mark should be a comma. Fill in circle J for Sample B in the answer rows at the bottom of the page. Make sure your answer circle is completely filled in with a dark mark.

Capitalization and Punctuation
Lesson 5b Punctuation

Directions: Fill in the space for the answer that has a mistake in punctuation. Fill in the last answer space if there is no mistake.

Sample A
* A "Trust me I wouldn't ask you to
  B do something that I would not feel
  C comfortable doing myself," said Bret.
  D (No mistakes)

Sample B
* J "What a great idea?" said Lise.
  K "I'll put my swimming suit on and
  L grab a towel. Then we can go."
  M (No mistakes)

- Skim each answer choice in an item. This will help you understand the meaning. Then go back and read the answer choices more carefully.

1. A Early umbrellas were made out
   * B of wood and oilcloth; which helped
   C them repel the rain and moisture.
   D (No mistakes)

2. * J After visiting the Grand Canyon
   K Ben finally had an idea of how big
   L and how spectacular the landmark is.
   M (No mistakes)

3. * A What's in a name? Some say a lot
   B People in Israel, India, and Africa still
   C give names with special meanings.
   D (No mistakes)

4. * J Kansas City the Heart of America
   K lies almost in the center of the country.
   L Its location has shaped its character.
   M (No mistakes)

5. A The influence of Louisiana's early
   B French and Spanish settlers is
   C especially noticeable in New Orleans.
   * D (No mistakes)

6. J A spotted skunk's diet consists
   * K of caterpillars and such "insects" as
   L beetles, crickets, and grasshoppers.
   M (No mistakes)

7. A The Taylor family had been on the
   B road for only a few minutes when the
   * C boys started to ask, Are we almost there?
   D (No mistakes)

8. J The activity known as letterboxing
   K is well known in England, but it
   * L hasnt spread to many other countries.
   M (No mistakes)

STOP

26 Answer rows
A ●BCD   1 A●CD   3 ●BCD   5 ABC●   7 AB●D
B ●KLM   2 ●KLM   4 ●KLM   6 J●LM   8 JK●M

Check to see that the students have filled in the correct answer circle.

 TIPS

Say Now let's look at the tip.

Have a volunteer read the tip aloud.

Say It is a good idea to skim the answer choices first. This will help you understand their meaning. Then you should go back and look at each answer choice more carefully so you can find the punctuation mistake.

Practice

Say Now you will do some Practice items. Remember to look carefully at all the answer choices. Skim the answer choices and then go back and read them more carefully. Make sure you fill in the circles in the answer rows with dark marks. Do not write anything except your answer choices in your books. Completely erase any marks for answers that you change. Work until you come to the STOP sign at the bottom of the page. Any questions? Start working now.

Allow time for the students to fill in their answers.

Say It's time to stop. You have finished Lesson 5b.

Review the answers with the students. It will be helpful to discuss the punctuation errors in the items. If any questions caused particular difficulty, work through each of the answer choices.

Have the students indicate completion of the lesson by entering their score for this activity on the progress chart at the beginning of the book.

Capitalization and Punctuation

Lesson 5b Punctuation

Directions: Fill in the space for the answer that has a mistake in punctuation. Fill in the last answer space if there is no mistake.

Sample A	* A	"Trust me I wouldn't ask you to	Sample B	* J	"What a great idea?" said Lise.
	B	do something that I would not		K	"I'll put my swimming suit on and
		feel		L	grab a towel. Then we can go."
	C	comfortable doing myself," said		M	(No mistakes)
		Bret.			
	D	(No mistakes)			

 • Skim each answer choice in an item. This will help you understand the meaning. Then go back and read the answer choices more carefully.

1 A Early umbrellas were made out
 * B of wood and oilcloth; which helped
   C them repel the rain and moisture.
   D (No mistakes)

2 * J After visiting the Grand Canyon
   K Ben finally had an idea of how big
   L and how spectacular the landmark is.
   M (No mistakes)

3 * A What's in a name? Some say a lot
   B People in Israel, India, and Africa still
   C give names with special meanings.
   D (No mistakes)

4 * J Kansas City the Heart of America
   K lies almost in the center of the country.
   L Its location has shaped its character.
   M (No mistakes)

5 A The influence of Louisiana's early
   B French and Spanish settlers is
   C especially noticeable in New Orleans.
 * D (No mistakes)

6 J A spotted skunk's diet consists
 * K of caterpillars and such "insects" as
   L beetles, crickets, and grasshoppers.
   M (No mistakes)

7 A The Taylor family had been on the
   B road for only a few minutes when the
 * C boys started to ask, Are we almost there?
   D (No mistakes)

8 J The activity known as letterboxing
   K is well known in England, but it
 * L hasnt spread to many other countries.
   M (No mistakes)

26 Answer rows   A   1   3  5   7
                  B 2 4 6 8

38 Unit 4 Lesson 5b Punctuation

Unit 4 Test Yourself: Capitalization and Punctuation

Focus

Language Skills
- identifying capitalization errors
- identifying punctuation errors

Test-taking Skills
- managing time effectively
- following printed directions
- working methodically
- understanding unusual item formats
- recalling error types
- indicating that an item has no mistakes
- analyzing answer choices
- using context to find an answer
- analyzing answer choices
- skimming answer choices

This lesson simulates an actual test-taking experience. Therefore, it is recommended that the directions be read verbatim and the suggested procedures and time allowances be followed.

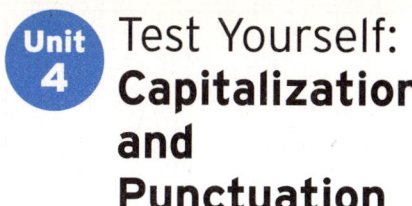

Unit 4 Test Yourself: Capitalization and Punctuation

Directions: Fill in the space for the answer that has a mistake in capitalization or punctuation. Fill in the last answer space if there is no mistake.

Sample A
- A My uncle was in the navy for
- B twenty years. He served on
- *C the aircraft carrier *enterprise*.
- D (No mistakes)

Sample B
- J Before we went to the amusement
- K park, Ms. Lincoln asked, "Did you
- *L remember your permission slips"
- M (No mistakes)

Directions: For numbers 1–8, fill in the space for the answer that has a mistake in capitalization. Fill in the last answer space if there is no mistake.

1
- A Two of my friends recently rode
- *B their bikes on the Santa Fe trail
- C from New Mexico to Kansas.
- D (No mistakes)

2
- J The water for our town comes from
- K a lake fifty miles away. The pipe
- L from the lake is about ten feet wide.
- *M (No mistakes)

3
- A It seems like science fiction,
- *B but an expedition to mars is
- C being planned for the near future.
- D (No mistakes)

4
- J "This project will be fun," insisted
- K our teacher. He smiled at us and said,
- *L "we are going to study pizza science."
- M (No mistakes)

5
- A The Middle Ages was the time
- B period before the Renaissance. It
- C is sometimes called the Dark Ages.
- *D (No mistakes)

6
- *J The U.S. department of defense
- K maintains a school system overseas
- L for children of military families.
- M (No mistakes)

7
- A The test is on Friday, but I
- B want to start studying now. Do
- C you want to study with me?
- *D (No mistakes)

8
- *J The Hotel's staff was wonderful.
- K They did everything possible to
- L make our stay in London enjoyable.
- M (No mistakes)

GO →

Directions

Administration Time: approximately 20 minutes

Say Turn to the Test Yourself lesson on page 27.

Point out to the students that this Test Yourself lesson is timed like a real test, but that they will score it themselves to see how well they are doing. Remind the students to pace themselves and to check the clock after they have finished the capitalization items to see how much time is left. This is about the halfway point in the lesson. Encourage the students to avoid spending too much time on any one item and to take their best guess if they are unsure of the answer.

Say There are two types of items in the Test Yourself lesson, so you will have to read the directions for each section and pay close attention to what you are doing. Remember to make sure that the circles in the answer rows are completely filled in. Press your pencil firmly so that your marks come out dark. Completely erase any marks for answers that you change. Do not write anything except your answer choices in your books.

Look at Sample A and listen carefully. Read the answer choices to yourself. Mark the circle for the answer that has a mistake in capitalization. Choose the last answer, *No mistakes*, if none of the answer choices has a mistake. Mark the circle for your answer.

Allow time for the students to fill in their answers.

Say The circle for answer C should be filled in because the name of the ship *Enterprise* should be capitalized. If you chose another answer, erase yours and fill in the circle for answer C now.

Check to see that the students have filled in the correct answer circle.

Say Now do Sample B. Read the answer choices to yourself. Mark the circle for the answer that has a mistake in punctuation. Choose the last answer, *No mistakes*, if none of the answer choices has a mistake in punctuation. Mark the circle for your answer.

Allow time for the students to fill in their answers.

Say The circle for answer L should be filled in. There should be a question mark after the word *slips*. If you chose another answer, erase yours and fill in the circle for answer L now.

Check to see that the students have filled in the correct answer circle.

Say Now you will do more items. Read the directions for each section. When you come to the GO sign at the bottom of the page, turn the page and continue working. Work until you come to the STOP sign on page 28. If you are not sure of an answer, fill in the circle for the answer you think might be right. Do you have any questions?

Answer any questions that the students have.

Say You may begin working. You will have 15 minutes.

Allow 15 minutes.

Say It's time to stop. You have finished the Test Yourself lesson. Check to see that you have completely filled in your answer circles with dark marks. Make sure that any marks for answers that you changed have been completely erased.

Unit 4 — Test Yourself: Capitalization and Punctuation

Directions: For numbers 9–18, fill in the space for the answer that has a mistake in punctuation. Fill in the last answer space if there is no mistake.

9   A   *A Hog on Ice*, written by Charles
   ∗B   Funk is a book about the origins of
     C   curious expressions and sayings.
     D   (No mistakes)

10   J   Shel Silverstein wrote popular
   ∗K   children's books but his work has a
     L   certain appeal for adults as well.
     M   (No mistakes)

11   A   "You paid full price for this book?"
     B   I said, shaking my head. "That's a
   ∗C   shame. Lilliana got her's on sale."
     D   (No mistakes)

12   J   In the 1970s, a popular fast-food
     K   company advertised with a song that
   ∗L   told its customers "Have it your way."
     M   (No mistakes)

13   A   When my sister started her new
     B   job, she discovered that she had to
   ∗C   pay federal state and local taxes.
     D   (No mistakes)

14   J   When I answered the phone,
     K   a familiar voice asked, "I'll bet
   ∗L   you cant guess who this is."
     M   (No mistakes)

15   A   The roadrunner, an unusual-
     B   looking bird, eats things like
     C   snakes, scorpions, and spiders.
   ∗D   (No mistakes)

16   J   The old car needed a lot of costly
   ∗K   repairs a new engine, a complete
     L   paint job, and a new interior.
     M   (No mistakes)

17 ∗A   Several pair's of shoes were on
     B   the floor. My mother asked us to
     C   pick them up before we went to bed.
     D   (No mistakes)

18   J   "You can't be serious about
   ∗K   getting up that early, laughed
     L   Onay. "We'll never be able to do it."
     M   (No mistakes)

28 Answer rows 9 A●C D 11 A B●D 13 A B●D 15 A B C● 17 ●B C D
                       10 J●L M 12 J K●M 14 J K●M 16 J●L M 18 J●L M

Go over the lesson with the students. Ask the students whether they read the directions for each section. Did they have enough time to finish all the items? Which items were most difficult? Work through any questions that caused difficulty.

Have the students indicate completion of the lesson by entering their score for this activity on the progress chart at the beginning of the book.

Unit 5

Background

This unit contains five lessons that deal with usage and expression skills.

- **In Lessons 6a and 6b,** students identify usage mistakes in written text. Students use context to find an answer, indicate that an item has no mistakes, and subvocalize answer choices. They work methodically, recall usage errors, and skip difficult items and return to them later.

- **In Lesson 7a,** students identify the best way to express an idea and answer questions about a paragraph. In addition to reviewing the test-taking skills learned in previous lessons, they learn the importance of following printed directions, understanding unusual item formats, and taking the best guess when unsure of the answer.

- **In Lesson 7b,** students choose the best word or words to complete a sentence, identify which paragraph best suits a stated purpose, answer questions about a paragraph, and identify correctly formed sentences. They review the test-taking skills learned in previous lessons.

- **In the Test Yourself lesson,** the usage and expression skills and test-taking skills introduced in Lessons 6a through 7b are reinforced and presented in a format that gives students the experience of taking an achievement test. Techniques for managing time effectively when taking a standardized test are reinforced.

Instructional Objectives

Lesson 6a **Usage** Lesson 6b **Usage**	Given text divided into three parts, students identify which part has a usage mistake or indicate that there is no mistake.
Lesson 7a **Expression** Lesson 7b **Expression**	Given a sentence with an underlined word or words, students identify which of three answer choices should replace the word or words or indicates that there should be no change.
	Given four paragraphs, the students identify which paragraph best suits a stated purpose.
	Given a paragraph and questions about it, students identify which of four answer choices is correct.
	Given four sentences, the students identify the best way to express the underlying idea.
Test Yourself	Given questions similar to those in Lessons 6a through 7b, students utilize usage and expression skills and test-taking strategies on achievement test formats.

Usage and Expression 41

Lesson 6a
Usage

Focus

Language Skill
- identifying mistakes in usage

Test-taking Skills
- using context to find an answer
- indicating that an item has no mistakes
- subvocalizing answer choices

Samples A and B

Say Turn to Lesson 6a on page 29. In this lesson you will look for mistakes in the correct use of English. Read the directions at the top of the page to yourself while I read them out loud.

Read the directions out loud to the students.

Say Let's begin with Sample A. It is a sentence divided into three parts. You are to find the part that has a mistake in English usage. If there is no mistake, choose the last answer, No mistakes. Read the answer choices to yourself. Does one of them have a mistake? *(no)* None of the answer choices has a mistake in English usage. Fill in circle D for Sample A in the answer rows at the bottom of the page. Check to make sure your answer circle is completely filled in with a dark mark.

Check to see that the students have filled in the correct answer circle.

Say Now do Sample B. Read the answer choices and look for a mistake in English usage. Choose the last answer if there is no mistake. *(pause)* Which answer did you choose? *(answer L)* The third answer choice has a mistake. The word *buying* should be *buy*. Fill in circle L for Sample B in the answer rows at the bottom of the page. Check to make sure the answer circle is completely filled in with a dark mark.

Check to see that the students have filled in the correct answer circle.

Usage and Expression
Lesson 6a Usage

Directions: Fill in the space for the answer that has a mistake in usage. Fill in the last answer space if there is no mistake.

| Sample A | A The ice on the lake was so
B thick this year that people could
C drive their cars across it.
∗ D (No mistakes) | Sample B | J The bicycle shop is having a
K sale next week. I think I'm going
∗ L to buying a new mountain bike.
M (No mistakes) |

- Say each answer choice carefully to yourself. Listen for the answer choice that doesn't sound right. This is usually the answer that has an error.

1 ∗ A   The Malaysian arts includes
    B   folk dances and puppet dramas that
    C   tell of adventure, war, and love.
    D   (No mistakes)

2   J   In the tale of Hansel and Gretel,
∗ K   the witch grows less and less kinder
    L   with the passing of each day.
    M   (No mistakes)

3   A   Rory finally realized that if he
    B   wanted the fence painted properly,
∗ C   he would just have to do it hisself.
    D   (No mistakes)

4   J   With mounting excitement, Melinda
∗ K   saw that she was gaining steady on
    L   the runners who were ahead of her.
    M   (No mistakes)

5   A   When the reporter asked who
    B   had come up with the brilliant idea,
∗ C   I pointed to Joe and said, "It was him."
    D   (No mistakes)

6 ∗ J   "We haven't got no time to
    K   waste," warned Zachary as he
    L   hopped on his mountain bike.
    M   (No mistakes)

7   A   Last spring the lake was
    B   overrun with a flock of Canada
∗ C   gooses and their many offspring.
    D   (No mistakes)

8   J   The postal worker delivers mail to
    K   residents on the west side of the block
∗ L   who chatted with her pleasantly.
    M   (No mistakes)

TIPS

Say Now let's look at the tips.

Have a volunteer read the tips aloud.

Say You might find it helpful to say the answer choices to yourself carefully. Choose the one that has a part that sounds incorrect. Mistakes in usage almost always sound a little unusual. This is a clue you can use to find the answer that has a usage mistake.

Practice

Say Let's do the Practice items now. Say the answer choices to yourself and listen for the one that sounds incorrect. Make sure you fill in the circles in the answer rows with dark marks. Do not write anything except your answer choices in your books. Completely erase any marks for answers that you change. When you come to the GO sign at the bottom of the page, turn the page and continue working. Work until you come to the STOP sign at the bottom of page 30. Any questions? Start working now.

Allow time for the students to fill in their answers.

Say It's time to stop. You have finished Lesson 6a.

Review the answers with the students. It will be helpful to discuss the error types that appear in the lesson and have the students read aloud the correct form of the sentences. If any questions caused particular difficulty, work through each of the answer choices.

Have the students indicate completion of the lesson by entering their score for this activity on the progress chart at the beginning of the book.

 Lesson 6a **Usage**

9   A   At the garage sale, I found
*B   a album from the 1970s that
   C   had never been played before.
   D   (No mistakes)

10   J   Yesterday, after the trainer taught
   K   us the basics of rock climbing, he
   L   said we were ready for a real cliff.
*M   (No mistakes)

11   A   Terry has locked the keys in his
*B   car at least for times this year, so
   C   it's a good thing he has a spare set.
   D   (No mistakes)

12   J   The teacher asked Rudy and
*K   I to stay late. She needed some
   L   help moving desks around.
   M   (No mistakes)

13 *A   A pile of leaves were under the tree.
   B   It was too good to pass up, so I ran
   C   as fast as I could and jumped into it.
   D   (No mistakes)

14   J   Marilyn couldn't wait to get home.
   K   She was expecting a package, and
   L   she was sure it would arrive today.
*M   (No mistakes)

15 *A   My sister found her a good pair
   B   of skis on sale. Now she is looking
   C   for boots and poles to go with them.
   D   (No mistakes)

16   J   A box full of used paperback books
*K   were on sale for a dollar. My older
   L   sister said she was going to buy them.
   M   (No mistakes)

17   A   The last time we had a neighborhood
   B   meeting, we had a potluck dinner. My
*C   father bringed a banana pie for dessert.
   D   (No mistakes)

18   J   Nat's parents liked his drawing
   K   so much they had it framed and
*L   hanged it on the living room wall.
   M   (No mistakes)

Answer rows 9 Ⓐ●ⒸⒹ 11 Ⓐ●ⒸⒹ 13 ●ⒷⒸⒹ 15 ●ⒷⒸⒹ 17 ⒶⒷ●Ⓓ
              10 ⒿⓀⓁ● 12 Ⓙ●ⓁⓂ 14 ⒿⓀⓁ● 16 Ⓙ●ⓁⓂ 18 ⒿⓀ●Ⓜ

Lesson 6a **Usage**

Lesson 6b
Usage

Focus

Language Skill
• identifying mistakes in usage

Test-taking Skills
• working methodically
• recalling usage errors
• indicating that an item has no mistakes
• skipping difficult items and returning to them later

Samples A and B

Say Turn to Lesson 6b on page 31. This is another lesson in which you will look for mistakes in the correct usage of English. Read the directions at the top of the page to yourself while I read them out loud.

Read the directions out loud to the students.

Say Sample A is two sentences divided into three parts. You are to find the part that has a mistake in English usage. If there is no mistake, choose the last answer, *No mistakes*. (pause) Answer B has a mistake. The word *tore* should be *torn*. Fill in answer circle B for Sample A in the answer rows at the bottom of the page. Check to make sure that the answer circle is completely filled in with a dark mark.

Check to see that the students have filled in the correct answer circle.

Say Now do Sample B. Read the answer choices and look for a mistake in English usage. Choose the last answer if there is no mistake. (pause) Which answer did you choose? (answer M) None of the answer choices has a usage mistake, so answer M is correct. Fill in circle M for Sample B in the answer rows at the bottom of the page. Make sure the circle is completely filled in with a dark mark.

Check to see that the students have filled in the correct answer circle.

Usage and Expression
Lesson 6b Usage

Directions: Fill in the space for the answer that has a mistake in usage. Fill in the last answer space if there is no mistake.

| Sample A | A I didn't realize my pants were
∗ B tore until I reached school. My
C friends really gave me the business.
D (No mistakes) | Sample B | J The street was crowded with
K people walking to work. Most of
L them didn't notice the artist.
∗ M (No mistakes) |

TIPS
• Pay attention to each word in an answer. Sometimes the mistake is a correct word used incorrectly.

1 ∗ A Most every day Mrs. Walters
   B runs six miles. The amazing thing
   C is that she is almost seventy.
   D (No mistakes)

2 J A bird got into our house
   K yesterday. It must have flown
   ∗ L in through a open window.
   M (No mistakes)

3 A The computer we just bought
   ∗ B is powerfuller than the old one.
   C It also has a CD-ROM drive.
   D (No mistakes)

4 J Australia is a wonderful place
   K to visit. It has a variety of climates,
   L from tropical forests to vast deserts.
   ∗ M (No mistakes)

5 ∗ A A book of ten stamps cost $3.70.
   B You will need at least three books
   C to send invitations to your friends.
   D (No mistakes)

6 ∗ J My brother yelled loud, but I
   K didn't hear him. He wanted me
   L to wait for him on the corner.
   M (No mistakes)

7 A Thank you for taking such good care
   B of my sister. She is doing well, and
   ∗ C her arm is beginning to feel more better.
   D (No mistakes)

8 ∗ J The team can't get no uniforms
   K because the school's budget has
   L been cut by the school board.
   M (No mistakes)

Answer rows A Ⓐ●©⓪ 1 Ⓐ●©⓪ 3 Ⓐ●©⓪ 5 ●ⒷⒸⒹ 7 ⒶⒷ●Ⓓ
             B ⒿⓀⓁ● 2 ⒿⓀ●Ⓜ 4 ⒿⓀⓁ● 6 ●ⓀⓁⓂ 8 ●ⓀⓁⓂ

31

★ **TIPS**

Say Now let's look at the tip.

Have a volunteer read the tip aloud.

Say When you read the answers, pay close attention to each word. In addition to looking for words that are incorrect, you should look for words that are used incorrectly.

Elaborate as necessary so the students understand that words such as *there* and *their* might sound alike, but they mean different things and are used differently in sentences.

44 Lesson 6b Usage

Practice

Say Let's do the Practice items now. Look for the answer that has a mistake in English usage. If an item seems difficult, skip it and go back to it later. Mark your answers in the rows at the bottom of the page. Make sure you fill in the circles in the answer rows with dark marks. Do not write anything except your answer choices in your books. Completely erase any marks for answers that you change. When you come to the GO sign at the bottom of the page, turn the page and continue working. Work until you come to the STOP sign at the bottom of page 32. Any questions? Start working now.

Allow time for the students to fill in their answers.

Say It's time to stop. You have finished Lesson 6b.

Review the answers with the students. It will be helpful to discuss the error types that appear in the lesson and have the students read aloud the correct form of the sentences. If any questions caused particular difficulty, work through each of the answer choices.

Have the students indicate completion of the lesson by entering their score for this activity on the progress chart at the beginning of the book.

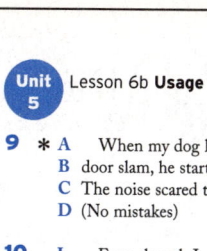 Lesson 6b **Usage**

9 *A When my dog heared the
   B door slam, he started barking.
   C The noise scared the cats.
   D (No mistakes)

10 J Even though I am much taller
   K than Warren, he can jump higher
*L than me when we play basketball.
   M (No mistakes)

11 A The doctor suggested to Linda
   B that she'd better take it easy for
   C a few days until she felt better.
*D (No mistakes)

12 *J "This ain't mine" said Marty.
   K "I think I must have grabbed
   L the wrong coat when we left."
   M (No mistakes)

13 A Because she didn't want to
   B bother anyone, Rita walked
*C quiet into the room.
   D (No mistakes)

14 J A group of Chinese visitors
*K are visiting our local school
   L sometime this winter.
   M (No mistakes)

15 A Our town has a nice park near
*B city hall. It was crowded with
   C visitors every weekend.
   D (No mistakes)

16 J Helen and I left early today.
   K We were already on the lake
*L when the sun rised this morning.
   M (No mistakes)

17 *A Mark called and talking about
   B the new bike he just got. He was
   C really excited about it.
   D (No mistakes)

18 J The crowd at the mall
   K would have been larger
*L accept for the weather.
   M (No mistakes)

32   Answer rows   9 ●BCD   11 ABC●   13 AB●D   15 A●CD   17 ●BCD
                          10 JK●M   12 ●KLM   14 J●LM   16 JK●M   18 JK●M

Lesson 6b **Usage**   45

Lesson 7a
Expression

Focus

Language Skills
- identifying correctly formed sentences
- identifying the sentence that does not fit in a paragraph
- identifying the best location for a sentence in a paragraph
- identifying the best closing sentence for a paragraph
- choosing the best word to complete a sentence

Test-taking Skills
- following printed directions
- understanding unusual item formats
- taking the best guess when unsure of the answer
- working methodically

Sample A

Say Turn to Lesson 7a on page 33. In this lesson, you will work with sentences and paragraphs. There are directions for each section of this lesson, so read them carefully before you answer questions.

Check to be sure the students have found the right page.

Say Look at Sample A. Read the four sentences. Find the answer choice that is the best way to express the idea. *(pause)* Which answer choice is correct? *(answer B)* Answer B is the best way to express the idea. Mark answer circle B for Sample A in the answer rows at the bottom of the page. Make sure the circle is completely filled in with a dark mark.

Check to see that the students have filled in the correct answer circle.

⭐ **TIPS**

Say Who will read the tip for us?

Have a volunteer read the tip aloud.

Usage and Expression
Lesson 7a Expression

Directions: Choose the best way to express the idea.

Sample A
A On the third floor, our apartment has a great view of the park.
∗ B Our apartment, which is on the third floor, has a great view of the park.
C With a great view of the park on the third floor is our apartment.
D Our apartment has a great view of the park on the third floor.

 • Pay attention to the directions for each section.

Directions: Use this paragraph to answer questions 1–4.

¹In 1908, Henry Ford was creating a car "for the great multitude." ²Ford paid his workers much more than other manufacturers. ³The Model T was a stripped-down car, but it was a great improvement over not having a car at all. ⁴Through assembly-line production, Ford was able to make a car that many working people could afford.

1 Which sentence should be left out of this paragraph?
A Sentence 1
∗ B Sentence 2
C Sentence 3
D Sentence 4

2 What is the best place for sentence 4?
J Where it is now
K Before sentence 1
∗ L Between sentences 2 and 3
M After sentence 4

3 Choose the best concluding sentence to add to this paragraph.
A The popular name for the car was the "Tin Lizzie."
B A Model T came in only one color, black, but people didn't seem to mind.
C The Model T had a four-cylinder engine.
∗ D Within just a few years, millions of Americans owned an automobile.

4 What is the best way to write the underlined part of sentence 1?
∗ J created
K have created
L to create
M (No change)

Answer rows A Ⓐ●ⒸⒹ 1 Ⓐ●ⒸⒹ 2 ⒿⓀ●Ⓜ 3 ⒶⒷⒸ● 4 ●ⓀⓁⓂ

33

Say In this lesson, you are looking for the best answer, not one that has a mistake. Read the directions for each section of the lesson carefully. There are different kinds of items, and if you don't pay attention to the directions, you may make a mistake.

46 Lesson 7a **Expression**

Practice

Say *Now we are ready for Practice. There are two types of items in this lesson, so be sure to read the directions for each section carefully. Choose the answer you think is correct for each item. If you are not sure which answer is correct, take your best guess. When you come to the GO sign at the bottom of the page, turn the page and continue working. Work until you come to the STOP sign at the bottom of page 34. Make sure your answer circles are completely filled in with dark marks. Do not write anything except your answer choices in your books. Completely erase any marks for answers that you change. Any questions? Start working now.*

Allow time for the students to fill in their answers. Walk around the room to be sure the students know how to answer the different item types in the lesson.

Say *It's time to stop. You have finished Lesson 7a.*

Review the answers with the students. If any questions caused particular difficulty, work through each of the answer choices.

Have the students indicate completion of the lesson by entering their score for this activity on the progress chart at the beginning of the book.

 Lesson 7a **Expression**

Directions: In questions 5–8, choose the best way to express the idea.

5 A Art historians said the paintings they were fakes, to everyone's dismay.
   B They were fakes, to everyone's dismay, said the art historians.
   C Art historians said they were fakes, to everyone's dismay.
 * D To everyone's dismay, art historians said the paintings were fakes.

6 * J My mother wore a confused look on her face.
   K My mother, she wore a confused and puzzled look on her face.
   L On her face, my mother a confused look she wore.
   M She was so confused and puzzled, my mother's face looked that way too.

7 A A computer isn't very useful and has the right software.
   B Having the right software making a computer very useful.
   C Although a computer isn't very useful, it has the right software.
 * D Without the right software, a computer isn't very useful.

8 J Jamie lined up with the other runners, hoping for a personal best at the starting line.
   K Hoping for a personal best at the starting line, Jamie lined up with the other runners.
   L At the starting line, Jamie lined up with the other runners, hoping for a personal best.
 * M Hoping for a personal best, Jamie lined up with the other runners at the starting line.

34 Answer rows 5 Ⓐ Ⓑ Ⓒ ●   6 ● Ⓚ Ⓛ Ⓜ   7 Ⓐ Ⓑ Ⓒ ●   8 Ⓙ Ⓚ Ⓛ ●

Lesson 7a **Expression**

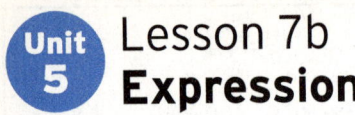

Lesson 7b
Expression

Focus

Language Skills
- choosing the best word to complete a sentence
- choosing the best paragraph for a given purpose
- identifying the sentence that does not fit in a paragraph
- identifying the best closing sentence for a paragraph
- identifying correctly formed sentences

Test-taking Skills
- following printed directions
- understanding unusual item formats
- skipping difficult items and returning to them later

Sample A

Say Turn to Lesson 7b on page 35. In this lesson, you will work with sentences and paragraphs. Read the directions for Sample A while I read them out loud.

Read the directions out loud to the students.

Say Let's look at Sample A. Read the sentence with the underlined part and each of the answer choices. Find the answer that is the best way to write the underlined part. If the underlined part is correct, choose the last answer, No change. *(pause)* Which answer choice is correct? *(answer C)* Mark answer circle C for Sample A in the answer rows at the bottom of the page. Make sure the circle is completely filled in with a dark mark.

Check to see that the students have filled in the correct answer circle. Explain why C is the best answer.

Usage and Expression
Lesson 7b Expression

Directions: Fill in the space for the answer that is the best way to write the underlined part of the sentence.

Sample A The zookeeper carried a monkey that <u>will cling</u> to her arm.
   A would cling
   B will have clung
 * C was clinging
   D (No change)

- If an item is too difficult, skip it and move on to the next item. Doing the easier items can help you understand the more difficult items.

Directions: For questions 1–4, choose the best way to write the underlined part of the sentence.

1 Jill was cold in a heavy sweatshirt, **so** Shari wore a T-shirt and was warm.
   A so that   B despite   * C but   D (No change)

2 A good crowd turned out for the game **in spite of** dreadful weather.
   J although   L however   K in addition to   * M (No change)

3 The First National Bank **will be located** in the same place for over one hundred years.
   A to be located   * B has been located   C being located   D (No change)

4 Which of these would be most appropriate at the end of a written report about the Revolutionary War?

J	The British were surprised to find how many of the colonists supported the Revolution. They expected people to support the crown and reject the ideas of the new government.	*L	The British were slowly being pushed into a corner and were outmanned. It became clear they had lost, and on October 19, 1781, the British general surrendered to George Washington.
K	The colonists had very few major victories. Instead, they used guerrilla warfare tactics for which the British were not prepared. Over the years of the war, they wore the British down.	M	In the early years of the war, things did not go well for the colonists. They were untrained and poorly equipped and were no match for the well-trained British forces.

★TIPS

Say Who will read the tip for us?

Have a volunteer read the tip aloud.

Say One of the most important test-taking strategies is skipping difficult items and returning to them later. This strategy saves time and gives you an opportunity to try all the items. If you waste too much time on difficult items, you might not have time to do easier ones.

Practice

Say Now we are ready for Practice. There are different types of items in this lesson. Read the directions for each section of the lesson. Choose the answer you think is correct for each item. When you come to the GO sign at the bottom of the page, turn the page and continue working. Work until you come to the STOP sign at the bottom of page 36. Make sure your answer circles are completely filled in with dark marks. Do not write anything except your answer choices in your books. Completely erase any marks for answers that you change. Any questions? Start working now.

Allow time for the students to fill in their answers. Walk around the room to be sure the students know how to answer the different item types in the lesson.

Say It's time to stop. You have finished Lesson 7b.

Review the answers with the students. If any questions caused particular difficulty, work through each of the answer choices. Discuss with the students any items they skipped and came back to.

Have the students indicate completion of the lesson by entering their score for this activity on the progress chart at the beginning of the book.

 Lesson 7b **Expression**

Directions: Use this paragraph to answer questions 5–8.

> ¹A surprising number of people like to assemble their own furniture. ²They buy kits that contain everything needed, from wood to screws. ³Furniture kits can be purchased from mail-order houses or walk-in retailers. ⁴These kits are less expensive than regular furniture, yet the quality of the finished product is high. ⁵Regular furniture can still be bought at stores, of course. ⁶And so, assembling a kit gives someone a sense of accomplishment.

5 Which sentence should be left out of this paragraph?
   A Sentence 2
   B Sentence 3
* C Sentence 5
   D Sentence 6

6 Choose the best concluding sentence to add to this paragraph.
   J Traditional furniture comes assembled from the factory.
   K People decorate their houses with different styles of furniture.
* L Because of these advantages, more and more people are buying furniture kits.
   M Many other products are also bought through mail order.

7 What is the best way to write the underlined part of sentence 3?
   A will be purchased
   B are purchasing
   C to be purchased
* D (No change)

8 What is the best way to write the underlined part of sentence 6?
   J Although
* K In addition
   L In respect to
   M Except

Directions: In question 9, choose the best way to express the idea.

9 * A Our teacher is also on the town council.
     B Our teacher, who is also on the town council.
     C The town council is something that our teacher is a member of.
     D Also on the town council is our teacher being.

36   Answer rows 5 Ⓐ Ⓑ ● Ⓓ 6 Ⓙ Ⓚ ● Ⓜ 7 Ⓐ Ⓑ Ⓒ ● 8 Ⓙ ● Ⓛ Ⓜ 9 ● Ⓑ Ⓒ Ⓓ

Unit 5 Test Yourself: Usage and Expression

Focus

Language Skills
- choosing the best word to complete a sentence
- identifying mistakes in usage
- identifying the best location for a sentence in a paragraph
- identifying the best opening sentence for a paragraph
- identifying the sentence that does not fit in a paragraph
- choosing the best paragraph for a given purpose
- identifying correctly formed sentences

Test-taking Skills
- managing time effectively
- following printed directions
- using context to find an answer
- indicating that an item has no mistakes
- subvocalizing answer choices
- working methodically
- recalling usage errors
- skipping difficult items and returning to them later
- following printed directions
- understanding unusual item formats
- taking the best guess when unsure of the answer

This lesson simulates an actual test-taking experience. Therefore, it is recommended that the directions be read verbatim and the suggested procedures and time allowances be followed.

Directions

Administration Time: approximately 30 minutes

Say Turn to the Test Yourself lesson on page 37.

Point out to the students that this Test Yourself lesson is timed like a real test, but that they will score it themselves to see how well they are doing. Remind the students to pace themselves and to check the clock after they have finished Number 13 to see how much time is left. This is about the halfway point in the lesson. Encourage the students to avoid spending too much time on any one item and to take their best guess if they are unsure of the answer.

Say There are different types of items in the Test Yourself lesson, so you will have to read the directions for each section and pay close attention to what you are doing. Remember to make sure that the circles in the answer rows are completely filled in. Press your pencil firmly so that your marks come out dark. Completely erase any marks for answers that you change. Do not write anything except your answer choices in your books.

Unit 5 Test Yourself: Usage and Expression

Directions: Choose the best way to write the underlined part of the sentence.

Sample Many people made suggestions about the park that <u>was built</u> next year.
A A will be builded   * B will be built   C is building   D (No change)

Directions: For questions 1–8, fill in the space for the answer that has a mistake in usage. Fill in the last answer space if there is no mistake.

1.   A The trees we planted last month
     B aren't doing well. My mother says
   * C we ought of watered them more often.
     D (No mistakes)

2.   J The movie had just started
     K when Vladimir said, "Oh no! I
     L forgot to turn the shower off!"
   * M (No mistakes)

3. * A Alexis growed three inches last year.
     B She's almost as tall as her mother,
     C and they can wear the same clothes.
     D (No mistakes)

4.   J The pond in the park was
   * K near full because of all the
     L rain we've had since January.
     M (No mistakes)

5.   A While his family was on vacation,
   * B Richmond hurt hisself. He was riding
     C his bike and fell on a rocky trail.
     D (No mistakes)

6.   J Because she works out almost
     K every day, Carlita thinks she is
   * L more stronger than she was before.
     M (No mistakes)

7.   A The delivery truck came to a stop
   * B in front of the Noonan's house.
     C The driver delivered a huge package.
     D (No mistakes)

8. * J Gina would of written to you
     K herself, but her writing arm is
     L in a cast. She broke it last week.
     M (No mistakes)

GO

Answer rows A ⓐ●ⓒⓓ 1 ⓐ●ⓒⓓ 3 ●ⓑⓒⓓ 5 ⓐ●ⓒⓓ 7 ⓐ●ⓒⓓ
                  2 ⓙⓚⓛ● 4 ⓙ●ⓛⓜ 6 ⓙⓚ●ⓜ 8 ●ⓚⓛⓜ

Say Look at Sample A and listen carefully. Read the sentence with the underlined part and the answer choices. Decide which answer answer is the best way to write the underlined part. If the underlined part is correct as it is, choose the last answer, *No change.*

Allow time for the students to fill in their answers.

Say The circle for answer B should be filled in. If you chose another answer, erase yours and fill in the circle for answer B now.

Check to see that the students have filled in the correct answer circle.

Say Now you will do more items. Read the directions for each section. When you come to the GO sign at the bottom of a page, continue working. Work until you come to the STOP sign at the bottom of page 40. If you are not sure of an answer, fill in the circle for the answer you think might be right. Do you have any questions?

Answer any questions the students have.

Say You may begin working. You will have 25 minutes.

Allow 25 minutes.

Test Yourself: Usage and Expression

Directions: Use this paragraph to answer questions 9–12.

> ¹Football began in medieval times as a game played by women and children as well as men. ²The members of one village tried to kick, carry, or throw a ball across fields and through forests to the church in a neighboring village. ³The rowdy game will be adopted and tamed by English schoolboys to become rugby. ⁴It was from English rugby that our football evolved. ⁵Today the Super Bowl is enjoyed by people around the world.

9 Where is the best place for sentence 3?
* A Where it is now
  B Between sentences 1 and 2
  C Between sentences 4 and 5
  D After sentence 5

10 Choose the best opening sentence to add to this paragraph.
  J Super Bowl Sunday is quickly becoming a national holiday.
  K Football is a fall tradition throughout America.
  L Americans are fond of their sports, especially football.
* M One of our most popular sports, football, has an unusual history.

11 Which sentence should be left out of this paragraph?
  A Sentence 1
  B Sentence 3
  C Sentence 4
* D Sentence 5

12 What is the best way to write the underlined part of sentence 3?
  J to be adopted
* K was adopted
  L having been adopted
  M (No change)

13 Which of these would be most useful in explaining how to use a personal computer?
* A The on/off switch is on the side of the computer. Most commands can be entered from the keyboard. The mouse moves the cursor around on the screen.
  B You can do lots of things with a computer. One of my favorites is communicating with my friends. We talk about lots of things.
  C The earliest computers were huge, often bigger than a room. They were slow and expensive and required special rooms that were extra clean and air-conditioned.
  D The price of computers has dropped quickly. Ten years ago a good computer cost $5,000. Today a more powerful computer can be bought for about $1,000.

Unit 5 Test Yourself: Usage and Expression

Directions: For questions 14–17, choose the best way to express the idea.

14 J My cousin, who is blind, although she loves skiing and ice skating.
    K Loving skiing and ice skating, my cousin is blind.
  * L Although she is blind, my cousin loves skiing and ice skating.
    M My cousin, although she is blind, loves skiing, and she loves ice skating.

15 A Doing the business news on a local television station, Felicia.
  * B Felicia does the business news on a local television station.
    C The business news is done on a local television station, and by Felicia.
    D Felicia does the business news, and she does it on a local television station.

16 J The books he borrowed from the library, Weldon can't find.
    K Weldon can't find them, the books he borrowed from the library.
  * L Weldon can't find the books he borrowed from the library.
    M The books Weldon can't find he borrowed them from the library.

17 A In the living room, the carpet, which was installed last year.
    B Last year in the living room, the carpet was installed.
  * C The carpet in the living room was installed last year.
    D The carpet was installed in the living room, and it was done last year.

18 **Which of these would be most appropriate in a friendly letter to someone you know?**

  * J The last time we had a neighborhood meeting, we had a potluck dinner. My father made a banana pie for dessert.

    K The traffic in our neighborhood is worse than ever. I'd like to suggest that we put in speed bumps to slow down traffic.

    L The skis I just bought are beginning to split. I'd like you to tell me how I can get them replaced.

    M The decision to build a new school doesn't make sense. Our school is fine, and taxes would have to be raised to pay for the new one.

Say It's time to stop. You have finished the Test Yourself lesson. Check to see that you have completely filled in your answer circles with dark marks. Make sure that any marks for answers that you changed have been completely erased.

Go over the lesson with the students. Ask the students whether they read the directions for each section. Did they have enough time to finish all the items? Which items were most difficult? Work through any questions that caused difficulty.

Have the students indicate completion of the lesson by entering their score for this activity on the progress chart at the beginning of the book.

Unit 5 Test Yourself: Usage and Expression

Directions: For questions 19–22, choose the best way to write the underlined part of the sentence.

19 Our electric bill was lower more than the weather was much colder.
* **A** even though
  B as if
  C in addition to
  D (No change)

20 The radio station has been playing nonstop music since six o'clock this morning.
  J will be playing
  K would have played
  L has been played
* **M** (No change)

21 The newspaper is usually delivered between six and seven in the morning.
  A is usually delivering
  B usually delivers
  C are usually delivered
* **D** (No change)

22 To arrive early is the only way to get good seats at the stadium.
* **J** Arriving early
  L Arrived early
  K Having arrived early
  M (No change)

23 Which of these would be most appropriate in the beginning of a report on the oil industry in America?

  A In 1901, a huge reservoir of oil was discovered near Beaumont, Texas. The strike was so large that within a year of the discovery, more than 1,500 oil companies were founded.

* **B** The first oil well in the United States was drilled in Titusville, Pennsylvania, in 1859. From this small beginning grew an important industry that changed the way of American life forever.

  C For many years, the most powerful oil company in America was the Standard Oil Company. John D. Rockefeller, the head of the company, was one of the most famous people in America.

  D Searching for oil is only a small part of the oil industry. The crude oil from the ground must be refined into more usable forms such as gasoline, heating oil, and jet fuel.

Unit 6

Background

This unit contains five lessons that deal with math concepts and estimation skills.

• **In Lessons 8a and 8b,** students solve problems involving math concepts. Students identify and use key words, numbers, and pictures. They refer to a graphic, find the answer without computing, work methodically, analyze answer choices, and reread questions.

• **In Lessons 9a and 9b,** students solve problems involving estimation. They review the test-taking skills introduced in the two previous lessons and evaluate answer choices.

• **In the Test Yourself lesson,** the math concepts and estimation skills and test-taking skills introduced in Lessons 8a through 9b are reinforced and presented in a format that gives students the experience of taking an achievement test. Techniques for managing time effectively when taking a standardized test are reinforced.

Instructional Objectives

Lesson 8a **Math Concepts** Lesson 8b **Math Concepts**	Given a problem involving math concepts, students identify which of four answer choices is correct.
Lesson 9a **Math Estimation** Lesson 9b **Math Estimation**	Given a problem involving estimation, students identify which of four answer choices is correct.
Test Yourself	Given questions similar to those in Lessons 8a through 9b, students utilize math concepts, estimation, and test-taking strategies on achievement test formats.

Unit 6 Lesson 8a Math Concepts

Focus

Mathematics Skills
- comparing and ordering whole numbers, decimals, fractions, and integers
- understanding scientific notation
- using a coordinate grid
- understanding congruence
- understanding lines and angles
- understanding probability
- recognizing transformations
- sequencing numbers or shapes
- identifying problem solving strategies
- solving measurement problems
- finding area
- understanding number sentences

Test-taking Skills
- identifying and using key words, numbers, and pictures
- referring to a graphic
- finding the answer without computing
- working methodically
- rereading a question

Samples A and B

Distribute scratch paper to the students.

Say Turn to Lesson 8a on page 41. In this lesson you will work on math problems. Read the directions at the top of the page to yourself.

Allow time for the students to read the directions.

Say Find Sample A. Read the question to yourselves. *(pause)* Which answer choice is correct? *(answer B, –3)* Yes, answer B is correct. Mark answer B for Sample A in the answer rows. Make sure the circle is completely filled in with a dark mark.

Check to see that the students have filled in the correct answer circle.

Say Now we'll do Sample B. Read the question to yourself. *(pause)* Think about the important words and numbers in the question that will help you find the answer. Which answer is correct? *(answer J)* Fill in answer J for Sample B in the answer rows at the bottom of the page. Be sure you fill in the circle with a dark mark.

Check to see that the students have filled in the correct answer circle. If necessary, elaborate on the solutions to the sample items.

★TIPS

Say Now let's look at the tips.

Have a volunteer read the tips aloud to the group.

Say You should look for key words, numbers, and pictures in a problem. They will help you find the answer. After you have chosen an answer, read the question again before you mark the space for your answer. Be sure your answer makes sense with the question.

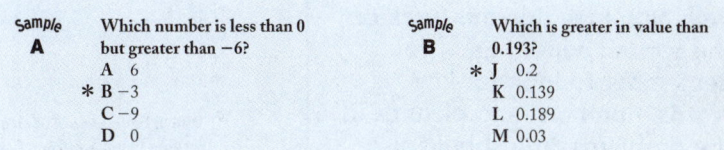

Lesson 8a **Math Concepts**

Directions: Read each mathematics problem. Choose the best answer.

Sample A	Which number is less than 0 but greater than –6?	Sample B	Which is greater in value than 0.193?
	A 6		*J 0.2
	*B –3		K 0.139
	C –9		L 0.189
	D 0		M 0.03

TIPS
- Read the question carefully. Look for key words and numbers so you know what the question is asking.
- Once you have chosen your answer, reread the question to be sure your answer makes sense.

1 The circumference of the earth is about 25,000 miles. Which of these is another way to show the circumference of the earth?
- A 2.5×10^2 miles
- B 2.5×10^3 miles
- *C 2.5×10^4 miles
- D 2.5×10^5 miles

2 What are the two coordinates of point D in the figure below?

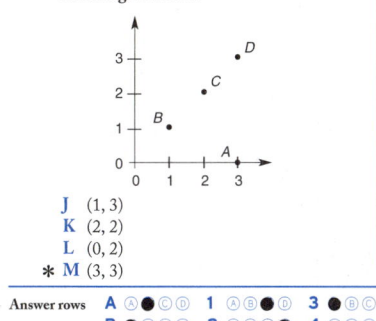

- J (1, 3)
- K (2, 2)
- L (0, 2)
- *M (3, 3)

3 In the figure below, line segment AB is parallel to line segment CD. What is the length of line segment AB?

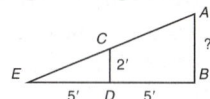

- *A 4′
- B 5′
- C 6′
- D It cannot be determined.

4 In which figure are the pairs of lines parallel?

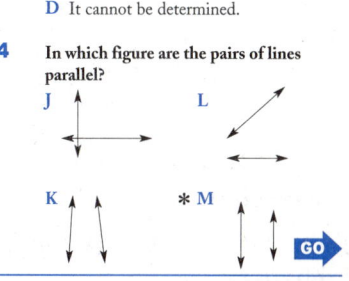

Lesson 8a Math Concepts 55

Practice

Say We are ready for Practice. You are going to do more problems in the same way that we did the samples. Do not write anything except your answer choices in your book. If you think it will help, you may do your work on the scratch paper I gave you. Remember to look for key words, numbers, and pictures in the problems. You should also remember that you don't have to compute to find some of the answers in this lesson. When you have finished working a problem, fill in the circle for your answer in the answer rows at the bottom of the page. Make sure that the circles for your answer choices are completely filled in with dark marks. Completely erase any marks for answers that you change. When you come to the GO sign at the bottom of a page, continue working. Work until you come to the STOP sign at the bottom of page 43. Do you have any questions? Start working now.

Allow time for the students to fill in their answers.

 Unit 6 Lesson 8a **Math Concepts**

5 One pen is randomly drawn from a jar containing 3 red, 4 blue, 4 black, and 2 green pens. What is the probability that the pen is either red or black?
  A $\frac{3}{13}$
  B $\frac{4}{13}$
  C $\frac{6}{13}$
  *D $\frac{7}{13}$

6 Which figure cannot be created by turning figure X without first lifting it off the paper?

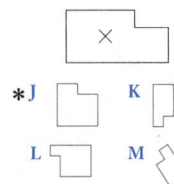

7 The number pattern 6, 12, 24, 48 … is formed by doubling the last number to get the next one. What is the 7th number in this pattern?
  A 70
  B 96
  C 280
  *D 384

8 One quarter of the way through a spelling test, Ben had spelled 5 words correctly. To find out how many words he would spell correctly overall if he continued spelling correctly at the same rate, Ben should
  J add 5 and $\frac{1}{4}$.
  *K multiply 5 by 4.
  L multiply 5 by $\frac{1}{4}$.
  M divide 5 by 4.

9 3.27 ÷ 0.01 = ☐ ?
  A 0.0327
  B 0.327
  C 32.7
  *D 327

10 Avni is measuring wood for an art project. One piece is $\frac{3}{4}$ of a meter long. The other piece is 40 centimeters long. How much longer is the first piece of wood than the second piece?
  J 10 centimeters
  K 30 centimeters
  *L 35 centimeters
  M 115 centimeters

11 Which point is most likely (4, −3)?

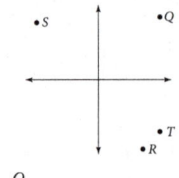

  A Q
  B R
  C S
  *D T

42 Answer rows   5 Ⓐ Ⓑ Ⓒ ●   7 Ⓐ Ⓑ Ⓒ ●   9 Ⓐ Ⓑ Ⓒ ●   11 Ⓐ Ⓑ Ⓒ ●
                 6 ● Ⓚ Ⓛ Ⓜ   8 Ⓙ ● Ⓛ Ⓜ   10 Ⓙ Ⓚ ● Ⓜ

GO

Say You may stop working now. You have finished Lesson 8a.

Review the answers with the students. If any problems caused particular difficulty, work through each of the answer choices. It may be helpful to have the students identify the key words and numbers in each problem. It is also a good idea to have volunteers solve each problem at the chalkboard and discuss the strategy they used.

Have the students indicate completion of the lesson by entering their score for this activity on the progress chart at the beginning of the book.

Unit 6 Lesson 8a **Math Concepts**

12 Which is closest in value to 7,459,326?
  J $7\frac{1}{4}$ million
✶ K $7\frac{1}{2}$ million
  L $7\frac{3}{5}$ million
  M $7\frac{3}{4}$ million

13 The area of the rectangle below is 35 square meters. What is the length of the missing side?

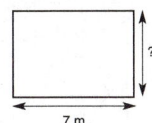

✶ A 5 m
  B 7 m
  C 10.5 m
  D 28 m

14 What is the 100th number in the sequence below?
3, 6, 9, 12, 15…
  J 30
  K 130
✶ L 300
  M 303

15 What is the area of the shaded part of the square below?

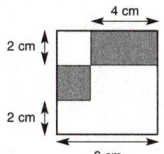

  A 8 cm²
  B 10 cm²
✶ C 12 cm²
  D 36 cm²

16 The workers in a factory wear red, blue, or gray uniforms, depending on where they work. In the cafeteria at noon, when all the workers eat, there are twice as many people wearing blue uniforms than red uniforms and three times as many people wearing gray uniforms than blue uniforms. If there are 15 people wearing red uniforms, how many people will be wearing gray uniforms?
✶ J 90
  L 100
  K 95
  M 115

17 What should replace the □ in the equation 5 □ $\frac{1}{4}$ = 20?
  A +
  B −
  C ×
✶ D ÷

Answer rows    43

Lesson 8a **Math Concepts**   57

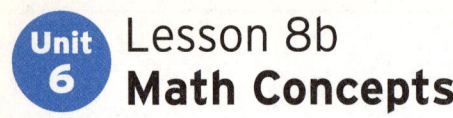

Lesson 8b
Math Concepts

Focus

Mathematics Skills
- finding squares and square roots
- solving measurement problems
- solving equations or expressions
- finding perimeter
- understanding characteristics of related numbers
- naming numerals
- understanding decimal operations
- using a coordinate grid
- understanding ratio and proportion
- recognizing fractional parts

Test-taking Skills
- analyzing answer choices
- referring to a graphic
- finding the answer without computing
- working methodically

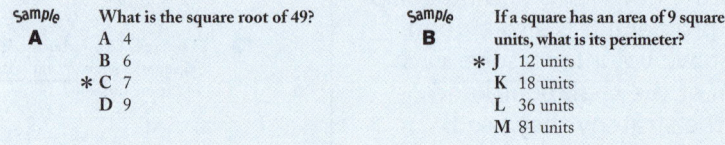

Lesson 8b Math Concepts

Directions: Read each mathematics problem. Choose the best answer.

Sample A What is the square root of 49?
A 4
B 6
*C 7
D 9

Sample B If a square has an area of 9 square units, what is its perimeter?
*J 12 units
K 18 units
L 36 units
M 81 units

 • Look carefully at the answer choices. Sometimes there is only a little difference between correct and incorrect answers.

1 Which expression has a negative value?
*A $-2 + (-5)$
B $-2 - (-5)$
C $-2 \times (-5)$
D $-2 \overline{) (-5)}$

2 If $a \times b = 400$, what is $\frac{400}{b}$ equal to?
*J a
K $400 \div a$
L $400 \times a$
M 400

3 What is the perimeter in feet of the figure below?

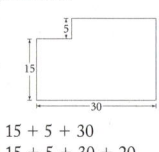

A $15 + 5 + 30$
B $15 + 5 + 30 + 20$
*C $15 + 5 + 30 + 30 + 20$
D $(15 \times 30) + (15 \times 5)$

4 Between what 2 whole numbers is $\sqrt{57}$?
J 5 and 6
K 6 and 7
*L 7 and 8
M 8 and 9

5 Suppose that the set of positive odd numbers {1, 3, 5, 7, 9, 11…} has every fourth number removed. Which of the following best describes the remaining numbers?
*A A set of positive odd numbers
B A set of positive even numbers
C A set of prime numbers
D A set of multiples of four

6 If $l + m = 20$ and $l < 10$, what must be true about m?
J $m < 10$
K $m = 10$
L $m < l$
*M $m > l$

44   Answer rows   A Ⓐ Ⓑ ● Ⓓ   1 ● Ⓑ Ⓒ Ⓓ   3 Ⓐ Ⓑ ● Ⓓ   5 ● Ⓑ Ⓒ Ⓓ
                   B ● Ⓚ Ⓛ Ⓜ   2 ● Ⓚ Ⓛ Ⓜ   4 Ⓙ Ⓚ ● Ⓜ   6 Ⓙ Ⓚ Ⓛ ●

Samples A and B

Distribute scratch paper to the students.

Say Turn to Lesson 8b on page 44. In this lesson you will work on more mathematics problems. Read the directions at the top of the page to yourself.

Allow time for the students to read the directions.

Say Look at Sample A at the top of the page. Read the question to yourself. *(pause)* Which answer choice is correct? *(answer C)* Yes, answer C is correct because the square root of 49 is 7. Mark answer C for Sample A in the answer rows. Make sure the circle is completely filled in with a dark mark.

Check to see that the students have filled in the correct answer circle.

Say Now we'll do Sample B. Read the question to yourself. *(pause)* Which answer is correct? *(answer J)* Fill in answer J for Sample B in the answer rows at the bottom of the page. Be sure you fill in the circle with a dark mark.

Check to see that the students have filled in the correct answer circle. Elaborate on the solutions to the sample items to be sure the students are familiar with the underlying concepts.

Say Now let's look at the tip.

Have a volunteer read the tip aloud to the group.

Say When you solve math problems, it is important that you look carefully at the answer choices. Sometimes they differ by only a single digit, decimal place, or important word. If you don't look carefully, you are more likely to make a mistake.

58   Unit 6   Lesson 8b Math Concepts

Practice

Say We are ready for Practice. You are going to do more problems in the same way that we did the samples. Do not write anything except your answer choices in your book. If you think it will help, you may do your work on scratch paper. When you have finished working a problem, fill in the circle for your answer in the answer rows at the bottom of the page. Make sure that the circles for your answer choices are completely filled in with dark marks. Completely erase any marks for answers that you change. When you come to the GO sign at the bottom of a page, continue working. Work until you come to the STOP sign at the bottom of page 46. Do you have any questions? Start working now.

Allow time for the students to fill in their answers.

Unit 6 Lesson 8b **Math Concepts**

7 A local corporation donated about 3 million dollars to a neighborhood school. Which of these figures could be the amount of the donation?
   A $319,425
 * B $3,210,565
   C $3,105,347,431
   D $3,113,542,324,903

8 If $e \times f = 274$, what is $274 \div e$ equal to?
 * J f
   K $274 \div f$
   L $274 \times f$
   M 274

9 $7.29 \div 0.001 = \square$?
   A 0.729
   B 72.9
   C 729
 * D 7,290

10 Calvin's cherry tree is $4\frac{1}{2}$ meters tall. His plum tree is 3 meters and 20 centimeters tall. How much taller is the cherry tree than the plum tree?
   J 30 centimeters
   K 1 meter 20 centimeters
 * L 1 meter 30 centimeters
   M 1 meter 50 centimeters

11 Which point is most likely $(-1, 3)$?

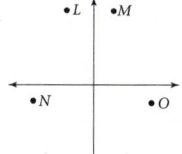

 * A L
   B M
   C N
   D O

12 Mr. Gordon reported that about three million people visited the Munro Museum of Art this year. Which of these figures could be the number of visitors at the museum?
   J 31,394
   K 295,049
 * L 2,849,048
   M 3,042,593,395

13 Which expression has a positive value?
   A $4 + (-8)$
 * B $4 - (-8)$
   C $4 \times (-8)$
   D $4 \div (-8)$

Answer rows 7 Ⓐ ● Ⓒ Ⓓ   9 Ⓐ Ⓑ Ⓒ ●   11 ● Ⓑ Ⓒ Ⓓ   13 Ⓐ ● Ⓒ Ⓓ
             8 ● Ⓚ Ⓛ Ⓜ   10 Ⓙ Ⓚ ● Ⓜ   12 Ⓙ Ⓚ ● Ⓜ

Say You may stop working now. You have finished Lesson 8b.

Review the answers with the students. If any problems caused particular difficulty, work through each of the answer choices. It may be helpful to have volunteers solve each problem at the chalkboard and discuss the strategy they used.

Have the students indicate completion of the lesson by entering their score for this activity on the progress chart at the beginning of the book.

Unit 6 Lesson 8b **Math Concepts**

14 What is the ratio of the number of squares to circles?

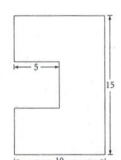

* J 1 to 1
  K 1 to 2
  L 1 to 3
  M 2 to 3

15 What is the perimeter in meters of the figure below?

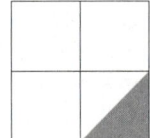

  A $5 + 10 + 15$
  B $5 + 10 + 10 + 15$
* C $5 + 5 + 10 + 10 + 15 + 15$
  D $(5 \times 10) + (5 \times 15)$

16 Between what 2 whole numbers is $\sqrt{87}$?
  J 7 and 8
  K 8 and 9
* L 9 and 10
  M 10 and 11

17 Suppose a set of positive even numbers {2, 4, 6, 8, 10, 12 …} has every fourth number removed. Which of the following best describes the <u>remaining</u> set of numbers?
* A A set of positive even numbers
  B A set of positive odd numbers
  C A set of prime numbers
  D A set of multiples of four

18 If $q + r = 80$ and $q > 40$, what must be true about r?
  J $r > 40$
  K $r = 40$
  L $r > q$
* M $r < 40$

19 What fraction of the figure is shaded?

* A $\frac{1}{8}$
  B $\frac{1}{6}$
  C $\frac{1}{4}$
  D $\frac{1}{2}$

STOP

46 Answer rows 14 ● K L M   16 J K ● M   18 J K L ●
                 15 A B ● D   17 ● B C D   19 ● B C D

---

60 Unit 6 Lesson 8b **Math Concepts**

Unit 6 Lesson 9a Math Estimation

Focus
Mathematics Skill
- estimating and rounding

Test-taking Skills
- working methodically
- finding the answer without computing
- evaluating answer choices

Samples A and B

Distribute scratch paper to the students.

Say Turn to Lesson 9a on page 47. In this lesson you will solve mathematics problems involving estimation. Read the directions at the top of the page to yourself.

Allow time for the students to read the directions.

Say Find Sample A. Read the question to yourselves. *(pause)* Think about how to solve the problem, then decide which answer is correct. *(answer C)* Yes, answer C is correct. The closest estimate of the solution is *between $2.25 and $2.50*. Mark answer C for Sample A in the answer rows. Make sure the circle is completely filled in with a dark mark.

Check to see that the students have filled in the correct answer circle.

Say Now we'll do Sample B. Read the question to yourself. Remember to round before you solve the problem. *(pause)* Which answer is correct? *(answer M)* Fill in answer M for Sample B in the answer rows at the bottom of the page. Be sure you fill in the circle with a dark mark.

Check to see that the students have filled in the correct answer circle. Elaborate on the solutions to the sample items.

Unit 6 Math Concepts and Estimation
Lesson 9a Math Estimation

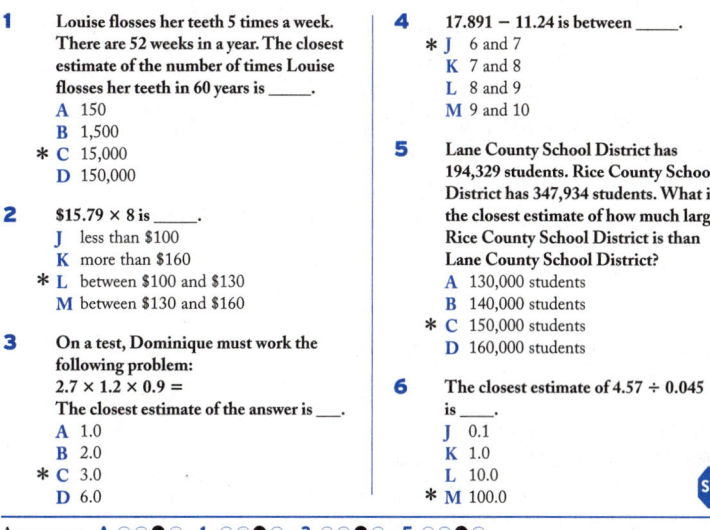

 **TIPS**

Say Now let's look at the tips.

Have a volunteer read the tips aloud to the group.

Say Estimation problems are different from other math problems because you do not have to find an exact answer. It is usually a good idea to solve the problems using two steps. First, round the numbers in the problem. Then, perform the operation. When you have finished, check your answer to be sure it makes sense with the question.

Review the rules for rounding with the students.

Practice

Say We are ready for Practice. You are going to do more problems in the same way that we did the samples. Do not write anything except your answer choices in your book. If you think it will help, you may do your work on scratch paper. Remember that you do not have to find an exact answer to the problems. When you have finished working a problem, fill in the circle for your answer in the answer rows at the bottom of the page. Make sure that the circles for your answer choices are completely filled in with dark marks. Completely erase any marks for answers that you change. Work until you come to the STOP sign at the bottom of the page. Do you have any questions? Start working now.

Allow time for the students to fill in their answers.

Say You may stop working now. You have finished Lesson 9a.

Review the answers with the students. If any problems caused particular difficulty, work through each of the answer choices. It may be helpful to have volunteers solve each problem at the chalkboard and discuss the rounding and estimation strategies they used.

Have the students indicate completion of the lesson by entering their score for this activity on the progress chart at the beginning of the book.

 Math Concepts and Estimation

Lesson 9a **Math Estimation**

Directions: Read each mathematics problem. Choose the answer that is the best estimate of the exact answer.

Sample A A set of 5 pens costs $12.00. The closest estimate of the cost of one pen is _____.
  A less than $2.00
  B between $2.00 and $2.25
*C between $2.25 and $2.50
  D more than $2.50

Sample B The closest estimate of $3,107 − $2,589 is _____.
  J $350
  K $400
  L $450
*M $500

- Remember, the correct answer is an estimate.
- Be sure your answer makes sense with the numbers in the problem.

1 Louise flosses her teeth 5 times a week. There are 52 weeks in a year. The closest estimate of the number of times Louise flosses her teeth in 60 years is _____.
  A 150
  B 1,500
*C 15,000
  D 150,000

2 $15.79 × 8 is _____.
  J less than $100
  K more than $160
*L between $100 and $130
  M between $130 and $160

3 On a test, Dominique must work the following problem: 2.7 × 1.2 × 0.9 = The closest estimate of the answer is ___.
  A 1.0
  B 2.0
*C 3.0
  D 6.0

4 17.891 − 11.24 is between _____.
*J 6 and 7
  K 7 and 8
  L 8 and 9
  M 9 and 10

5 Lane County School District has 194,329 students. Rice County School District has 347,934 students. What is the closest estimate of how much larger Rice County School District is than Lane County School District?
  A 130,000 students
  B 140,000 students
*C 150,000 students
  D 160,000 students

6 The closest estimate of 4.57 ÷ 0.045 is ___.
  J 0.1
  K 1.0
  L 10.0
*M 100.0

Answer rows A ⒶⒷ●Ⓓ 1 ⒶⒷ●Ⓓ 3 ⒶⒷ●Ⓓ 5 ⒶⒷ●Ⓓ
            B ⒿⓀⓁ● 2 ⒿⓀ●Ⓜ 4 ●ⓀⓁⓂ 6 ⒿⓀⓁ●

Lesson 9b
Math Estimation

Focus

Mathematics Skill
- estimating and rounding

Test-taking Skills
- finding the answer without computing
- working methodically

Samples A and B

Distribute scratch paper to the students.

Say Turn to Lesson 9b on page 48. In this lesson you will solve more problems involving estimation. Read the directions at the top of the page to yourself.

Allow time for the students to read the directions.

Say Find Sample A. Read the question to yourselves. *(pause)* Remember to round before you solve the problem. Which answer choice is correct? *(answer A)* Yes, answer A is correct. The closest estimate of the exact answer is *16,000.* Mark answer A for Sample A in the answer rows. Make sure the circle is completely filled in with a dark mark.

Check to see that the students have filled in the correct answer circle.

Say Now we'll do Sample B. Read the question to yourself. Think about how to solve the problem. *(pause)* Which answer is correct? *(answer K)* Fill in answer K for Sample B in the answer rows at the bottom of the page. Be sure you fill in the circle with a dark mark.

Check to see that the students have filled in the correct answer circle. Elaborate on the solutions to the sample items, emphasizing rounding and then solving.

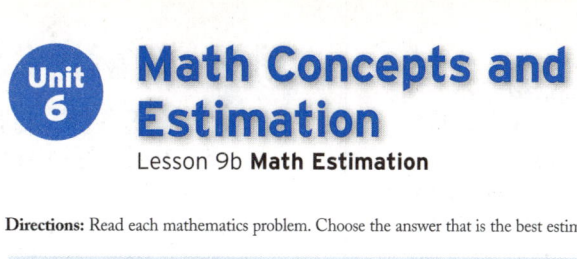

Math Concepts and Estimation
Lesson 9b **Math Estimation**

Directions: Read each mathematics problem. Choose the answer that is the best estimate of the exact answer.

Sample A The closest estimate of 19,786 − 4,029 is ____.
* A 16,000
  B 17,000
  C 18,000
  D 19,000

Sample B Three friends share the cost of renting a canoe for a day. The canoe costs $14.80 in all. The closest estimate of each person's share is ____.
  J $4.50
* K $5.00
  L $5.50
  M $6.00

TIPS • Round the numbers first and then solve the problem.

1. Patrick bought these items:
   toothbrush $0.89
   dental floss $2.15
   mouthwash $5.90
   toothpaste $4.29

   The closest estimate of the amount of change from $15 is ____.
   A $1
   * B $2
   C $3
   D $4

2. $6\frac{1}{3} \times 12$ is ____.
   J less than 68
   K more than 80
   L between 68 and 74
   * M between 74 and 80

3. The Marion County Library has 849 shelves of books. On each shelf, there are 21 books. The closest estimate of the number of books in the library is ____.
   A 2,000
   * B 20,000
   C 200,000
   D 2,000,000

4. Which best shows how to get the closest estimate of 4.2 × 7.9?
   J 5 × 8
   * K 4 × 8
   L 4 × 7
   M 5 × 7

48   Answer rows   A ●BCD   1 A●CD   3 A●CD
                   B J●LM   2 JK L●   4 J●LM

TIPS

Say Now let's look at the tip.

Have a volunteer read the tip aloud to the group.

Say The most important thing to remember when you solve estimation problems is to round numbers first. Once you round numbers correctly, it is easy to find the answer. Think about the rules for rounding so you know when to round up or down.

Review rounding rules with the students, emphasizing when to round up and when to round down. Include a discussion of fractions and decimals as well as whole numbers.

Practice

Say We are ready for Practice. You are going to do more problems in the same way that we did the samples. Do not write anything except your answer choices in your book. If you think it will help, you may do your work on scratch paper. Remember that you do not have to find an exact answer to the problems. When you have finished working a problem, fill in the circle for your answer in the answer rows at the bottom of the page. Make sure that the circles for your answer choices are completely filled in with dark marks. Completely erase any marks for answers that you change. Work until you come to the STOP sign at the bottom of the page. Do you have any questions? Start working now.

Allow time for the students to fill in their answers.

Say You may stop working now. You have finished Lesson 9b.

Review the answers with the students. If any problems caused particular difficulty, work through each of the answer choices. It may be helpful to have volunteers solve each problem at the chalkboard and discuss the strategy they used.

Have the students indicate completion of the lesson by entering their score for this activity on the progress chart at the beginning of the book.

Math Concepts and Estimation

Lesson 9b Math Estimation

Directions: Read each mathematics problem. Choose the answer that is the best estimate of the exact answer.

Sample A The closest estimate of 19,786 − 4,029 is ____.
* A 16,000
  B 17,000
  C 18,000
  D 19,000

Sample B Three friends share the cost of renting a canoe for a day. The canoe costs $14.80 in all. The closest estimate of each person's share is ____.
  J $4.50
* K $5.00
  L $5.50
  M $6.00

 TIPS • Round the numbers first and then solve the problem.

1 Patrick bought these items:
toothbrush	$0.89
dental floss	$2.15
mouthwash	$5.90
toothpaste	$4.29

The closest estimate of the amount of change from $15 is ____.
  A $1
* B $2
  C $3
  D $4

2 $6\frac{1}{3} \times 12$ is ____.
  J less than 68
  K more than 80
  L between 68 and 74
* M between 74 and 80

3 The Marion County Library has 849 shelves of books. On each shelf, there are 21 books. The closest estimate of the number of books in the library is ____.
  A 2,000
* B 20,000
  C 200,000
  D 2,000,000

4 Which best shows how to get the closest estimate of 4.2×7.9?
  J 5×8
* K 4×8
  L 4×7
  M 5×7

 STOP

48 Answer rows   A ●ⓑⓒⓓ   1 ⓐ●ⓒⓓ   3 ⓐ●ⓒⓓ
                 B ⓐ●ⓒⓜ   2 ⓙⓚⓛ●   4 ⓙ●ⓛⓜ

Unit 6 Test Yourself: Math Concepts and Estimation

Focus

Mathematics Skills
- estimating and rounding
- recognizing equivalent fractions and decimals
- understanding average (mean)
- understanding variability
- understanding ratio and proportion
- solving measurement problems
- recognizing alternate forms of a number
- solving equations or expressions
- identifying the best measurement unit
- understanding probability
- sequencing numbers or shapes

Test-taking Skills
- managing time effectively
- following printed directions
- identifying and using key words, numbers, and pictures
- referring to a graphic
- finding the answer without computing
- working methodically
- rereading a question
- analyzing answer choices
- evaluating answer choices

Unit 6 Test Yourself: Math Concepts and Estimation

Directions: Read each mathematics problem. Choose the best answer.

Sample A The closest estimate of $23.16 − $15.97 is _____.
- A $5
- B $6
- *C $7
- D $8

Sample B Which fraction is not equal to 0.5?
- J $\frac{1}{2}$
- *K $\frac{4}{10}$
- L $\frac{50}{100}$
- M $\frac{25}{50}$

1 There were 46, 48, 53, and 61 pennies in 4 jars. The average (mean) of these 4 numbers of pennies is about
- A 42.
- *B 52.
- C 57.
- D 210.

2 Which of the following is not the same as $\frac{5}{25}$?
- J $\frac{1}{5}$
- *K $5\frac{1}{25}$
- L $\frac{20}{100}$
- M $\frac{25}{125}$

3 Which set of numbers shows the greatest variability?
- *A {1, 8, 14}
- B {13, 13, 13}
- C {10, 12, 14}
- D {7, 9, 10, 12}

4 What is the ratio of squares to triangles?

- J 2 to 4
- *K 4 to 2
- L 4 to 6
- M 2 to 6

5 Mr. Paine wants to buy 5 containers of cottage cheese. One container weighs 1 pound 8 ounces. How much would 5 containers of cottage cheese weigh?
- A 5 pounds 8 ounces
- B 7 pounds 5 ounces
- *C 7 pounds 8 ounces
- D 7 pounds 10 ounces

6 What number is expressed by $(4 \times 10^3) + (9 \times 10^2) + (6 \times 10) + (2 \times 1)$?
- J 496.2
- *K 4,962
- L 104,962
- M 496,200

This lesson simulates an actual test-taking experience. Therefore, it is recommended that the directions be read verbatim and that the suggested procedures and time allowances be followed.

Directions

Administration Time: approximately 30 minutes

Distribute scratch paper to the students.

Say Turn to the Test Yourself lesson on page 49.

Point out to the students that this Test Yourself lesson is timed like a real test, but that they will score it themselves to see how well they are doing. Encourage them to read each question carefully, to think about what they are supposed to do, and to work carefully on scratch paper when necessary. They should skip difficult problems and return to them later and take their best guess when they are unsure of the answer.

Say This lesson will check how well you can solve mathematics problems. Remember to make sure that the circles for your answer choices are completely filled in. Press your pencil firmly so that your marks come out dark. Completely erase any marks for answers that you change. Do not write anything except your answer choices in your books.

Look at Sample A. Read the question and the answer choices. Mark the circle for the answer you think is correct.

Allow time for the students to fill in their answers.

Say The circle for answer C should be filled in because the correct answer is *$7*. If you chose another answer, erase yours and fill in circle C now.

Check to see that the students have filled in the correct answer circle.

Say Now read Sample B and the answer choices. Fill in the circle for the answer you think is correct.

Allow time for the students to fill in their answers.

Say The circle for answer K should be filled in because the right answer is *four-tenths*. If you chose another answer, erase yours and fill in circle K now.

Check to see that the students have filled in the correct answer circle.

Say Now you will do more mathematics problems. You may use the scratch paper I gave you. When you come to the GO sign at the bottom of a page, continue working. Work until you come to the STOP sign at the bottom of page 52. Make sure that the circles for your answers are completely filled in with dark marks. Be sure to fill in the circle in the answer row for the problem you are working on. Completely erase any marks for answers that you change. You will have 25 minutes to solve the problems. You may begin.

Allow 25 minutes.

Unit 6 — Test Yourself: Math Concepts and Estimation

7 Which is the value of b if $\frac{16}{(b+3)} = 2$?
  A 0
  B 2
  C 3
 *D 5

8 Which of the following is another name for $2\frac{1}{5}$?
  J $\frac{2}{5}$
  K $\frac{3}{5}$
  L $\frac{10}{5}$
 *M $\frac{11}{5}$

9 The length of a car was measured by rounding up or down to the nearest meter. The largest difference between the measurement and the actual length would be
  A 1 centimeter.
 *B 50 centimeters ($\frac{1}{2}$ meter).
  C 1 meter.
  D 2 meters.

10 In the equation $5y - 3 = 17$, what is the value of y?
  J 2
  K 3
 *L 4
  M 4.5

11 The length of time needed to paint a classroom is best measured by
  A minutes.
 *B days.
  C months.
  D years.

12 A shirt is randomly drawn from a drawer containing 4 purple shirts, 2 red shirts, 3 green shirts, and 5 blue shirts. What is the probability that the shirt is either red or green?
  J $\frac{2}{14}$
  K $\frac{3}{14}$
  L $\frac{4}{14}$
 *M $\frac{5}{14}$

13 The number pattern 160, 80, 40, 20… is formed by dividing the last number in half to get the next one. What is the 6th number in this pattern?
  A 0
  B 2
 *C 5
  D 10

14 One quarter of the way through a free-throw shooting contest, Regina had made 7 baskets. To find out how many baskets she would make in the whole contest if she continued making baskets at the same rate, Regina should
  J add 7 and $\frac{1}{4}$.
 *K multiply 7 by 4.
  L multiply 7 by $\frac{1}{4}$.
  M divide 7 by 4.

GO

50 Answer rows 7 Ⓐ Ⓑ Ⓒ ●   9 Ⓐ ● Ⓒ Ⓓ   11 Ⓐ ● Ⓒ Ⓓ   13 Ⓐ Ⓑ ● Ⓓ
                 8 Ⓙ Ⓚ Ⓛ ● 10 Ⓙ Ⓚ ● Ⓜ   12 Ⓙ Ⓚ Ⓛ ●   14 Ⓙ ● Ⓛ Ⓜ

Unit 6 Test Yourself: Math Concepts and Estimation

Directions: For questions 15–26, choose the answer that is the best estimate of the exact answer.

15 Rachel has $15.21 in her piggy bank. Her little sister Anna has $\frac{2}{3}$ as much money in her piggy bank. The closest estimate of how much money Anna has in her piggy bank is _____.
- A $9
- *B $10
- C $12
- D $22

16 The closest estimate of $9\frac{5}{7} - 5\frac{1}{10}$ is _____.
- J 3
- K 4
- *L 5
- M 6

17

Customers in 42nd Street Post Office	
MONDAY	438
TUESDAY	693
WEDNESDAY	320
THURSDAY	194
FRIDAY	379

The closest estimate of the total customers in the 42nd Street Post Office for the week is _____.
- A 1,700
- B 1,800
- *C 2,000
- D 2,200

18 The closest estimate of 34,917 ÷ 352 is _____.
- *J 100
- K 1,000
- L 10,000
- M 100,000

19 There are 5,280 feet in 1 mile. There are 12 inches in a foot. The number of inches in a mile is between _____.
- A 20,000 and 35,000 inches
- B 35,000 and 50,000 inches
- *C 50,000 and 70,000 inches
- D 70,000 and 100,000 inches

20 $492 \div 7\frac{1}{5}$ is _____.
- J less than 60
- *K between 60 and 70
- L between 70 and 80
- M more than 80

Say It's time to stop. You have finished the Test Yourself lesson. Check to see that you have completely filled in your answer circles. Make sure that any marks for answers that you changed have been completely erased.

Go over the lesson with the students. Ask whether they had enough time to finish the lesson. Did they work carefully on scratch paper? Which questions required them to guess? What were some of the problems they experienced? Work through any problems that caused difficulty.

Have the students indicate completion of the lesson by entering their score for this activity on the progress chart at the beginning of the book. If necessary, provide additional practice problems similar to the ones in this unit.

 Test Yourself: Math Concepts and Estimation

21 The closest estimate of 40% of $145.98 is _____.
  A $30
  B $40
  C $50
 *D $60

22  Flippers $42.99 Sale ¼ off

The closest estimate of the amount saved by buying the flippers on sale is between _____.
  J $1 and $10
 *K $10 and $20
  L $20 and $30
  M $30 and $40

23

Number of Miles Traveled	
MONDAY	240
TUESDAY	90
WEDNESDAY	160
THURSDAY	70
FRIDAY	410
SATURDAY	180
SUNDAY	220

The closest estimate of the total distance traveled is _____.
  A 1,100 miles
  B 1,200 miles
 *C 1,400 miles
  D 1,500 miles

24  Tickets to the basketball game cost $10.50.

The closest estimate of how much it would cost for 3 people to go to a basketball game is between _____.
  J $27 and $30
 *K $30 and $33
  L $33 and $36
  M $36 and $39

25 The closest estimate of 19.85 × 2.04 is _____.
  A 30
  B 35
 *C 40
  D 45

26 The closest estimate of $2.95 + $7.15 + $1.89 + $3.30 is between _____.
 *J $15 and $16
  K $16 and $17
  L $17 and $18
  M $18 and $19

52 Answer rows 21 Ⓐ Ⓑ Ⓒ ● 23 Ⓐ Ⓑ ● Ⓓ 25 Ⓐ Ⓑ ● Ⓓ
              22 Ⓙ ● Ⓛ Ⓜ 24 Ⓙ ● Ⓛ Ⓜ 26 ● Ⓚ Ⓛ Ⓜ

---

68 Unit 6 **Test Yourself Math Concepts and Estimation**

Background

This unit contains five lessons that deal with math problem solving and data interpretation skills.

• **In Lessons 10a and 10b,** students solve word problems. They work methodically, indicate that the correct answer is not given, and practice converting items to a workable format. They also estimate an answer and take their best guess when unsure of the answer.

• **In Lessons 11a and 11b,** students solve problems involving data interpretation. Students use charts and graphs and practice finding the answer without computing. They evaluate answer choices, transfer numbers accurately, perform the correct operation, and compute carefully.

• **In the Test Yourself lesson,** the math problem solving, data interpretation, and test-taking skills introduced in Lessons 10a through 11b are reinforced and presented in a format that gives students the experience of taking an achievement test. Techniques for managing time effectively when taking a standardized test are reinforced.

Instructional Objectives

| Lesson 10a | **Math Problem Solving** | Given a word problem students identify which of three answer choices is correct or indicates that the correct answer is not given. |
| Lesson 10b | **Math Problem Solving** | |

| Lesson 11a | **Data Interpretation** | Given a problem involving a chart, diagram, or graph, students identify which of three answer choices is correct or indicates that the correct answer is not given. |
| Lesson 11b | **Data Interpretation** | |

| | **Test Yourself** | Given questions similar to those in Lessons 10a through 11b, students utilize problem solving, data interpretation, and test-taking strategies on achievement test formats. |

Lesson 10a
Math Problem Solving

Focus
Mathematics Skill
- solving word problems

Test-taking Skills
- indicating that the correct answer is not given
- working methodically
- converting items to a workable format
- estimating an answer

Sample A

Distribute scratch paper to the students.

Say Turn to Lesson 10a on page 53. In this lesson you will solve word problems. Read the directions at the top of the page to yourself.

Allow time for the students to read the directions.

Say Find Sample A. Read the question to yourselves. *(pause)* Find the best answer. *(answer C)* Yes, answer C is correct. Mark answer C for Sample A in the answer rows. Make sure the circle is completely filled in with a dark mark.

Check to see that the students have filled in the correct answer circle. Elaborate on the solution to the problem.

★TIPS

Say Now let's look at the tip.

Have a volunteer read the tip aloud to the group.

Say When you solve word problems, be sure to read them carefully. It may also help to estimate about how big the answer should be. This will help you find the right answer.

Math Problem Solving and Data Interpretation
Lesson 10a Math Problem Solving

Directions: Read each mathematics problem. Choose the best answer.

Sample A On Friday afternoon, Miguel received a phone call saying the computer software he had ordered would be delivered in five days. On which day will his computer software be delivered?

- A Monday
- B Tuesday
- *C Wednesday
- D Thursday

 • Read the question carefully. Think about how big the answer should be. Then solve the problem.

1 The Monton family went on a week-long vacation to the Oregon beach. They drove to the beach in two days. The first day they drove 495 miles, and on the second day, they drove 640 miles farther. How many miles farther was the Montons' second day of driving?
- *A 145
- B 640
- C 1,135
- D Not given

2 One night the 6 members of the Monton family went to dinner with their 3 friends and 4 relatives who lived at the beach. At the restaurant, no more than 5 people could sit at each table. Based on this information, at least how many tables did the group need?
- J 2
- *K 3
- L 13
- M Not given

3 A store at the beach rents 2 kinds of kites. The dragon kites rent for $7 a day, and the box kites rent for $5 a day. One day the Montons and another family rented out $55 worth of kites. Mrs. Monton will know how many kites the group rented if she
- A divides $55 by $5.
- B knows how many people were in the group.
- C multiplies $7 by $5 and subtracts the product from $55.
- *D knows how many dragon kites the group rented.

4 Mr. and Mrs. Monton bought a sand pail and shovel for each of their 4 children. They also bought 2 folding chairs for themselves. A sand pail and shovel costs $3, and a folding chair costs $7. How much did the Montons spend to buy the chairs and sand pails?
- J $12
- K $17
- L $20
- *M $26

Answer rows

Practice

Say We are ready for Practice. You are going to do more problems in the same way that we did the samples. Do not write anything except your answer choices in your book. If you think it will help, you may do your work on scratch paper. When you have finished working a problem, fill in the circle for your answer in the answer rows at the bottom of the page. If the answer you find is not one of the choices, choose the last answer, Not given. Make sure that the circles for your answer choices are completely filled in with dark marks. Completely erase any marks for answers that you change. Work until you come to the STOP sign at the bottom of the page. Do you have any questions? Start working now.

Allow time for the students to fill in their answers.

Say You may stop working now. You have finished Lesson 10a.

Review the answers with the students. If any problems caused particular difficulty, work through each of the answer choices. It may be helpful to have volunteers solve each problem at the chalkboard and discuss the strategy they used.

Have the students indicate completion of the lesson by entering their score for this activity on the progress chart at the beginning of the book.

 Unit 7

Math Problem Solving and Data Interpretation

Lesson 10a **Math Problem Solving**

Directions: Read each mathematics problem. Choose the best answer.

Sample A On Friday afternoon, Miguel received a phone call saying the computer software he had ordered would be delivered in five days. On which day will his computer software be delivered?

A Monday
B Tuesday
∗ C Wednesday
D Thursday

 • Read the question carefully. Think about how big the answer should be. Then solve the problem.

1 The Monton family went on a week-long vacation to the Oregon beach. They drove to the beach in two days. The first day they drove 495 miles, and on the second day, they drove 640 miles farther. How many miles farther was the Montons' second day of driving?
∗ A 145
B 640
C 1,135
D Not given

2 One night the 6 members of the Monton family went to dinner with their 3 friends and 4 relatives who lived at the beach. At the restaurant, no more than 5 people could sit at each table. Based on this information, at least how many tables did the group need?
J 2
∗ K 3
L 13
M Not given

3 A store at the beach rents 2 kinds of kites. The dragon kites rent for $7 a day, and the box kites rent for $5 a day. One day the Montons and another family rented out $55 worth of kites. Mrs. Monton will know how many kites the group rented if she
A divides $55 by $5.
B knows how many people were in the group.
C multiplies $7 by $5 and subtracts the product from $55.
∗ D knows how many dragon kites the group rented.

4 Mr. and Mrs. Monton bought a sand pail and shovel for each of their 4 children. They also bought 2 folding chairs for themselves. A sand pail and shovel costs $3, and a folding chair costs $7. How much did the Montons spend to buy the chairs and sand pails?
J $12
K $17
L $20
∗ M $26

Answer rows A ⒶⒷ●Ⓓ 1 ●ⒷⒸⒹ 2 Ⓙ●ⓁⓂ 3 ⒶⒷⒸ● 4 ⒿⓀⓁ●

53

Lesson 10a Math Problem Solving

Lesson 10b
Math Problem Solving

Focus

Mathematics Skill
• solving word problems

Test-taking Skills
• working methodically
• taking the best guess when unsure of the answer

Samples A and B

Distribute scratch paper to the students.

Say Turn to Lesson 10b on page 54. In this lesson you will solve more word problems. Read the directions at the top of the page to yourself.

Allow time for the students to read the directions.

Say Find Sample A. Read the question to yourselves and find the answer. You may use scratch paper to solve the problem. *(pause)* Which answer choice is correct? *(answer A)* Answer A is correct because Helen could spend exactly $23. Mark answer A for Sample A in the answer rows. Make sure the circle is completely filled in with a dark mark.

Check to see that the students have filled in the correct answer circle. Elaborate on the solution to the problem.

Say Now do Sample B. Read the problem to yourself. Think about what you should do before you solve the problem. *(pause)* Which answer is correct? *(answer L)* Answer L is correct because the 3 senior tickets would cost $30. Fill in answer L for Sample B in the answer rows at the bottom of the page. Be sure you fill in the circle with a dark mark.

Check to see that the students have filled in the correct answer circle. Elaborate on the solution to the problem.

Math Problem Solving and Data Interpretation

Lesson 10b **Math Problem Solving**

Directions: Read each mathematics problem. Choose the best answer.

Sample A
Helen had $23 to buy sandwiches for her family. Sandwiches cost either $4 or $5 each. Could Helen spend exactly $23 for sandwiches?
* A Yes.
  B No, she would have $1 left over.
  C No, she would have $2 left over.
  D No, she would have $3 left over.

Sample B
Senior tickets to a play cost $\frac{2}{3}$ of the adult price. For his grandparents, Eugene bought 3 senior tickets that cost $15 for adults. How much were 3 senior tickets?
  J $10
  K $20
* L $30
  M $45

TIPS
• It may help to outline a solution on scratch paper before you start to solve the problem.

1 The Evergreen Scenic Tour Train can hold 350 people. On a summer weekend, 298 people were on board the train. All but 13 of the people who purchased tickets came on the tour. How many tickets were sold in all?
  A 52
  B 285
* C 311
  D 337

2 Tickets to the Saturday tour cost $15. Tickets to the Sunday tour cost $\frac{2}{3}$ as much. All 350 tickets were bought for the Sunday tour. How much money did the owner make from the Sunday tour? To find out,
  J multiply $15 by 350.
  K multiply $15 by $\frac{2}{3}$.
  L multiply $15 by 3 and then multiply the product by 350.
* M multiply $15 by $\frac{2}{3}$ and then multiply the product by 350.

3 The Evergreen Scenic Tour Train usually makes about $3,500 for its special Fourth of July tour (with a special ticket price). Ticket prices are cut in half for the New Year's Eve tour, and usually about 175 people attend. How much does attendance change from the Fourth of July tour to the New Year's Eve tour?
* A It is impossible to tell without knowing the Fourth of July ticket price.
  B It is impossible to tell without knowing the New Year's Eve ticket price.
  C Attendance decreases by half.
  D Attendance doubles.

★**TIPS**

Say Now let's look at the tip.

Have a volunteer read the tip aloud to the group.

Say Sometimes it will help if you outline the solution to a problem on scratch paper before you try to solve it. This will help you decide which numbers to use and which operation to perform. It may even help you estimate the size of the answer.

Practice

Say We are ready for Practice. You are going to do more problems in the same way that we did the samples. Do not write anything except your answer choices in your book. If you think it will help, you may do your work on scratch paper. If you are not sure which answer is correct, take your best guess. When you have finished working a problem, fill in the circle for your answer in the answer rows at the bottom of the page. Make sure that the circles for your answer choices are completely filled in with dark marks. Completely erase any marks for answers that you change. Work until you come to the STOP sign at the bottom of the page. Do you have any questions? Start working now.

Allow time for the students to fill in their answers.

Say You may stop working now. You have finished Lesson 10b.

Review the answers with the students. If any problems caused particular difficulty, work through each of the answer choices. It may be helpful to have volunteers solve each problem at the chalkboard and discuss the strategy they used.

Have the students indicate completion of the lesson by entering their score for this activity on the progress chart at the beginning of the book.

Math Problem Solving and Data Interpretation

Lesson 10b **Math Problem Solving**

Directions: Read each mathematics problem. Choose the best answer.

Sample A Helen had $23 to buy sandwiches for her family. Sandwiches cost either $4 or $5 each. Could Helen spend exactly $23 for sandwiches?
* A Yes.
  B No, she would have $1 left over.
  C No, she would have $2 left over.
  D No, she would have $3 left over.

Sample B Senior tickets to a play cost $\frac{2}{3}$ of the adult price. For his grandparents, Eugene bought 3 senior tickets that cost $15 for adults. How much were 3 senior tickets?
  J $10
  K $20
* L $30
  M $45

 • It may help to outline a solution on scratch paper before you start to solve the problem.

1. The Evergreen Scenic Tour Train can hold 350 people. On a summer weekend, 298 people were on board the train. All but 13 of the people who purchased tickets came on the tour. How many tickets were sold in all?
   A 52
   B 285
* C 311
   D 337

2. Tickets to the Saturday tour cost $15. Tickets to the Sunday tour cost $\frac{2}{3}$ as much. All 350 tickets were bought for the Sunday tour. How much money did the owner make from the Sunday tour? To find out,
   J multiply $15 by 350.
   K multiply $15 by $\frac{2}{3}$.
   L multiply $15 by 3 and then multiply the product by 350.
* M multiply $15 by $\frac{2}{3}$ and then multiply the product by 350.

3. The Evergreen Scenic Tour Train usually makes about $3,500 for its special Fourth of July tour (with a special ticket price). Ticket prices are cut in half for the New Year's Eve tour, and usually about 175 people attend. How much does attendance change from the Fourth of July tour to the New Year's Eve tour?
* A It is impossible to tell without knowing the Fourth of July ticket price.
   B It is impossible to tell without knowing the New Year's Eve ticket price.
   C Attendance decreases by half.
   D Attendance doubles.

54 Answer rows A ●BCD B JK●M 1 AB●D 2 JKL● 3 ●BCD

Unit 7 Lesson 11a
Data Interpretation

Focus

Mathematics Skill
- interpreting tables and graphs

Test-taking Skills
- finding the answer without computing
- evaluating answer choices
- performing the correct operation
- computing carefully
- using charts and graphs
- transferring numbers accurately

Sample A

Distribute scratch paper to the students.

Say Turn to Lesson 11a on page 55. In this lesson you will solve problems involving a graph or chart. Read the directions at the top of the page to yourself.

Allow time for the students to read the directions.

Say Find Sample A. Look at the chart and read the question for Sample A to yourselves. Use the information in the chart to find the answer. *(pause)* Which answer choice is correct? *(answer D)* Yes, answer D is correct. *New York* has the largest area of the cities in the chart. Mark answer D for Sample A in the answer rows. Make sure the circle is completely filled in with a dark mark.

Check to see that the students have filled in the correct answer circle.

★ TIPS

Say Now let's look at the tips.

Have a volunteer read the tips aloud to the group.

Unit 7 Math Problem Solving and Data Interpretation

Lesson 11a **Data Interpretation**

Directions: Read each mathematics problem. Choose the best answer.

Sample A Which city has the largest area?
- A Tokyo
- B Mumbai
- C Moscow
- ∗ D New York

City	Area Sq. Mi.	Number of People	Density*
Beijing, China	151	5,736,000	38
Mumbia, India	95	11,777,000	124
Moscow, Russia	379	10,367,000	27
New York, U.S.A	1,274	14,622,000	11
Tokyo, Japan	1,089	26,952,000	25

*Thousands of people per square mile

TIPS
- Look at the graph or chart, and then read the questions. Look at the graph or chart when you solve the problem.
- When you solve the problem, transfer numbers carefully from the graph or chart.

Directions: Use the graph below to answer questions 1–4.

Kasota County Athlete Participation

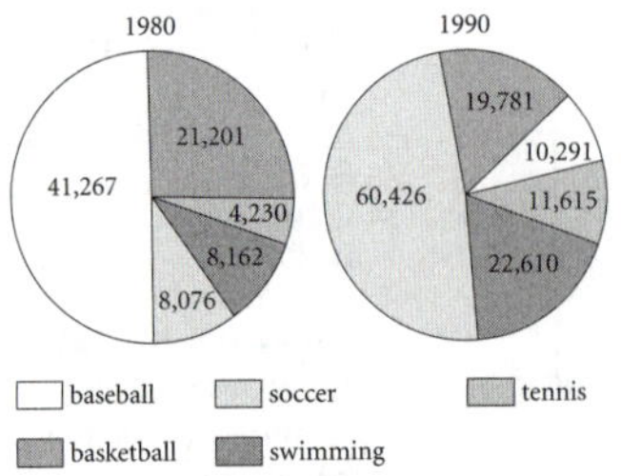

1980: 41,267; 21,201; 4,230; 8,162; 8,076
1990: 60,426; 19,781; 10,291; 11,615; 22,610

□ baseball □ soccer □ tennis
□ basketball □ swimming

1 What percentage of Kasota County athletes played soccer in 1980?
- ∗ A 10%
- B 25%
- C 50%
- D 90%

2 Which sport had the largest participation in Kasota County in 1990?
- J Baseball
- K Basketball
- ∗ L Soccer
- M Swimming

3 About what portion of athletes participated in either swimming or tennis in 1990 in Kasota County?
- A $\frac{1}{10}$
- B $\frac{1}{5}$
- ∗ C $\frac{1}{3}$
- D $\frac{1}{2}$

4 About how many athletes participated in basketball in 1980 in Kasota County?
- J 19,000
- ∗ K 21,000
- L 40,000
- M There is not enough information given to answer this question.

STOP

Say A good way to solve problems involving charts or graphs is to look at the chart or graph, read the question, then look back at the chart or graph when you solve the problem. Also, be sure to transfer numbers accurately from the graph or chart.

Practice

Say *We are ready for Practice. You are going to do more problems in the same way that we did the sample. Be sure to look at the graph when you solve the problems. Do not write anything except your answer choices in your book. If you think it will help, you may do your work on scratch paper. When you have finished working a problem, fill in the circle for your answer in the answer rows at the bottom of the page. Make sure that the circles for your answer choices are completely filled in with dark marks. Completely erase any marks for answers that you change. Work until you come to the STOP sign at the bottom of the page. Do you have any questions? Start working now.*

Allow time for the students to fill in their answers.

Say *You may stop working now. You have finished Lesson 11a.*

Review the answers with the students. If any problems caused particular difficulty, work through each of the answer choices. It may be helpful to have volunteers solve each problem at the chalkboard and discuss the strategy they used. You may also want to review the information in the graph to be sure the students understand how to interpret a circle graph.

Have the students indicate completion of the lesson by entering their score for this activity on the progress chart at the beginning of the book.

Math Problem Solving and Data Interpretation

Lesson 11a Data Interpretation

Directions: Read each mathematics problem. Choose the best answer.

Sample A Which city has the largest area?
A Tokyo
B Mumbai
C Moscow
* D New York

City	Area Sq. Mi.	Number of People	Density*
Beijing, China	151	5,736,000	38
Mumbia, India	95	11,777,000	124
Moscow, Russia	379	10,367,000	27
New York, U.S.A	1,274	14,622,000	11
Tokyo, Japan	1,089	26,952,000	25

*Thousands of people per square mile

- Look at the graph or chart, and then read the questions. Look at the graph or chart when you solve the problem.
- When you solve the problem, transfer numbers carefully from the graph or chart.

Directions: Use the graph below to answer questions 1–4.

Kasota County Athlete Participation

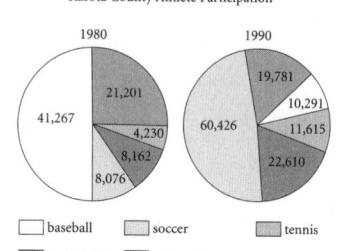

□ baseball   □ soccer   □ tennis
■ basketball ■ swimming

1 What percentage of Kasota County athletes played soccer in 1980?
* A 10%
B 25%
C 50%
D 90%

2 Which sport had the largest participation in Kasota County in 1990?
J Baseball
K Basketball
* L Soccer
M Swimming

3 About what portion of athletes participated in either swimming or tennis in 1990 in Kasota County?
A $\frac{1}{10}$
B $\frac{1}{5}$
* C $\frac{1}{3}$
D $\frac{1}{2}$

4 About how many athletes participated in basketball in 1980 in Kasota County?
J 19,000
* K 21,000
L 40,000
M There is not enough information given to answer this question.

Answer rows   A Ⓐ Ⓑ Ⓒ ●   1 ● Ⓑ Ⓒ Ⓓ   2 Ⓙ Ⓚ ● Ⓜ   3 Ⓐ Ⓑ ● Ⓓ   4 Ⓙ ● Ⓛ Ⓜ

Lesson 11b
Data Interpretation

Focus

Mathematics Skill
- interpreting graphs

Test-taking Skills
- working methodically
- finding the answer without computing
- using charts and graphs

Say Turn to Lesson 11b on page 56. In this lesson you will solve problems involving a graph.

Check to see that the students have found the right page.

Practice

Say For the Practice items in this lesson, you are going to do more problems in the same way that we did in Lesson 11a. Read the directions at the top of the page and look at the graph when you solve the problems. Do not write anything except your answer choices in your book. If you think it will help, you may do your work on scratch paper. When you have finished working a problem, fill in the circle for your answer in the answer rows at the bottom of the page. Make sure that the circles for your answer choices are completely filled in with dark marks. Completely erase any marks for answers that you change. Work until you come to the STOP sign at the bottom of the page. Do you have any questions? Start working now.

Allow time for the students to fill in their answers.

Say You may stop working now. You have finished Lesson 11b.

Math Problem Solving and Data Interpretation

Lesson 11b **Data Interpretation**

Directions: Use the graph below to answer questions 1–4.

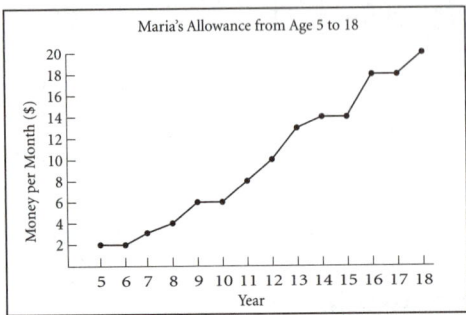

Maria's Allowance from Age 5 to 18

1 How much did Maria receive for her allowance when she was ten and a half?
- A $5
- B $6
- C $6.50
- * D $7

2 How old was Maria the last time her allowance was not increased?
- * J 17
- K 15
- L 10
- M 6

3 What was the largest increase in dollars in Maria's allowance?
- A $1
- B $2
- C $3
- * D $4

4 Which statement best describes Maria's allowance from ages 5 to 18?
- J Maria's allowance held fairly constant until she was 12 and then increased steadily.
- * K Maria's allowance increased gradually throughout this period.
- L Maria's allowance increased until she was 10 and then held fairly constant.
- M Maria's allowance decreased until she was 10 and then increased rapidly.

56 Answer rows 1 Ⓐ Ⓑ Ⓒ ●   2 ● Ⓚ Ⓛ Ⓜ   3 Ⓐ Ⓑ Ⓒ ●   4 Ⓙ ● Ⓛ Ⓜ

Review the answers with the students. If any problems caused particular difficulty, work through each of the answer choices. It may be helpful to have volunteers solve each problem and discuss the strategy they used.

Have the students indicate completion of the lesson by entering their score for this activity on the progress chart at the beginning of the book.

Unit 7 Test Yourself: Math Problem Solving and Data Interpretation

Focus

Mathematics Skills
- solving word problems
- interpreting tables and graphs

Test-taking Skills
- managing time effectively
- following printed directions
- indicating that the correct answer is not given
- working methodically
- converting items to a workable format
- estimating an answer
- taking the best guess when unsure of the answer
- finding the answer without computing
- evaluating answer choices
- performing the correct operation
- computing carefully
- using charts and graphs
- transferring numbers accurately

Unit 7 Test Yourself: Math Problem Solving and Data Interpretation

Directions: Read each mathematics problem. Choose the best answer.

Sample A
Dr. Proctor arrives at the hospital at 6 A.M. She does rounds until 10 A.M., then takes an hour to eat lunch and work out at the gym. She arrives at her office at 11 A.M. and sees patients until 4 P.M. Dr. Proctor goes home for a few hours, then returns to the hospital for 2 hours in the emergency room, starting at 8 P.M.

For how many hours does Dr. Proctor see patients in her office?
- A 4 hours
- *B 5 hours
- C 6 hours
- D Not given

Directions: Use the table below to answer questions 1–4.

Model	Price	MPG* Highway/City	Resale Rank
Venture	$16,000	32/24	5
Jetfire	$24,000	30/24	2
Lowboy	$21,000	28/22	6
Ultima	$35,000	22/16	1
Trakker	$17,500	26/24	4
Roadster	$32,000	20/14	3

*miles per gallon

1 Gerry is planning on buying a car. She has decided to buy a Trakker. The salesperson says the Trakker is on sale for 10% off. How much will she have to pay for the car she wants?
- A $15,570
- B $16,750
- C $17,500
- *D Not given

2 Gerry's parents own a Jetfire. They are going on a trip of 180 miles, all of which is highway. Gasoline costs $1.20 a gallon. How can they calculate how much they will spend on gas on the trip?
- *J 180 ÷ 30 × $1.20
- K 180 ÷ 24 × $1.20
- L $1.20 × 30 × 180
- M $1.20 × 24 × 180

3 Which car under $25,000 has the highest resale rank?
- A Roadster
- *B Jetfire
- C Ultima
- D Venture

GO

Answer rows A ⒶB●Ⓓ 1 ⒶⒷⒸ● 2 ●ⓀⓁⓂ 3 Ⓐ●ⒸⒹ

57

This lesson simulates an actual test-taking experience. Therefore, it is recommended that the directions be read verbatim and that the suggested procedures and time allowances be followed.

Directions

Administration Time: approximately 20 minutes

Distribute scratch paper to the students.

Say Turn to the Test Yourself lesson on page 57.

Point out to the students that this Test Yourself lesson is timed like a real test, but that they will score it themselves to see how well they are doing. Encourage them to read each question carefully, to think about what they are supposed to do, and to work carefully on scratch paper when necessary. They should skip difficult problems and return to them later and take their best guess when they are unsure of the answer.

Say This lesson will check how well you can solve mathematics problems like the ones we practiced before. Remember to make sure that the circles for your answer choices are completely filled in. Press your pencil firmly so that your marks come out dark. Completely erase any marks for answers that you change. Do not write anything except your answer choices in your books.

Look at Sample A. Read the story, the question, and the answer choices. Mark the circle for the answer you think is correct.

Allow time for the students to fill in their answers.

Unit 7 Test Yourself Math Problem Solving and Data Interpretation   77

Say The circle for answer B should be filled in. Dr. Proctor sees patients in her office for 5 hours. If you chose another answer, erase yours and fill in circle B now.

Check to see that the students have filled in the correct answer circle.

Say Now you will solve more problems. You may use the scratch paper I gave you. When you come to the GO sign at the bottom of the page, turn the page and continue working. Work until you come to the STOP sign at the bottom of page 58. Make sure that the circles for your answer choices are completely filled in with dark marks. Be sure to fill in the circle in the answer row for the problem you are working on. Completely erase any marks for answers that you change. You will have 15 minutes to solve the problems. You may begin.

Allow 15 minutes.

Say It's time to stop. You have finished the Test Yourself lesson. Check to see that you have completely filled in your answer circles. Make sure that any marks for answers that you changed have been completely erased.

Go over the lesson with the students. Ask whether they had enough time to finish the lesson. Did they work carefully on scratch paper? Which questions required them to guess? What were some of the problems they experienced? Work through any problems that caused difficulty.

Have the students indicate completion of the lesson by entering their score for this activity on the progress chart at the beginning of the book. If necessary, provide additional practice problems similar to the ones in this unit.

Unit 7 Test Yourself: Math Problem Solving and Data Interpretation

4 When the software arrives, Miguel discovers that it is on 2 disks. One disk has programs that take up 947 kilobytes of space, and the other has programs that take up 643 kilobytes of space. His hard disk drive has 5000 kilobytes of space left. How can Miguel find out how much space will be left on his disk drive after he copies the contents of the two disks onto it?
  J Add 947 and 643, multiply by 2, then subtract the total from 5,000.
  K Add 947, 643, and 5,000.
  L Subtract 643 from 947 and divide by 2.
* M Add 947 and 643, then subtract the total from 5,000.

Directions: Use the graph below to answer questions 5–8.

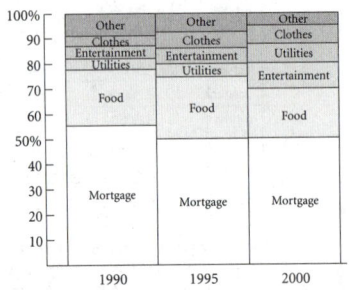

Dunn Family Expenses

5 Which expense increased the most from 1990 to 2000?
  A Food
  B Utilities
* C Entertainment
  D Mortgage

6 For each of the three years, which expense has about the same percentage of the total as entertainment?
* J Clothes
  K Food
  L Utilities
  M Other

7 In 1995, mortgage payments and food accounted for what percent of the Dunn family's total expenses?
  A 20%
  B 50%
* C 70%
  D 85%

8 The family spent more on entertainment each year. From which category did this increase probably come?
  J Clothes
* K Mortgage
  L Utilities
  M Other

58 Answer rows 4 ⓙⓀⓁ● 5 ⒶⒷ●Ⓓ 6 ●ⓀⓁⓂ 7 ⒶⒷ●Ⓓ 8 Ⓙ●ⓁⓂ

Unit 8

Background

This unit contains five lessons that deal with math computation skills.

• **In Lessons 12a and 12b,** students solve problems involving addition and subtraction of whole numbers, fractions, and decimals. Students practice performing the correct operation, computing carefully, and transferring numbers accurately. They indicate that the correct answer is not given, convert items to a workable format, work methodically, and take their best guess when unsure of the answer.

• **In Lessons 13a and 13b,** students solve problems involving multiplication and division. In addition to reviewing the test-taking skills introduced in the previous lessons, students learn to skip difficult items and return to them later.

• **In the Test Yourself lesson,** the math computation skills and test-taking skills introduced in Lessons 12a through 13b are reinforced and presented in a format that gives students the experience of taking an achievement test. Techniques for managing time effectively when taking a standardized test are reinforced.

Instructional Objectives

Lesson 12a	**Adding and Subtracting**	Given a problem involving adding or subtracting, students identify which of three answer choices is correct or indicates that the correct answer is not given.
Lesson 12b	**Adding and Subtracting**	
Lesson 13a	**Multiplying and Dividing**	Given a problem involving multiplying or dividing, students identify which of three answer choices is correct or indicates that the correct answer is not given.
Lesson 13b	**Multiplying and Dividing**	
	Test Yourself	Given questions similar to those in Lessons 12a through 13b, students utilize computation and test-taking strategies on achievement test formats.

Lesson 12a
Adding and Subtracting

Focus

Mathematics Skill
- adding and subtracting whole numbers, fractions, and decimals

Test-taking Skills
- performing the correct operation
- computing carefully
- transferring numbers accurately
- indicating that the correct answer is not given
- converting items to a workable format
- working methodically

Samples A and B

Distribute scratch paper to the students.

Say Turn to Lesson 12a on page 59. In this lesson you will solve addition and subtraction problems. Read the directions at the top of the page to yourself while I read them out loud.

Read the directions out loud to the students.

Say Let's do Sample A. Read the problem and find the answer. You may work on the scratch paper I gave you. If you do work on scratch paper, be sure to transfer numbers accurately and compute carefully. *(pause)* Which answer choice is correct *(answer C)* What answer did you get? *(890,295)* Mark answer circle C for Sample A in the answer rows at the bottom of the page. Make sure the circle is completely filled in with a dark mark.

Check to see that the students have filled in the correct answer circle. Demonstrate the solution to the problem on the chalkboard.

Say Do Sample B yourself. Read the problem and choose the answer you think is correct. If the correct answer is not one of the choices, choose the last answer, N. *(pause)* What answer should you choose? *(answer M)* Yes, the solution to the problem, *0.44,* is not one of the choices. Fill in circle M for Sample B in the answer rows. Make sure it is completely filled in with a dark mark.

Check to see that the students have filled in the correct answer circle.

★ **TIPS**

Say Now let's look at the tips.

Have a volunteer read the tips aloud to the group.

Say When you work on scratch paper, be sure you transfer numbers accurately and work carefully. It's a good idea to solve the problem on scratch paper before you look at the answer choices. Once you have solved the problem, you can compare your answer with the answer choices.

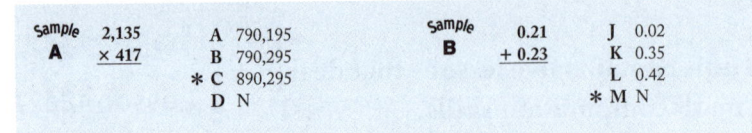

Page 59 student workbook showing Math Computation Lesson 12a with Sample A (2,135 × 417, answer C 890,295), Sample B (0.21 + 0.23, answer M N), and problems 1–8:

1. 67 + 8 + 124 + 53 = (C 252)
2. 17/32 − 13/32 = (J 1/8)
3. 8.7 + 2.3 = (C 11.0)
4. 0.69 − 0.3 = (M N)
5. 0.51 + 7 + 3.8 = (C 11.31)
6. 8/10 + 4/10 = (M N)
7. 7,423 − 2,968 = (A 4,455)
8. 3 − 0.72 = (K 2.28)

Practice

Say We are ready for Practice. You are going to do more problems in the same way that we did the samples. Do not write anything in your book except your answer choices. If you need to, use scratch paper to work the problems. Transfer numbers accurately to scratch paper and be sure to compute carefully. Pay careful attention to the operation sign for each problem. If the answer you find is not one of the choices, choose the last answer, *N*. Work until you come to the STOP sign at the bottom of the page. Make sure that the circles for your answer choices are completely filled in with dark marks. Erase any marks for answers that you change. You may begin.

Allow time for the students to fill in their answers.

Say It's time to stop. You have finished Lesson 12a.

Review the answers with the students. If any problems caused particular difficulty, work through each of the answer choices. Be sure to demonstrate each computation process in detail.

Have the students indicate completion of the lesson by entering their score for this activity on the progress chart at the beginning of the book.

 Unit 8 **Math Computation**
Lesson 12a **Adding and Subtracting**

Directions: Solve each problem. Choose the answer you think is correct. If the correct answer is not given, fill in the space for the last answer, N.

| Sample A | 2,135 × 417 | A 790,195
B 790,295
*C 890,295
D N | Sample B | 0.21 + 0.23 | J 0.02
K 0.35
L 0.42
*M N |

 **TIPS**
- Transfer numbers carefully to scratch paper, and be sure to perform the correct operation.
- Work the problem on scratch paper before you look at the answer choices.

1. 67
   8
   124
   + 53

   A 152
   B 242
   *C 252
   D N

2. $\frac{17}{32} - \frac{13}{32} =$

   *J $\frac{1}{8}$
   K $\frac{1}{16}$
   L $\frac{30}{32}$
   M N

3. 8.7 + 2.3 =

   A 10.0
   B 10.10
   *C 11.0
   D N

4. 0.69 − 0.3 =

   J 0.0039
   K 0.36
   L 0.66
   *M N

5. 0.51 + 7 + 3.8 =

   A 0.96
   B 10.59
   *C 11.31
   D N

6. $\frac{8}{10} + \frac{4}{10} =$

   J $\frac{2}{5}$
   K $\frac{4}{5}$
   L $\frac{5}{10}$
   *M N

7. 7,423
   − 2,968

   *A 4,455
   B 4,465
   C 4,565
   D N

8. 3 − 0.72 =

   J 0.69
   *K 2.28
   L 2.72
   M N

Answer rows   A ⓐⓑ●ⓓ   1 ⓐⓑ●ⓓ   3 ⓐⓑ●ⓓ   5 ⓐⓑ●ⓓ   7 ●ⓑⓒⓓ
              B ⓙⓚⓛ●   2 ●ⓚⓛⓜ   4 ⓙⓚⓛ●   6 ⓙⓚⓛ●   8 ⓙ●ⓛⓜ

Lesson 12b
Adding and Subtracting

Focus

Mathematics Skill
- adding and subtracting whole numbers, fractions, and decimals

Test-taking Skills
- performing the correct operation
- computing carefully
- transferring numbers accurately
- indicating that the correct answer is not given
- taking the best guess when unsure of the answer

Samples A and B

Distribute scratch paper to the students.

Say Turn to Lesson 12b on page 60. In this lesson you will solve more addition and subtraction problems. Read the directions at the top of the page to yourself while I read them out loud.

Read the directions out loud to the students.

Say Let's do Sample A. Read the problem and find the answer. You may work on the scratch paper I gave you. *(pause)* Which answer choice is correct? *(answer C, 1.7)* Mark answer circle C for Sample A in the answer rows at the bottom of the page. Make sure the circle is completely filled in with a dark mark.

Check to see that the students have filled in the correct answer circle.

Say Now do Sample B. Read the problem and choose the answer you think is correct. *(pause)* What is the correct answer? *(answer K)* Answer K is correct because *five-ninths* is the solution to the problem. Fill in circle K for Sample B in the answer rows. Make sure it is completely filled in with a dark mark.

Check to see that the students have filled in the correct answer circle. Review the solution to each of the sample items on the chalkboard.

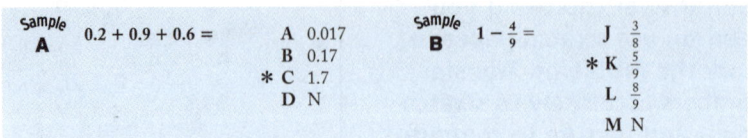

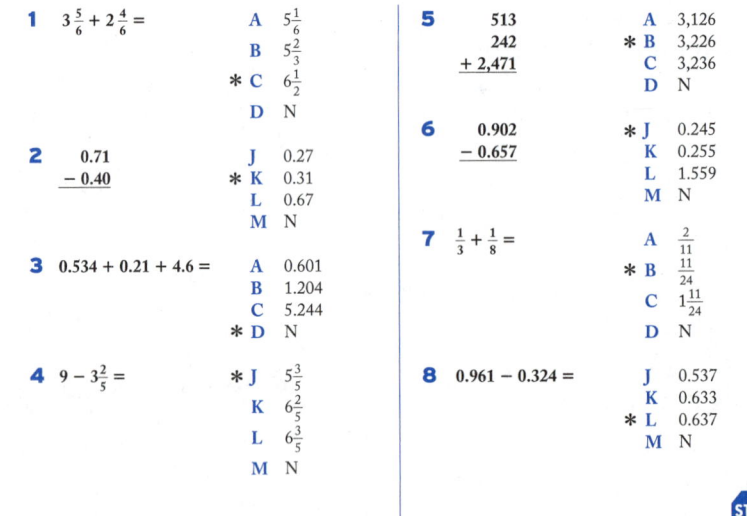

★ TIPS

Say Now let's look at the tip.

Have a volunteer read the tip aloud to the group.

Say When you solve computation problems that involve fractions and decimals, be sure to look at the numbers in the problem carefully. It is easy to make mistakes when you transfer and calculate with fractions and decimals.

82   Lesson 12b Adding and Subtracting

Practice

Say We are ready for Practice. You are going to do more problems in the same way that we did the samples. Do not write anything in your book except your answer choices. If necessary, use scratch paper to work the problems. Pay careful attention to the operation sign for each problem, and rearrange the problem on scratch paper in a way that will help you solve it. If you are not sure which answer is correct, be sure to take your best guess. Work until you come to the STOP sign at the bottom of the page. Make sure that the circles for your answer choices are completely filled in with dark marks. Erase any marks for answers that you change. You may begin.

Allow time for the students to fill in their answers.

Say It's time to stop. You have finished Lesson 12b.

Review the answers with the students. If any problems caused particular difficulty, work through each of the answer choices.

Have the students indicate completion of the lesson by entering their score for this activity on the progress chart at the beginning of the book.

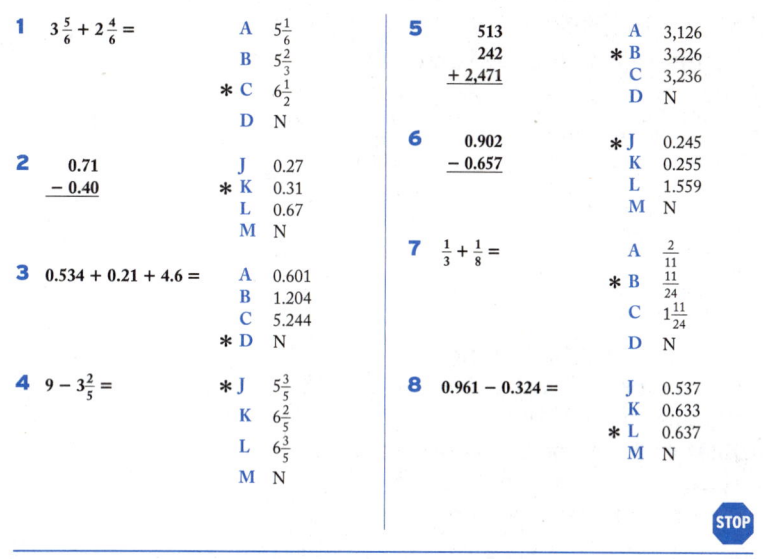

Unit 8 Lesson 12b **Adding and Subtracting**   83

Unit 8 Lesson 13a
Multiplying and Dividing

Focus

Mathematics Skill
- multiplying and dividing whole numbers, fractions, and decimals

Test-taking Skills
- performing the correct operation
- computing carefully
- transferring numbers accurately
- indicating that the correct answer is not given
- converting items to a workable format
- working methodically

Samples A and B

Distribute scratch paper to the students.

Say Turn to Lesson 13a on page 61. In this lesson you will solve multiplication and division problems. Read the directions at the top of the page to yourself while I read them out loud.

Read the directions out loud to the students.

Say Let's do Sample A. Read the problem and find the answer. You may work on the scratch paper I gave you. *(pause)* Which answer choice is correct? *(answer B, 25,200)* Mark answer circle B for Sample A in the answer rows at the bottom of the page. Make sure the circle is completely filled in with a dark mark.

Check to see that the students have filled in the correct answer circle.

Say Do Sample B yourself. Read the problem and choose the answer you think is correct. *(pause)* What is the correct answer? *(answer J)* Yes, answer J is correct because the solution to the problem is *one-thirtieth*. Fill in circle J for Sample B in the answer rows. Make sure it is completely filled in with a dark mark.

Check to see that the students have filled in the correct answer circle. Review the solution to each sample item on the chalkboard.

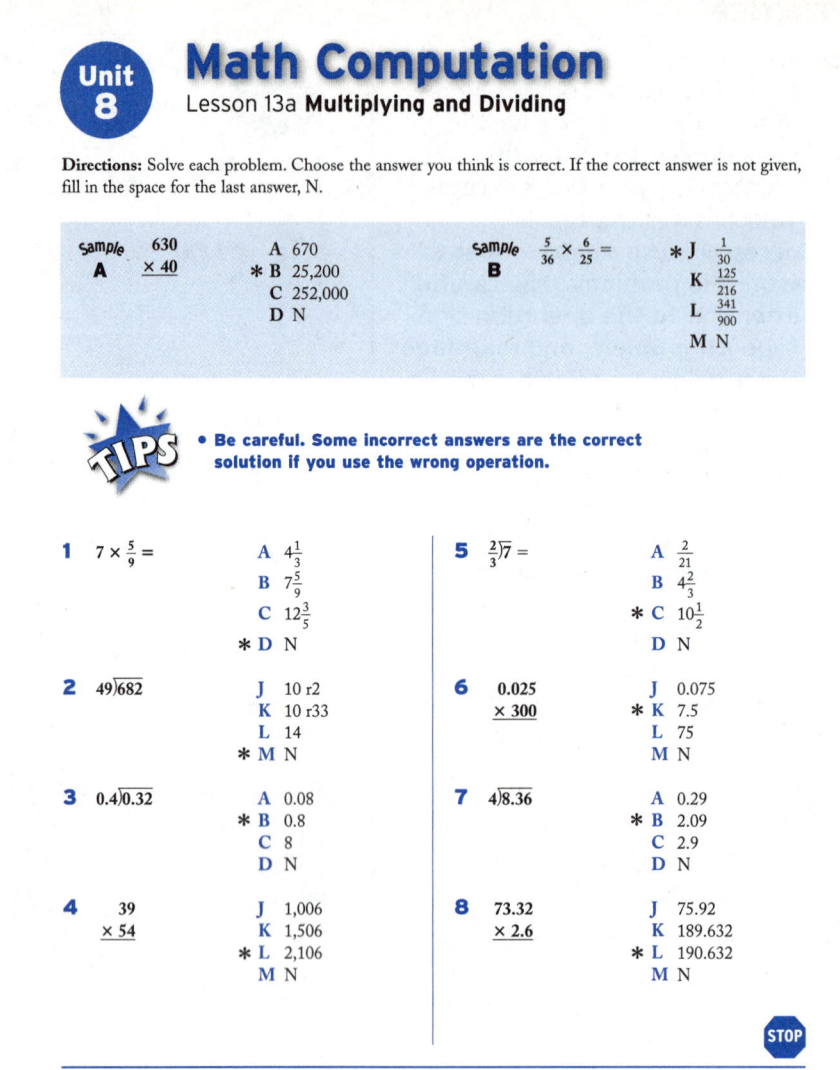

Say Now let's look at the tip.

Have a volunteer read the tip aloud to the group.

Say On an achievement test, one of the incorrect answers is sometimes the solution to a problem using the same numbers but a different operation. Be careful because you might choose this answer by mistake if you don't pay close attention to the operation sign in a problem.

Point out that answer A of Sample A is the correct solution to an addition problem involving the two numbers in Sample A. The students might choose this answer if they did not pay close attention to the operation sign.

84 Unit 8 Lesson 13a **Multiplying and Dividing**

Practice

Say We are ready for Practice. You are going to do more problems in the same way that we did the samples. Do not write anything in your book except your answer choices. If you need to, use scratch paper to work the problems. Pay careful attention to the operation sign for each problem, and rearrange the problem on scratch paper in a way that will help you solve it. If you are not sure which answer is correct, be sure to take your best guess. Work until you come to the STOP sign at the bottom of the page. Make sure that the circles for your answer choices are completely filled in with dark marks. Erase any marks for answers that you change. You may begin.

Allow time for the students to fill in their answers.

Say It's time to stop. You have finished Lesson 13a.

Review the answers with the students. If any problems caused particular difficulty, work through each of the answer choices.

Have the students indicate completion of the lesson by entering their score for this activity on the progress chart at the beginning of the book.

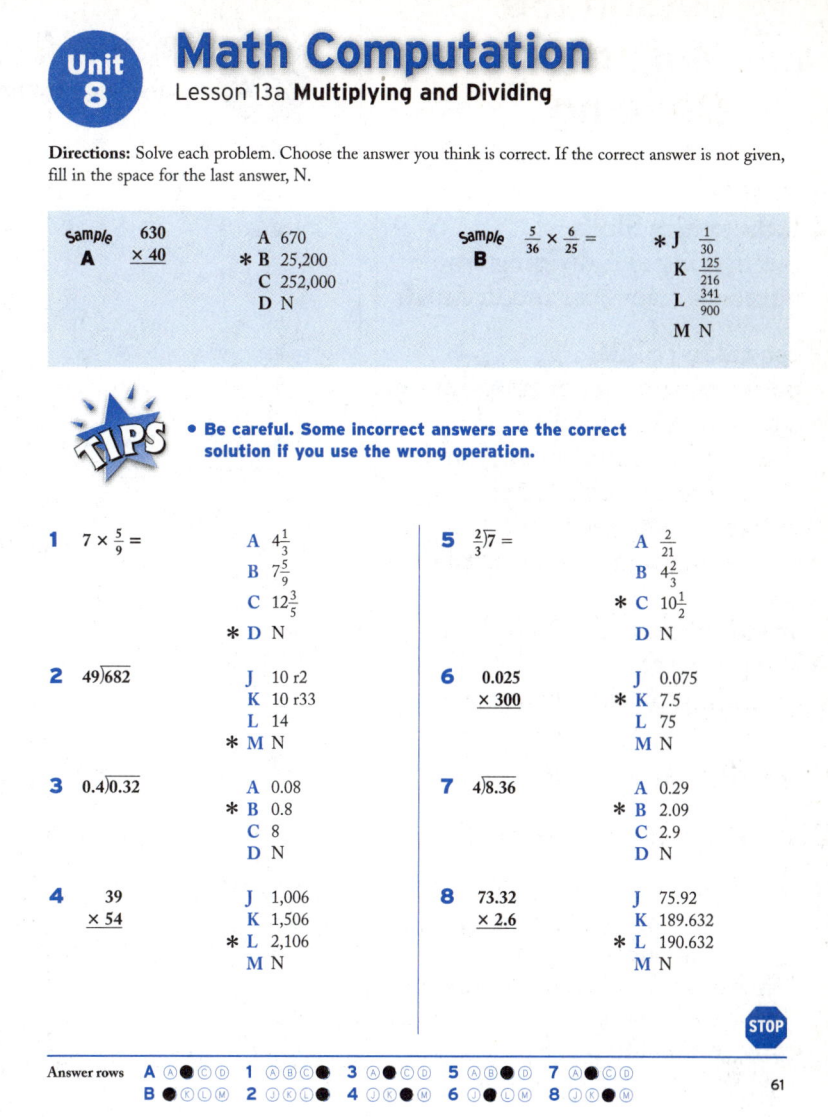

Unit 8 Lesson 13b
Multiplying and Dividing

Focus

Mathematics Skills
- multiplying and dividing whole numbers, fractions, and decimals

Test-taking Skills
- performing the correct operation
- computing carefully
- transferring numbers accurately
- indicating that the correct answer is not given
- converting items to a workable format
- working methodically
- skipping difficult items and returning to them later

Samples A and B

Distribute scratch paper to the students.

Say Turn to Lesson 13b on page 62. In this lesson you will solve more multiplication and division problems. Read the directions at the top of the page to yourself while I read them out loud.

Read the directions out loud to the students.

Say Let's do Sample A. Read the problem and find the answer. You may work on the scratch paper I gave you. *(pause)* Which answer choice is correct? *(answer A)* The correct answer is *one-fourth*. Mark answer circle A for Sample A in the answer rows at the bottom of the page. Make sure the circle is completely filled in with a dark mark.

Check to see that the students have filled in the correct answer circle.

Say Do Sample B yourself. Read the problem and choose the answer you think is correct. *(pause)* What is the correct answer? *(answer L)* Yes, answer L is correct because the solution to the division problem is *0.08*. Fill in circle L for Sample B in the answer rows. Make sure it is completely filled in with a dark mark.

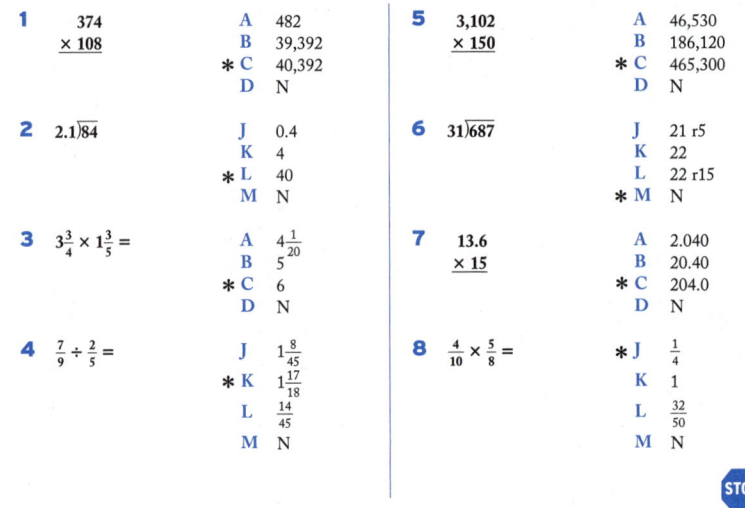

Check to see that the students have filled in the correct answer circle.

★TIPS

Say Now let's look at the tip.

Have a volunteer read the tip aloud to the group.

Say When you solve problems involving fractions and decimals, pay extra attention. It is easy to make mistakes if you are not careful, expecially when you are multiplying and dividing. These operations require special rules when they involve fractions and decimals.

Solve the sample items on the chalkboard. Emphasize each step of the solution, particularly those associated with operations involving fractions and decimals.

86 Unit 8 Lesson 13b **Multiplying and Dividing**

Practice

Say We are ready for Practice. You are going to do more problems in the same way that we did the samples. Do not write anything in your book except your answer choices. If you need to, use scratch paper to work the problems. Pay careful attention to the operation sign for each problem, and rearrange the problem on scratch paper in a way that will help you solve it. If an item seems difficult, skip it and come back to it later. Work until you come to the STOP sign at the bottom of the page. Make sure that the circles for your answer choices are completely filled in with dark marks. Erase any marks for answers that you change. You may begin.

Allow time for the students to fill in their answers.

Say It's time to stop. You have finished Lesson 13b.

Review the answers with the students. If any problems caused particular difficulty, work through each of the answer choices. Pay extra attention to the items involving fractions and decimals.

Have the students indicate completion of the lesson by entering their score for this activity on the progress chart at the beginning of the book.

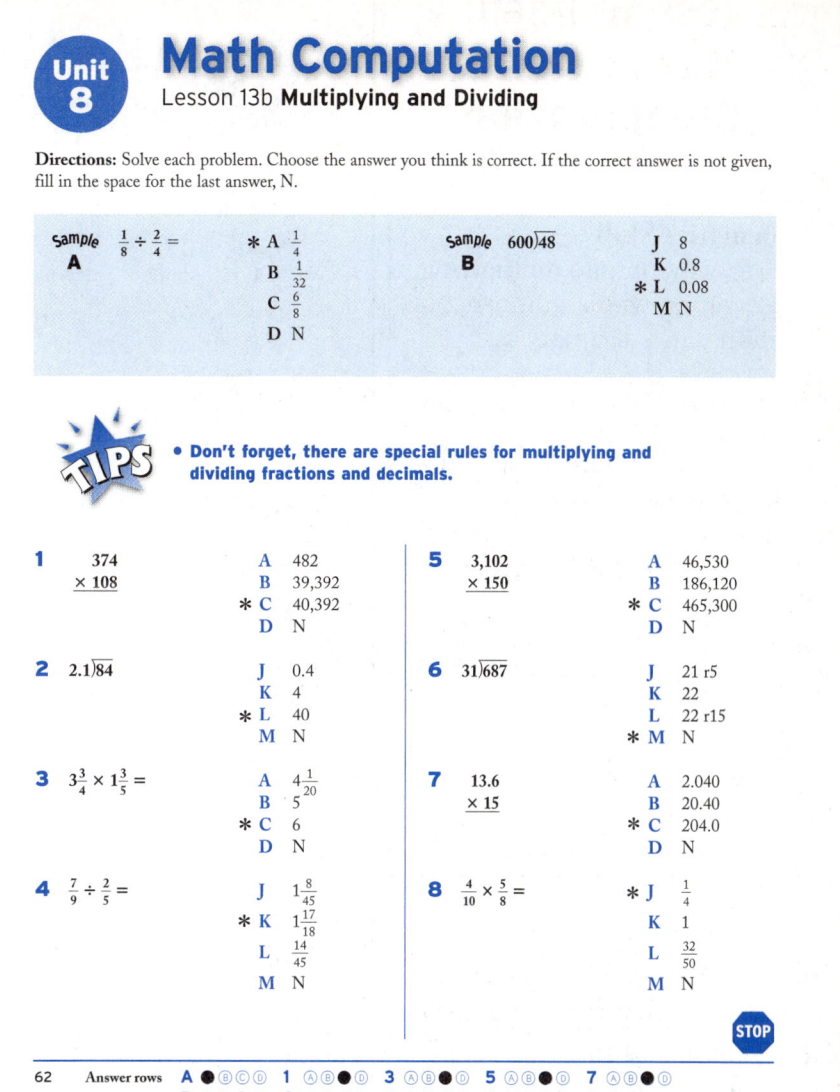

Lesson 13b **Multiplying and Dividing** 87

Unit 8 Test Yourself: Math Computation

Focus

Mathematics Skill
- adding, subtracting, multiplying, and dividing whole numbers, fractions, and decimals

Test-taking Skills
- managing time effectively
- performing the correct operation
- computing carefully
- transferring numbers accurately
- indicating that the correct answer is not given
- converting items to a workable format
- working methodically
- taking the best guess when unsure of the answer
- skipping difficult items and returning to them later

This lesson simulates an actual test-taking experience. Therefore, it is recommended that the directions be read verbatim and that the suggested procedures and time allowances be followed.

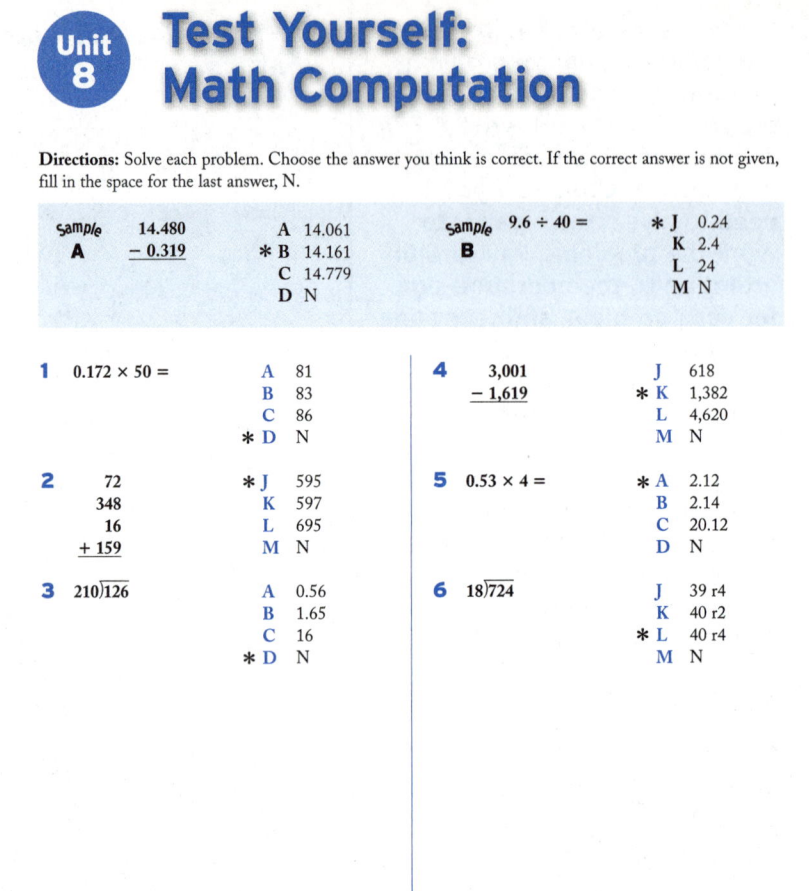

Directions

Administration Time: approximately 20 minutes

Distribute scratch paper to the students.

Say Turn to the Test Yourself lesson on page 63.

Point out to the students that this Test Yourself lesson is timed like a real test, but that they will score it themselves to see how well they are doing. Encourage them to read each question carefully, to think about what they are supposed to do, and to work carefully on scratch paper when necessary. They should skip difficult problems and return to them later and take their best guess when they are unsure of the answer.

Say This lesson will check how well you can solve computation problems. Remember to make sure that the circles for your answer choices are completely filled in. Press your pencil firmly so that your marks come out dark. Completely erase any marks for answers that you change. Do not write anything except your answer choices in your books.

Look at Sample A. Read the question and the answer choices. Mark the circle for the answer you think is correct.

Allow time for the students to fill in their answers.

Say The circle for answer B should be filled in. If you chose another answer, erase yours and fill in circle B now.

Check to see that the students have filled in the correct answer circle.

Say Now do Sample B. Solve the problem and fill in the circle for the answer you think is correct.

Allow time for the students to fill in their answers.

Say The circle for answer J should be filled in. If you chose another answer, erase yours and fill in circle J now.

Check to see that the students have filled in the correct answer circle.

Say Now you will do more mathematics problems. You may use the scratch paper I gave you. Remember, for some items, the correct answer is not given. When this happens, choose the last answer. When you come to the GO sign at the bottom of the page, turn the page and continue working. Work until you come to the STOP sign at the bottom of page 64. Make sure that the circles for your answer choices are completely filled in with dark marks. Be sure to fill in the circle in the answer row for the problem you are working on. Completely erase any marks for answers that you change. You will have 15 minutes to solve the problems. You may begin.

Allow 15 minutes.

Say It's time to stop. You have finished the Test Yourself lesson. Check to see that you have completely filled in your answer circles. Make sure that any marks for answers that you changed have been completely erased.

Go over the lesson with the students. Ask whether they had enough time to finish the lesson. Did they work carefully on scratch paper? Which questions required them to guess? What were some of the problems they experienced? Work through any problems that caused difficulty.

Have the students indicate completion of the lesson by entering their score for this activity on the progress chart at the beginning of the book. If necessary, provide additional practice problems similar to the ones in this unit.

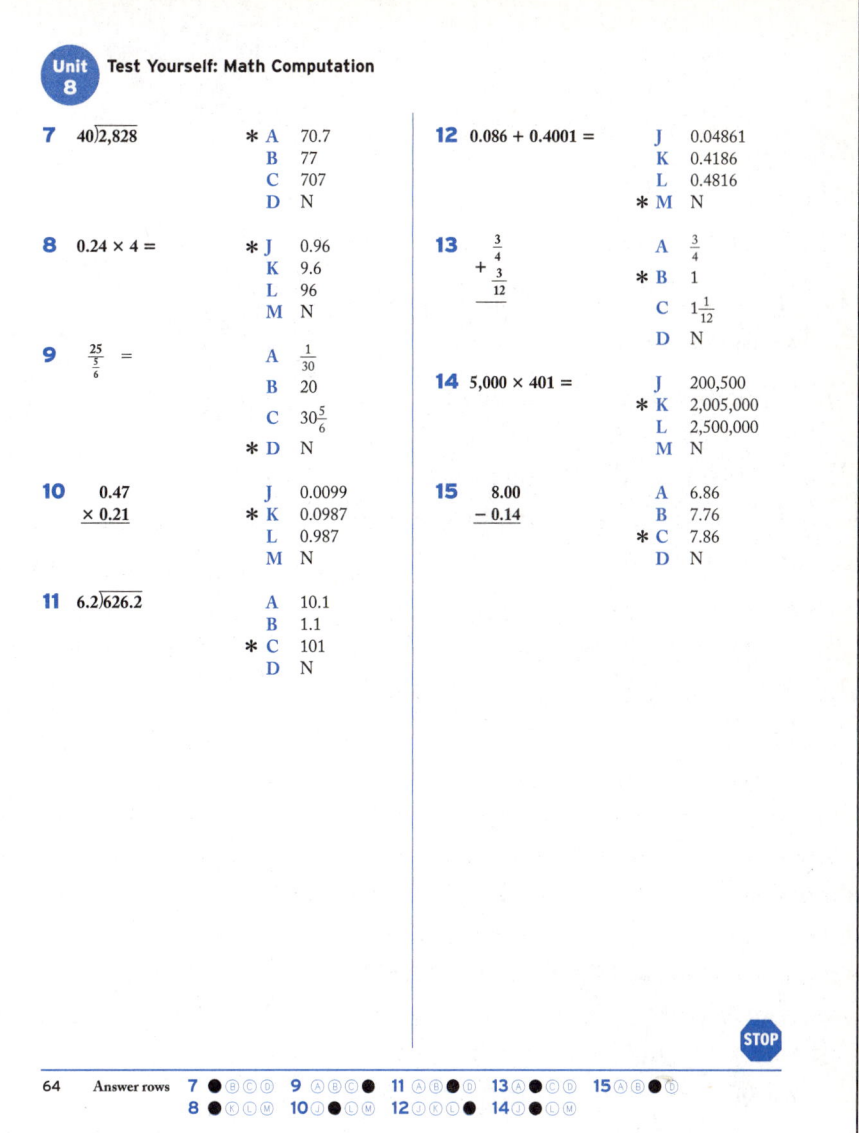

Unit 9

Background

This unit contains seven lessons that deal with study skills.

- **In Lessons 14a and 14b,** students answer questions about a diagram or map. They work methodically, refer to a reference source, skim a reference source, and evaluate answer choices.

- **In Lessons 15a through 16b,** students answer questions about the Dewey decimal classification system and *Reader's Guide to Periodical Literature*. They use a dictionary and an index, differentiate among reference sources, and use key words. In addition to reviewing the test-taking skills introduced in earlier lessons, the students recall prior knowledge, restate a question, take their best guess when unsure of the answer, and skip difficult items and return to them later. They also learn to mark the right answer as soon as it is found.

- **In the Test Yourself lesson,** the study skills and test-taking skills introduced and used in Lessons 14a through 16b are reinforced and presented in a format that gives students the experience of taking an achievement test. Techniques for managing time effectively when taking a standardized test are reinforced.

Instructional Objectives

Lesson 14a **Maps and Diagrams** Lesson 14b **Maps and Diagrams**	Given a question about a map or diagram, students identify which of four answer choices is correct.
Lesson 15a **Reference Materials** Lesson 15b **Reference Materials** Lesson 16a **Reference Materials** Lesson 16b **Reference Materials**	Given a question about a reference source, index, dictionary, key words, the Dewey decimal classification system, or the *Reader's Guide to Periodical Literature*, students identify which of four answer choices is correct.
Test Yourself	Given questions similar to those in Lessons 14a through 16b, students utilize study skills and test-taking strategies on achievement test formats.

Lesson 14a
Maps and Diagrams

Focus

Reference Skills
- understanding a map
- understanding a diagram

Test-taking Skills
- working methodically
- skimming a reference source
- referring to a reference source
- evaluating answer choices

Sample A

Say Turn to Lesson 14a on page 65. In this lesson you will practice using maps and diagrams. Read the directions at the top of the page to yourself.

Allow time for the students to read the directions.

Say Look at the map at the top of the page and read the question for Sample A. What is the correct answer to the question? *(pause)* Answer D is correct. Mark circle D for Sample A in the answer rows at the bottom of the page. Make sure the circle is completely filled in. Press your pencil firmly so that your mark comes out dark.

Check to see that the students have filled in the correct answer circle.

★TIPS

Say Now let's look at the tips.

Have a volunteer read the tips aloud.

Say Whenever you answer questions about a reference source, it is a good idea to skim the reference source and then read the questions. Don't try to remember the information in the reference source. Instead, look back at it to find the answer. Once you decide which answer is correct, check your answer against the reference source to be sure it makes sense.

Lesson 14a **Maps and Diagrams**

Directions: Read each question. Choose the best answer.

Which county in the imaginary state on the left is in the northeast corner?
A A
B B
C C
*D D

TIPS
- Skim the map or diagram; then read the questions. Sometimes reading the questions will help you understand better.
- After you choose your answer, check it against the map or diagram to make sure it is correct.

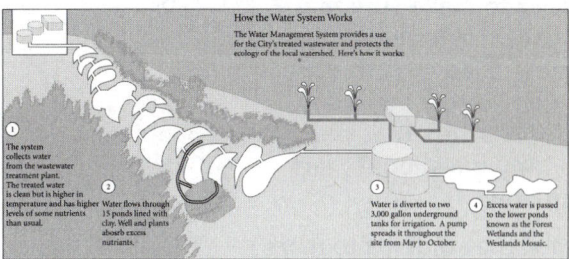

Directions: The diagram above illustrates how the water management system at the Kalapooia Garden uses the city of Pinau's treated wastewater. Use the diagram and key to answer questions 1–4.

1   Which sequence of steps is used in this water management system?
  A Pouring, lining, covering, spreading
  B Dripping, passing, flowing, filling
*C Collecting, flowing, diverting, passing
  D Treating, absorbing, pushing, soaking

2   Which of these happens to the water before it reaches the Kalapooia Garden?
  J It is sent to two 3,000 gallon tanks.
*K It is treated.
  L It is passed into the lower ponds.
  M It is absorbed.

GO

Answer rows   A Ⓐ Ⓑ Ⓒ ●   1 Ⓐ Ⓑ ● Ⓓ   2 Ⓙ ● Ⓛ Ⓜ

Lesson 14a Maps and Diagrams   91

Practice

Say Let's do the Practice items now. There are different kinds of items in this lesson. Be sure to read the directions for each section when you answer the questions. Think about what the questions are asking and be sure to refer to the map or diagram to answer the questions. When you come to the GO sign at the bottom of the page, turn the page and continue working. Work until you come to the STOP sign at the bottom of page 66. Remember to make sure that your answer circles are completely filled in with dark marks. Completely erase any marks for answers that you change. Any questions? Start working now.

Allow time for the students to mark their answers.

Say It's time to stop. You have finished Lesson 14a.

Review the answers with the students. If any questions caused particular difficulty, work through each of the answer choices.

Have the students indicate completion of the lesson by entering their score for this activity on the progress chart at the beginning of the book.

Unit 9 Lesson 14a **Maps and Diagrams**

3 Why must the water flow through fifteen clay-lined ponds?
   A To raise the temperature of the water
   B To create a natural-looking waterfall
 ∗ C To allow excess nutrients to be absorbed
   D To make sure the ponds are full all year

4 What happens to the water that does not fit in the 3,000-gallon tanks?
   J It is pumped throughout the site.
 ∗ K It is passed to the lower ponds.
   L It is stored for the dry season.
   M It is returned to the city's treatment plant.

Directions: The diagram below describes how electricity gets from the source to the consumer. Use the diagram to answer questions 5–10.

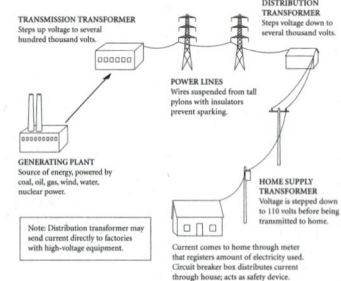

5 Which three terms best describe the path shown in this diagram?
   A Generation, use, current
   B Current, source, voltage
   C Voltage, transformation, current
 ∗ D Generation, transmission, use

6 Which source of energy is not mentioned?
   J Coal
 ∗ K Solar
   L Wind
   M Water

7 What is the purpose of the home supply transformer?
 ∗ A To step down current to 110 volts
   B To insulate the house
   C To measure electric use
   D To create electricity as close to homes as possible

8 At which point is the voltage in the system the highest?
   J Just before it reaches a home
   K Just after it leaves the generating plant
 ∗ L Just after it leaves the transmission transformer
   M Just after it leaves the distribution transformer

9 The power lines are suspended from
   A transmission transformers.
 ∗ B tall pylons.
   C distribution transformers.
   D generating plants.

10 What can you infer about some factories from the diagram?
   J They receive power after it goes through a home.
   K They receive power right from the generating plant.
 ∗ L They have equipment that can run on high voltage.
   M They don't need any kind of electricity.

66   Answer rows   3 Ⓐ Ⓑ Ⓒ ●   5 Ⓐ Ⓑ Ⓒ ●   7 ● Ⓑ Ⓒ Ⓓ   9 Ⓐ ● Ⓒ Ⓓ
                   4 Ⓙ ● Ⓛ Ⓜ   6 Ⓙ ● Ⓛ Ⓜ   8 Ⓙ Ⓚ ● Ⓜ   10 Ⓙ Ⓚ ● Ⓜ

Lesson 14b
Maps and Diagrams

Focus

Reference Skill
- understanding a map

Test-taking Skills
- working methodically
- referring to a reference source

Say Turn to Lesson 14b on page 67. In this lesson you will answer more questions about maps and diagrams. Read the directions at the top of the page to yourself.

Allow time for the students to read the directions.

Say Look at the map at the top of the page and read the question for Sample A. What is the correct answer to the question? *(pause)* Answer C is correct. Mark circle C for Sample A in the answer rows at the bottom of the page. Make sure the circle is completely filled in. Press your pencil firmly so that your mark comes out dark.

Check to see that the students have filled in the correct answer circle.

★ TIPS

Say Now let's look at the tip.

Have a volunteer read the tip aloud.

Say Even if you understand the information in a map or diagram well, you should be sure to use it to find the answer. You should also check your answers against the reference source to be sure they are correct. It is easy to make a mistake if you don't look at the reference source for each question.

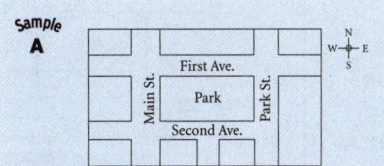

Lesson 14b **Maps and Diagrams**

Directions: Read each question. Choose the best answer.

Based on the map, which of these statements is false?
A First Avenue crosses Main Street.
B First Avenue crosses Park Street.
∗ C Second Avenue crosses First Avenue.
D Second Avenue runs east and west.

TIPS
- Don't try to answer a question without looking at the map or diagram. Even if you are sure which answer is correct, check your answer against the map or diagram.

Directions: The top map is part of a larger road map. The bottom map is a city map of Hicks, showing the main streets. Use these maps to answer questions 1–3.

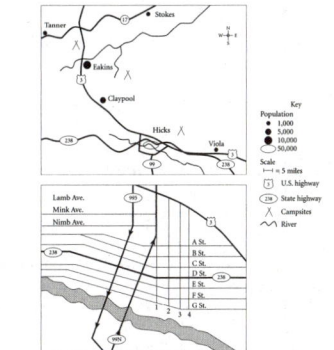

1 Which of these towns probably has the largest population?
A Stokes
B Tanner
∗ C Eakins
D Claypool

2 Jacob lives on the corner of 4th and A Streets. About how many miles must he drive to get on Highway 3?
J $\frac{1}{2}$ ∗ L 20
K 4   M 50

3 Where would you see a sign that said 40 miles east to Stokes?
∗ A Just outside of Tanner
B Near the city of Eakins
C Between Viola and Hicks
D In the city of Claypool

Answer rows   A Ⓐ Ⓑ ● Ⓓ   1 Ⓐ Ⓑ ● Ⓓ   2 Ⓙ Ⓚ ● Ⓜ   3 ● Ⓑ Ⓒ Ⓓ

67

Practice

Say Let's do the Practice items now. There are different kinds of items in this lesson, so be sure to read the directions for each section. Look at the map or diagram and then read the questions. Think about what the questions are asking and be sure to refer to the reference source to answer the questions. When you come to the GO sign at the bottom of the page, turn the page and continue working. Work until you come to the STOP sign at the bottom of page 68. Remember to make sure that your answer circles are completely filled in with dark marks. Completely erase any marks for answers that you change. Any questions? Start working now.

Allow time for the students to mark their answers.

Say It's time to stop. You have finished Lesson 14b.

Review the answers with the students. If any questions caused particular difficulty, work through each of the answer choices.

Have the students indicate completion of the lesson by entering their score for this activity on the progress chart at the beginning of the book.

Unit 9 Lesson 14b **Maps and Diagrams**

Directions: These are three different maps of one area of a country. There are five states featured on the map. The area's main cities, highways, and industries as well as annual snowfall are shown. Use these maps to answer questions 4–10.

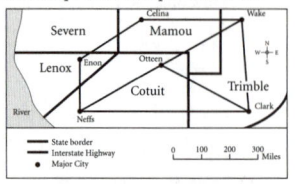

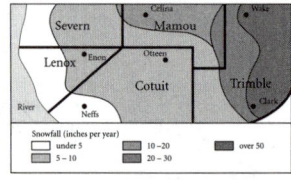

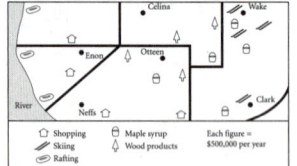

4 What is the shortest route by interstate highway from Celina to Otteen?
  J 200 miles
  K 250 miles
  *L 600 miles
  M 1,100 miles

5 Which city probably has the most tourists?
  A Celina
  B Otteen
  C Clark
  *D Wake

6 What is the total value of wood products made in Cotuit each year?
  J $500,000
  *K $1,000,000
  L $1,500,000
  M $5,000,000

7 Which of these would a tourist visiting Clark most likely bring home as a gift for a friend?
  A New skis
  *B Maple syrup
  C A wood carving
  D A T-shirt

8 Which state would probably appear most mountainous from the window of a plane?
  *J Trimble
  K Cotuit
  L Lenox
  M Severn

9 Which of these is the best estimate of the average yearly snowfall in Enon?
  A 4 inches
  *B 7 inches
  C 11 inches
  D 15 inches

10 Which of the following businesses would you expect to find in Mamou?
  J Ski resorts
  *K Lumber mills
  L Tourism
  M Pancake shops

68 Answer rows 4 ⓙⓀ●Ⓜ 6 ⓙ●ⓁⓂ 8 ●ⓀⓁⓂ 10 ⓙ●ⓁⓂ
                 5 ⒶⒷⒸ● 7 Ⓐ●ⒸⒹ 9 Ⓐ●ⒸⒹ

---

94 Unit 9 Lesson 14b **Maps and Diagrams**

Lesson 15a
Reference Materials

Focus

Reference Skills
- differentiating among reference sources
- using a dictionary

Test-taking Skills
- working methodically
- skimming a reference source
- restating a question
- referring to a reference source

Sample A

Say Turn to Lesson 15a on page 69. In this lesson you will practice using study skills. Read the directions at the top of the page to yourself.

Allow time for the students to read the directions.

Say Look at the question for Sample A. Which answer is correct? *(pause)* Answer C is correct because *a dictionary* is the best place to find out how to pronounce a word. Mark circle C for Sample A in the answer rows at the bottom of the page. Make sure the circle is completely filled in. Press your pencil firmly so that your mark comes out dark.

Check to see that the students have filled in the correct answer circle.

Say Now do Sample B. Read the question and decide which answer is best. *(pause)* Answer M is correct because *an encyclopedia* is most likely to have a picture of the rings of Saturn. Mark circle M for Sample B in the answer rows at the bottom of the page. Make sure the circle is completely filled in. Press your pencil firmly so that your mark comes out dark.

Check to see that the students have filled in the correct answer circle.

Maps, Diagrams, and Reference Materials
Lesson 15a Reference Materials

Directions: Read each question. Choose the best answer.

Sample A Which of these would tell you if *chai* sounds most like *high* or *stay*?
- A   A thesaurus
- B   An atlas
- *C   A dictionary
- D   An English grammar book

Sample B A picture of the rings of Saturn would probably be found in
- J   a thesaurus.
- K   a science fiction book.
- L   a dictionary.
- *M   an encyclopedia.

- Skim the reference source. Read each question and the answer choices. Refer back to the reference source to answer the questions.
- If a question seems confusing, read it again. Try to restate the question in a way that is easier for you to understand.

Directions: Questions 1–4 are about using library materials. Choose the best answer for each question.

1 Which of these would help you decide which bicycle tires are best for your bike and the way you ride?
- A   *Time*
- *B   *Consumer Reports*
- C   *National Geographic*
- D   *Science Weekly*

2 Which of these should you use to find a story about a forest fire in your area that occurred yesterday?
- *J   Your local newspaper
- K   A weekly news magazine
- L   *National Geographic*
- M   *Scientific American*

3 Which of these would you find in a thesaurus?
- A   The distance from Boston to Dublin
- B   The Latin name for a blue jay
- *C   A synonym for *excellent*
- D   A list of books about raising rabbits

4 If you were looking for information on the energy efficiency of fluorescent lights, which key term should you use if your first choice, *fluorescent*, didn't work?
- J   Electricity
- *K   Lighting
- L   Energy
- M   Efficiency

TIPS

Say Now let's look at the tips.

Have a volunteer read the tips aloud.

Say If a reference source is part of a question, begin by skimming it. Read the questions and then look back at the reference source to find the answers. If a question seems confusing, try reading it a second time. You might also try to restate the question in words that are easier for you to understand. When you understand a question, you are more likely to find the right answer.

Practice

Say Let's do the Practice items now. Read the questions carefully, and if a reference source is part of the question, be sure to use it to find the answer. If a question seems confusing, try saying it in words you understand better. When you come to the GO sign at the bottom of the page, turn the page and continue working. Work until you come to the STOP sign at the bottom of page 70. Remember to make sure that your answer circles are completely filled in with dark marks. Completely erase any marks for answers that you change. Any questions? Start working now.

Allow time for the students to mark their answers.

Say It's time to stop. You have finished Lesson 15a.

Review the answers with the students. If any questions caused particular difficulty, work through each of the answer choices.

Have the students indicate completion of the lesson by entering their score for this activity on the progress chart at the beginning of the book.

 Unit 9 Lesson 15a **Reference Materials**

for•feit (fôr´ fĭt) *n.* A fine or penalty. —*v.* To lose as the result of a failure or penalty
forge (fôrj) *n.* 1. The fireplace or furnace in which metal is heated before shaping —*v.* 2. To form by heating and hammering 3. To form in any way
for•ger•y (fôr´ jə rē) *n., pl.* **ies** 1. An imitation of a signature for illegal purposes
for•get (fər gĕt´) *v.* 1. To cease or fail to remember 2. To leave something behind unintentionally
for•give (fər gĭv´) *v.* 1. To pardon an offense
for•lorn (fôr lôrn´) *adj.* 1. A feeling of misery or unhappiness 2. Deserted or forsaken
for•te (fôr´ tā) *or* (fôr´ tē) *adj.* A musical direction meaning loud or with force
for•ti•fi•ca•tion (fôr´ tə fə kā´ shən) *n.* 1. The act of strengthening 2. Often **fortifications**, a military position
for•ti•tude (fôr´ tĭ tōōd) *n.* Strength under difficult conditions

1. **Pronunciation Guide:**

ă	sat	ŏ	lot	ə	represents
ā	day	ō	so	a	in alone
ä	calm	ōō	look	e	in open
â	pare	ōō	root	i	in easily
ĕ	let	ô	ball	o	in gallop
ē	me	ŭ	cut	u	in circus
ĭ	sit	û	purr		
ī	lie				

2. **Abbreviations:** *n.*, noun; *v.*, verb; *adj.*, adjective; *pl.*, plural

Directions: Use the dictionary and the guides on the left to answer questions 5–10.

5. How would you spell the word that means "strength under difficult conditions"?
   A fortatude
   ∗ B fortitude
   C fortitood
   D fortititude

6. The *y* in *forgery* sounds like the
   J *e* in *let.*
   ∗ K *e* in *me.*
   L *i* in *lie.*
   M *a* in *day.*

7. Which word fits best in this sentence? "Judy felt _____ when she learned Roshani would be moving."
   A forget   C forte
   B fortitude   ∗ D forlorn

8. What is the plural of *forgery*?
   ∗ J forgeries   L forgeryes
   K forgerys   M forgeryies

9. In which sentence is the word *forfeit* used correctly?
   A We will forfeit the team to get ready for the game.
   B The key to winning the game will be to practice, forfeit, and concentrate.
   ∗ C Unless more players show up, we'll have to forfeit the game.
   D If we forfeit, it will improve our record.

10. How do the two pronunciations of *forte* differ?
    J The number of syllables is different.
    K The accent is on different syllables.
    ∗ L The *e* is pronounced differently.
    M The *o* is pronounced differently.

70 Answer rows   5 Ⓐ ● Ⓒ Ⓓ   7 Ⓐ Ⓑ Ⓒ ●   9 Ⓐ Ⓑ ● Ⓓ
                  6 Ⓙ ● Ⓛ Ⓜ   8 ● Ⓚ Ⓛ Ⓜ   10 Ⓙ Ⓚ ● Ⓜ

Lesson 15b
Reference Materials

Focus
Reference Skills
- using an index
- using the *Reader's Guide to Periodical Literature*
- using key words

Test-taking Skills
- working methodically
- referring to a reference source
- taking the best guess when unsure of the answer

Sample A

Say Turn to Lesson 15b on page 71. In this lesson you will show how well you can use different reference sources. Read the directions at the top of the page to yourself.

Allow time for the students to read the directions.

Say Look at the part of an index and the questions for Sample A. Which answer is correct? *(pause)* Answer B is correct because information about instant pictures would be found on page 145. Mark circle B for Sample A in the answer rows at the bottom of the page. Make sure the circle is completely filled in. Press your pencil firmly so that your mark comes out dark.

Check to see that the students have filled in the correct answer circle. If necessary, explain why answer B is correct.

TIPS

Say Now let's look at the tip.

Have a volunteer read the tip aloud.

 Unit 9 Maps, Diagrams, and Reference Materials
Lesson 15b Reference Materials

Directions: Read each question. Choose the best answer.

Film, 142-157; additive color, 143; availability, 148; cartridge, 149; contrast, 144-145; early types, 142-143; formats, 149; instant picture, 143-147; speed, 103, 132

Sample A Which page from this part of an index would tell you about the film needed for instant pictures?
- A 142
- *B 145
- C 151
- D 157

 • Look carefully at the reference sources. They contain a lot of information and can be confusing.

Directions: Use the entries from the *Readers' Guide to Periodical Literature* to answer questions 1–2.

> Photography
> An introduction to the camera. F. Blanchard. il *Camera and Darkroom*. 15:34-41 F '94
> Action photos. R. Shawn & M. Oliver. il *Sports Photography*. 7:5-9+ At '91
> The candid moment. [preparation makes candid photography easier and better] B. Jennings. il *Photographer*. 47:19-23 Jy '93
> Annual review of film. [judges rate twenty film types] staff il *The Photography Professional*. 33:14-20 O '95

1 Which article is most recent?
- A The first
- B The second
- C The third
- *D The fourth

2 What is the word "Photography"?
- J The section of the classified ads where you would find this information
- *K The subject of all four entries
- L The title of the first entry
- M The title of the last magazine

Directions: Before you use certain reference materials, you need to decide exactly which word or phrase to use to find the information you want. We call this word or phrase the *key term*. In questions 3–5, select the best key term.

3 Which key term should you use to learn about the architecture of the ancient Maya culture?
- *A Maya
- B Ancient
- C Culture
- D Architecture

4 Which key term should you use to learn more about hurling, a sport like lacrosse played in Ireland?
- J Ireland
- K Sport
- *L Hurling
- M Lacrosse

5 Which key term should you use to find out how to create a school newspaper using desktop publishing software?
- A Newspaper
- B School
- *C Desktop publishing
- D Publishing

Answer rows A ⓐ ● ⓒ ⓓ   2 ⓙ ● ⓛ ⓜ   4 ⓙ ⓚ ● ⓜ
1 ⓐ ⓑ ⓒ ●   3 ● ⓑ ⓒ ⓓ   5 ⓐ ⓑ ● ⓓ

Say Information sources often contain a lot of information. You should be sure to look at the reference source carefully to answer questions. The best way to do this is to refer back to the reference source after reading each question. Don't try to memorize the reference source. This will waste time and maybe even confuse you. Just look back at the reference source carefully to answer the questions.

Practice

Say Let's do the Practice items now. Read the questions and choose the answers you think are best. Be sure to look back at the reference source to answer the questions. If you are not sure which answer is correct, take your best guess. When you come to the GO sign at the bottom of the page, turn the page and continue working. Work until you come to the STOP sign at the bottom of page 72. Remember to make sure that your answer circles are completely filled in with dark marks. Completely erase any marks for answers that you change. Any questions? Start working now.

Allow time for the students to mark their answers.

Say It's time to stop. You have finished Lesson 15b.

Review the answers with the students. If any questions caused particular difficulty, work through each of the answer choices.

Have the students indicate completion of the lesson by entering their score for this activity on the progress chart at the beginning of the book.

 Unit 9 Lesson 15b **Reference Materials**

This is an index from a book called *Photography Made Easy*. Use the index to answer questions 6–9.

Advertising photography, 314-318
Aperture, 101-125; automatic, 118; controls, 101-102; and depth of field, 118-123; f-number system, 117; principle of, 100
Automatic cameras, See Cameras
Backgrounds, black, 174; for glass, 174; in natural photography, 300-303; in studios, 167-169; white, 172
Black and white film, 144-157; availability, 148; characteristic curve, 155; developer, 144-145, 222; infrared, 157, 312; processing, 144, 214-216, 224-226
Camera, 98-111; automatic, 105, 134-135; basic principles, 100-101; development of, 98-99; electronic scanning, 292-293; single lens reflex, 102, 106, 111, 205-206
Color, additive, 143; balance, 78-79; complementary, 70; contrast, 26-27; subtractive, 242; and weather, 23, 28, 30
Darkroom, equipment, 220-221; layout, 234-235
Development, 217-226; agitation, 221, 225-226; chemicals, 144-146; and grain, 223; temperature, 224

Exposure, in close-up work, 197; and color, 132; controls, 101, 106, 110; problems, 137, 306; timers, 237
Film, 142-157; additive color, 143; availability, 148; cartridge, 149; contrast, 144-145; early types, 142-143; formats, 149; instant picture, 143-147; speed, 103, 132
High-speed cameras, 209, 324
Image quality, and agitation, 226; black and white negatives, 228-229; color negatives, 230; and development time, 224; prints, 240-242
Lens, 113-127; autofocus, 115, 121; close-up, 195-196; fixed focus, 114; for natural history photography, 300
Light, and color, 26-27; and contrast, 24-27; moonlight, 31; natural, 14-32, 160; and time of day, 16-18, 23
Magnification, 277-278
Perspective, and depth, 81; and telephoto lens, 189; and wide-angle lens, 186, 187
Scientific photography, aerial, 296; astronomical, 295; high-speed, 275; medical, 285-290, 291-295
Telescopes, 290-291

6 Which page would explain the relationship between aperture and depth of field?
  J 101   L 197
*K 122   M 314

7 Which page would show you an illustration of the effects of magnification?
  A 177   *C 278
  B 178   D 287

8 Which page would tell you about automatic cameras?
*J 105   L 292
  K 111   M 295

9 Which page would probably tell you how cameras and telescopes are alike?
  A 100   *C 290
  B 135   D 295

72   Answer rows 6 Ⓙ ● Ⓛ Ⓜ 7 Ⓐ Ⓑ ● Ⓓ 8 ● Ⓚ Ⓛ Ⓜ 9 Ⓐ Ⓑ ● Ⓓ

Lesson 16a
Reference Materials

Focus

Reference Skills
- using a dictionary
- understanding the Dewey decimal classification system
- differentiating among reference sources

Test-taking Skills
- working methodically
- recalling prior knowledge

Sample A and B

Say Turn to Lesson 16a on page 73. In this lesson you will show how well you understand how to use different reference sources. Read the directions at the top of the page to yourself.

Allow time for the students to read the directions.

Say Read the question for Sample A and the part of a dictionary. Which answer is correct? *(pause)* Answer C is correct because you might use *a pick* to grub for something. Mark circle C for Sample A in the answer row at the bottom of the page. Make sure the circle is completely filled in. Press your pencil firmly so that your mark comes out dark.

Check to see that the students have filled in the correct answer circle.

 TIPS

Say Now let's look at the tip.

Have a volunteer read the tip aloud.

 Maps, Diagrams, and Reference Materials

Lesson 16a **Reference Materials**

Directions: Read each question. Choose the best answer.

grub (grəb) *n.* 1. the larva of certain insects 2. a dull person 3. food –*v.* 3. to dig up, particularly roots

Sample A Which tool might you use to *grub*?
A A screwdriver
B A hammer
* C A pick
D A pair of pliers

 • You may know some answers without looking at the reference source. Mark these answers only if you are sure you are correct.

Directions: Use the dictionary and the guides to answer questions 1–8 on page 74.

dec•a•dent (děk´ ə dənt) or (dĭ kād´nt) *adj.* Corrupt; immoral; self-indulgent: *a decadent life of excessive money and no responsibility*
de•cant•er (dĭ kăn´ tər) *n.* A vessel, usually an ornamental glass bottle used to hold liquid beverages
dec•i•bel (děs´ ə bəl, bĕl´) *n.* A unit used to express the intensity of a sound wave
de•coy (dē´ koi´) or (dĭ koi´) *n.* Something or someone used to lure a person or thing into danger or a trap
de•face (dĭ fās´) *v.* To ruin or disfigure the appearance of something –*adj.* **defaced**
de•feat•ist (dĭ fē ´tĭst) *n.* A person who surrenders easily –*adj.* marked by the qualities of defeatism
de•file (dĭ fīl´) *v.* To make dirty or unclean –*n.* A narrow passage, especially between mountains
de•fin•i•tive (dĭ fĭn´ ĭ tĭv) *adj.* Most reliable or complete: *the definitive biography of Abraham Lincoln*

de•ism (dē´ ĭz əm) *n.* Belief in the existence of God on the evidence of reason
de•lib•er•ate (dĭ lĭb´ ər ĭt) *v.* Carefully considering something before making a decision –*n.* **deliberation**
de•men•tia (dĭ měn´ shə) *n.* The loss of intellectual ability due to loss of or damage to neurons in the brain
dem•i•god (děm´ ē gŏd) *n.* A mythological being, part divine and part human

1. **Pronunciation Guide:**

ă	sat	ŏ	lot	ə represents
ā	day	ō	so	a in alone
ä	calm	ōō	look	e in open
â	pare	ōō	root	i in easily
ĕ	let	ô	ball	o in gallop
ē	me	ŭ	cut	u in circus
ĭ	sit	û	purr	
ī	lie			

2. **Abbreviations:** *n.*, noun; *v.*, verb; *adj.*, adjective; *pl.*, plural

GO ➡

Answer rows   A Ⓐ Ⓑ ● Ⓓ

73

Say It is usually a good idea to look at a reference source to answer a question. Sometimes, however, you might know the answer to a question without looking at the source. This is most often true with a reference source like a dictionary. When this happens, you can mark the answer and move on to the next item. This will save you some time on an achievement test, but you should do it only if your are sure you know the right answer.

Practice

Say Let's do the Practice items now. There are different kinds of items in this lesson, so be sure to read the directions for each section. When you come to a GO sign at the bottom of a page, continue working. Work until you come to the STOP sign at the bottom of page 75. Remember to make sure that your answer circles are completely filled in with dark marks. Completely erase any marks for answers that you change. Any questions? Start working now.

Allow time for the students to mark their answers.

 Lesson 16a **Reference Materials**

1. How should you spell the word that means to be without morals?
   - A decadant
   - * B decadent
   - C decedant
   - D decadant

2. The *i* in *decibel* sounds like the *i* in
   - J defeatist.
   - K defile.
   - * L dementia.
   - M demigod.

3. How do the two pronunciations of *decoy* differ?
   - A The *oy* is pronounced differently.
   - B The *d* is pronounced differently.
   - * C The *e* is pronounced differently.
   - D The *c* is pronounced differently.

4. What is the plural of *decanter*?
   - J decanter
   - * K decanters
   - L decanteres
   - M decanters'

5. Which word fits best in this sentence? "The jury _____ for several hours before reaching a verdict."
   - A defiled
   - * B deliberated
   - C defaced
   - D defeatist

6. Which word fits best in this sentence? "The battle was over quickly because of the soldiers' _____ attitudes."
   - J decadent
   - K definitive
   - * L defeatist
   - M defaced

7. Which word fits best in this sentence? "A hunter will often use a _____ in order to capture prey."
   - * A decoy
   - B decanter
   - C decibel
   - D demigod

8. In which sentence is the word *definitive* used correctly?
   - J A definitive scientist researched the mysteries of space.
   - K The definitive of civilization is how life began.
   - L Larry Welch is the most definitive of any coach I've had.
   - * M Ken Burns's documentary is the definitive history of jazz.

74   Answer rows   1 Ⓐ●ⒸⒹ   3 ⒶⒷ●Ⓓ   5 Ⓐ●ⒸⒹ   7 ●ⒷⒸⒹ
                   2 ⒿⓀ●Ⓜ   4 Ⓙ●ⓁⓂ   6 ⒿⓀ●Ⓜ   8 ⒿⓀⓁ●

Say It's time to stop. You have finished Lesson 16a.

Review the answers with the students. If any questions caused particular difficulty, work through each of the answer choices.

Have the students indicate completion of the lesson by entering their score for this activity on the progress chart at the beginning of the book.

 Lesson 16a **Reference Materials**

Directions: The Dewey decimal classification system arranges nonfiction library books in ten major categories according to subject. Use the categories below to answer questions 9–12.

000-099	General works (encyclopedias, magazines, newspapers)
100-199	Philosophy (psychology, ethics)
200-299	Religion (world religions, mythology)
300-399	Social sciences (customs, law, economics, government, education)
400-499	Languages (dictionaries, grammars)
500-599	Pure sciences (math, biology, chemistry, physics)
600-699	Applied sciences (medicines, business, engineering, farming, homemaking)
700-799	Arts and recreation (music, sports, painting, dance)
800-899	Literature (poetry, plays, essays)
900-999	History (biography, travel, geography)

9 Where would a book about schools in Germany be shelved?
   A 100–199
* B 300–399
   C 400–499
   D 900–999

10 How would a book about growing fig trees be categorized?
   J General
   K Social sciences
   L Pure sciences
* M Applied sciences

11 Where would a book about the world's largest bridges be shelved?
   A 300–399
   B 500–599
* C 600–699
   D 700–799

12 How would a book about aviation pioneers be categorized?
   J Philosophy
   K Social Sciences
   L Applied Sciences
* M History

Directions: Questions 13–15 are about using library materials. Choose the best answer for each question.

13 Which of these should you use to find pictures of different types of deciduous trees?
   A An atlas
   B A dictionary
* C An encyclopedia
   D A glossary

14 How could you find out which books by Robert Cormier your local library has?
   J Look in the R section of the biographies
   K Look in the P section of the biographies
* L Search the catalog system for "Cormier" as an author
   M Search the catalog system for "Robert" as an author

15 Under which label on a library shelf would you most likely find the book *Maria Mitchell: First Woman Astronomer* by Lena Tanaguchi?
   A Chemistry
* B Biography
   C Autobiography
   D Current Events

Answer rows **9** Ⓐ●ⒸⒹ **11** ⒶⒷ●Ⓓ **13** ⒶⒷ●Ⓓ **15** Ⓐ●ⒸⒹ
               10 ⒿⓀⓁ● **12** ⒿⓀⓁ● **14** Ⓙ●ⓁⓂ

75

 Lesson 16a **Reference Materials**   101

Lesson 16b
Reference Materials

Focus

Reference Skill
- understanding the Dewey decimal classification system
- using a dictionary

Test-taking Skills
- marking the right answer as soon as it is found
- working methodically
- referring to a reference source

Samples A and B

Say Turn to Lesson 16b on page 76. In this lesson you will answer questions about reference sources. Read the directions at the top of the page to yourself.

Allow time for the students to read the directions.

Say Look at the chart showing the Dewey decimal classification system below the tips. Now read the question for Sample A. Which answer is correct? *(pause)* Yes, answer B is correct because *history* is a social science. Mark circle B for Sample A in the answer rows at the bottom of the page. Make sure the circle is completely filled in. Press your pencil firmly so that your mark comes out dark.

Check to see that the students have filled in the correct answer circle.

Say Read Sample B and think about what the question is asking. Which answer is correct? *(pause)* Answer L is correct because *a local newspaper* would contain the most news about where you live. Mark circle L for Sample B in the answer rows at the bottom of the page. Make sure the circle is completely filled in. Press your pencil firmly so that your mark comes out dark.

Check to see that the students have filled in the correct answer circle.

Maps, Diagrams, and Reference Materials

Lesson 16b Reference Materials

Directions: Read each question. Choose the best answer.

| Sample A | Which of these is a social science?
A Biology
∗ B History
C Mathematics
D Spanish | Sample B | The most news about your hometown would be found in
J a weekly news magazine.
K an Internet site.
∗ L a local newspaper.
M the national news. |

TIPS • As soon as you know which answer is correct, mark it and move on to the next item. If you have time after trying all the items, go back and check the answers you were unsure about.

Directions: The Dewey decimal classification system arranges nonfiction library books in ten major categories according to subject. Use the categories below to answer questions 1–3.

000-099	General works (encyclopedias, magazines, newspapers)
100-199	Philosophy (psychology, ethics)
200-299	Religion (world religions, mythology)
300-399	Social sciences (customs, law, economics, government, education)
400-499	Languages (dictionaries, grammars)
500-599	Pure sciences (math, biology, chemistry, physics)
600-699	Applied sciences (medicine, business, engineering, farming, homemaking)
700-799	Arts and recreation (music, sports, painting, dance)
800-899	Literature (poetry, plays, essays)
900-999	History (biology, travel, geography)

1 How would a book about paintings by American artists be shelved?
A 100–199
B 200–299
∗ C 700–799
D 900–999

2 How would the book *An Introduction to Business Law* be categorized?
J 200–299
∗ K 300–399
L 600–699
M 900–999

3 How would a book about geometry be categorized?
∗ A Pure sciences
B Philosophy
C Social sciences
D Applied sciences

GO

★ TIPS

Say Now let's look at the tip.

Have a volunteer read the tip aloud.

Say One way to save time on an achievement test is to mark answers as soon as you decide which one is correct. Then you can move on to the next item. You should do this only when you are sure about the correct answer. Once you have tried all the items, you can check the answers you weren't sure about. Working this way saves time and lets you check your answers.

Practice

Say Let's do the Practice items now. Read the questions and answer choices carefully, and be sure to use the reference source to find the answers. As soon as you know which answer is correct, mark your choice and move on to the next item. When you come to the GO sign at the bottom of the page, continue working. Work until you come to the STOP sign at the bottom of page 77. Remember to make sure that your answer circles are completely filled in with dark marks. Completely erase any marks for answers that you change. Any questions? Start working now.

Allow time for the students to mark their answers.

Say It's time to stop. You have finished Lesson 16b.

Review the answers with the students. If any questions caused particular difficulty, work through each of the answer choices.

Have the students indicate completion of the lesson by entering their score for this activity on the progress chart at the beginning of the book.

 Unit 9 Lesson 16b **Reference Materials**

gar•ble (gär´ bəl) *v.* to confuse unintentionally; to jumble –*adj.* **garbleable** –*n.* **garbler**
gar•ru•lous (gâr´ ə ləs) *adj.* excessively talkative in a rambling, roundabout manner
gauche (gōsh) *adj.* lacking social grace, sensitivity; awkward; crude
gen•try (jĕn´ trē) *n.* wellborn and well-bred people; in England, the class below the nobility
ger•mane (jər mān´) *adj.* closely or significantly related; relevant
gir•der (gûr´ dər) *n.* a large beam, as of steel, reinforced concrete, or timber for supported masonry
gist (jĭst) *n.* the main or essential part of a matter
gon•do•la (gŏn´ dl ə) or (gŏn dō´ lə) *n.* a long, narrow, flat boat used especially on the canals of Venice
gra•di•ent (grā´ dē ənt) *n.* the degree of inclination, or rate of ascent or descent
gra•tu•i•ty (grə tōō´ ĭ tē) *n.* a gift of money over and above payment due for service
gros•grain (grō´ grān´) *n.* a heavy corded ribbon or cloth of silk or rayon
gump•tion (gŭmp´ shən) *n.* initiative; aggressiveness; courage; spunk
gut•tur•al (gŭt´ ər əl) *adj.* of or pertaining to the throat; harsh; throaty

1. **Pronunciation Guide:**

ă	sat	ŏ	lot	ə	represents
ā	day	ō	so		a in alone
ä	calm	ōō	look		e in open
â	pare	ōō	root		i in easily
ĕ	let	ô	ball		o in gallop
ē	me	ŭ	cut		u in circus
ĭ	sit	û	purr		
ī	lie				

2. **Abbreviations:** *n.*, noun; *v.*, verb; *adj.*, adjective; *pl.*, plural

Directions: Use the dictionary and the guides on the left to answer questions 4–8.

4 How would you spell the word that means "a harsh, throaty sound"?
  J guteral
✱ K guttural
  L guturral
  M gutteral

5 The *gros* in *grosgrain* best rhymes with the word
  A nose.
  B moss.
✱ C stow.
  D ghoul.

6 How do the two pronunciations of *gondola* differ?
  J The *g* is pronounced differently.
  K The first *o* is pronounced differently.
  L The second *a* is pronounced differently.
✱ M The accent is on different syllables.

7 What is the plural of *gradient*?
✱ A gradients
  B gradience
  C gradiences
  D gradiencis

8 Which word fits best in this sentence? "The leader _____ the instructions in such a way that no one knew what to do."
  J garble
  K garbler
✱ L garbled
  M garbleable

Answer rows 4 ⓙ●ⓛⓜ 5 ⓐⓑ●ⓓ 6 ⓙⓚⓛ● 7 ●ⓑⓒⓓ 8 ⓙⓚ●ⓜ   77

Unit 9 Test Yourself: Maps, Diagrams, and Reference Materials

Focus

Reference Skills
- using a dictionary
- understanding a map
- understanding a diagram
- using a chart
- understanding the Dewey decimal classification system
- differentiating among reference sources
- using key words
- using the *Reader's Guide to Periodical Literature*

Test-taking Skills
- managing time effectively
- following printed directions
- working methodically
- skimming a reference source
- referring to a reference source
- evaluating answer choices
- restating a question
- taking the best guess when unsure of the answer
- recalling prior knowledge
- marking the right answer as soon as it is found

Test Yourself: Maps, Diagrams, and Reference Materials

Directions: Read each question. Choose the best answer.

Aperture, 101-125; automatic, 118; controls, 101-102; and depth of field, 118-123; f-number system, 117; principle of, 100
Backgrounds, black, 174; for glass, 174; in natural photography, 300-303; in studios, 167-169; white, 172
Black and white film, 144-157; availability, 148; characteristic curve, 155; developer, 144-145, 222; infrared, 157, 312; processing, 144, 214-216, 224-226
Camera, 98-111; automatic, 105, 134-135; basic principles, 100-101

Sample A Which page would tell you how to process black and white film?
- A 118
- B 157
- C 210
- *D 215

Directions: This map is part of a road map. Use it to answer questions 1–4.

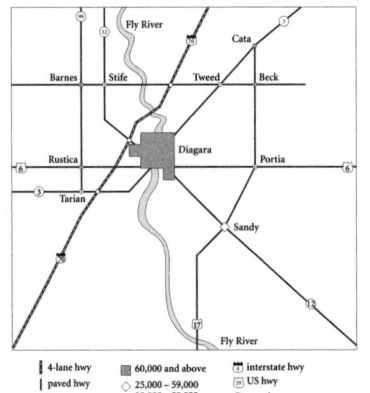

1. Where would you see a sign that said 15 miles east to Beck and 50 miles west to Stife?
   - A In Barnes
   - *B In Tweed
   - C In Diagara
   - D In Cata

2. Which of these towns has a population similar to Portia's population?
   - *J Tarian
   - K Sandy
   - L Rustica
   - M Cata

3. When traveling from Barnes to Diagara, about how many miles are saved by going through Stife instead of Rustica?
   - *A 10
   - B 20
   - C 40
   - D 60

78 Answer rows A ⓐⓑⓒ● 1 ⓐ●ⓒⓓ 2 ●ⓚⓛⓜ 3 ●ⓑⓒⓓ

This lesson simulates an actual test-taking experience. Therefore it is recommended that the directions be read verbatim and that the suggested procedures and time allowances be followed.

Directions

Administration Time: approximately 45 minutes

Say Turn to the Test Yourself lesson on page 78.

Point out to the students that this Test Yourself lesson is timed like a real test, but that they will score it themselves to see how well they are doing. Remind the students to work quickly and not to spend too much time on any one item. Encourage them to compare their answers with the reference material and to take their best guess when they are unsure of the answer.

Say This lesson will check how well you learned the reference skills you practiced in other lessons. Remember to make sure that the circles for your answer choices are completely filled in. Press your pencil firmly so that your marks come out dark. Completely erase any answers that you change. Do not write anything except your answer choices in your books.

Look at the index and question for Sample A. What is the correct answer to the question? Mark the circle for your answer.

Allow time for the students to mark their answers.

Say The circle for answer D should have been filled in. If you chose another answer, erase yours and fill in circle D now.

Check to see that the students have marked the correct answer circle.

---

104 Unit 9 Test Yourself Maps, Diagrams, and Reference Materials

Say Now you will do more items. Do not spend too much time on any one question and pay attention to the directions for each section of the lesson. If you are not sure of an answer, take your best guess and mark the circle for the answer you think might be right. When you come to the GO sign at the bottom of a page, continue working. Work until you come to the STOP sign at the bottom of page 85. When you have finished, you can check over your answers to this lesson. Then wait for the rest of the group to finish. Do you have any questions? You will have 40 minutes. Begin working now.

Allow 40 minutes.

 Unit 9 Test Yourself: Maps, Diagrams, and Reference Materials

4 Which of these is the largest city northeast of Diagara?
   J Sandy
   K Portia
 * L Cata
   M Barnes

6 How wide is the entertainment center with the doors closed?
   J 18 inches
   K 26 inches
 * L 36 inches
   M 72 inches

Directions: The diagram below is for an entertainment center. Use the diagram to answer questions 5–8.

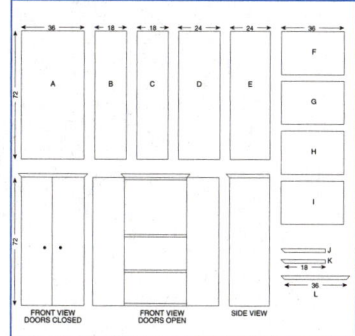

7 Which piece is not connected to piece A?
 * A B
   B D
   C E
   D F

8 What is the purpose of pieces J, K, and L?
   J Trim around the bottom
 * K Trim around the top
   L Trim for the doors
   M Shelves inside

5 Which of these is the best description of piece E?
   A It is the front.
   B It is the back.
   C It is the top.
 * D It is the side.

GO

Answer rows 4   5   6   7   8

Unit 9 Test Yourself: Maps, Diagrams, and Reference Materials

Directions: The map below shows a continent and several islands on a planet like Earth. Use this map to answer questions 9–15.

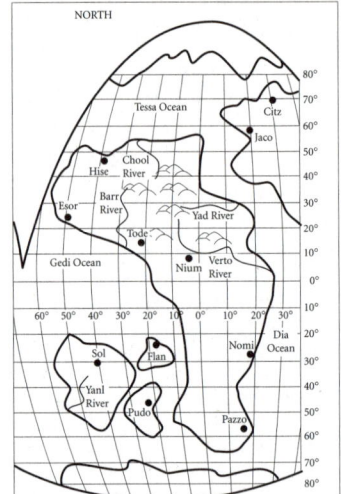

9 How many degrees south is Pazzo from Jaco?
- A About 25
- B About 50
- C About 75
- ✱D About 100

10 During which trip would you probably experience a change of time zones?
- ✱J Sol to Nomi
- K Esor to Hise
- L Flan to Pudo
- M Nium to Pazzo

11 Where can the mouth of the Verto River be found?
- A 10°N and 35°W
- B 22°S and 19°E
- ✱C 3°N and 27°E
- D 15°S and 8°W

12 When it is midnight in Hise, about what time is it in Sol?
- J Noon
- ✱K Midnight
- L Several hours earlier
- M Several hours later

13 Where is the point of 40°S, 45°W located?
- A Near Pudo
- B In the Gedi Ocean
- ✱C Near the start of the Yanl River
- D Near the start of the Barr River

14 Which of these probably has a climate most suited for year-round winter sports activities?
- J Nium
- K Esor
- L Tode
- ✱M Citz

15 Which river flows southeast?
- A Yad River
- ✱B Verto River
- C Barr River
- D Yanl River

Unit 9 Test Yourself: Maps, Diagrams, and Reference Materials

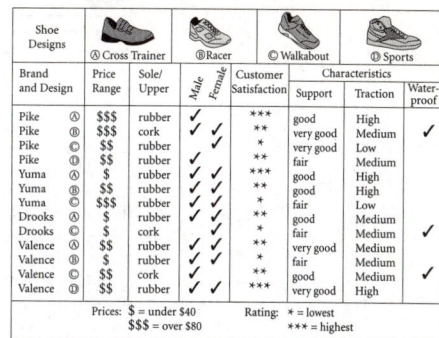

Shoe Designs		Ⓐ Cross Trainer	Ⓑ Racer	Ⓒ Walkabout	Ⓓ Sports		
Brand and Design	Price Range	Sole/Upper	Male	Female	Customer Satisfaction	Characteristics		
						Support	Traction	Water-proof
Pike Ⓐ	$$$	rubber	✓		***	good	High	
Pike Ⓑ	$$$	cork	✓		**	very good	Medium	✓
Pike Ⓒ	$$	rubber		✓	*	very good	Low	
Pike Ⓓ	$$	rubber	✓		**	fair	Medium	
Yuma Ⓐ	$	rubber	✓	✓	***	good	High	
Yuma Ⓑ	$$	rubber	✓	✓	**	good	High	
Yuma Ⓒ	$$$	rubber	✓	✓	*	fair	Low	
Drooks Ⓑ	$	rubber	✓		**	good	Medium	
Drooks Ⓒ	$	cork		✓	*	fair	Medium	✓
Valence Ⓐ	$$	rubber	✓	✓	**	very good	Medium	
Valence Ⓑ	$	rubber	✓	✓	*	fair	Medium	
Valence Ⓒ	$$	cork	✓		**	good	Medium	✓
Valence Ⓓ	$$	rubber	✓	✓	***	very good	High	

Prices: $ = under $40   Rating: * = lowest
$$$ = over $80   *** = highest

Directions: This chart was made to help customers at a sporting goods store compare different athletic shoes that are available. Use the chart to answer questions 16–22.

16 Which brand makes the least expensive racer shoe?
- J Pike
- K Yuma
- L Drooks
- *M Valence

17 If you needed as much support as possible, which of these would be the best walking shoe for you?
- A Valence walkabouts
- B Drooks walkabouts
- *C Pike walkabouts
- D Yuma walkabouts

18 How do the Yuma racers differ from the other brands of racers?
- J They cost more.
- K They have rubber soles.
- L They provide less support.
- *M They offer better traction.

19 How are the Valence and Drooks walkabouts similar?
- A In their price range
- *B In the materials they are made of
- C In how well they are rated
- D In the support they provide

20 Which of these seems most closely related to soles made of cork?
- *J Being waterproof
- K Having traction
- L High customer satisfaction
- M Being expensive

21 Which brand makes the highest-rated cross trainer for women?
- A Pike
- *B Yuma
- C Drooks
- D Valence

22 How is this chart organized?
- J By price range
- K By customer rating
- *L By brand name
- M By sport activity

Unit 9 Test Yourself: Maps, Diagrams, and Reference Materials

haugh•ty (hô´tē) *adj.* Disdainfully proud; snobbish; arrogant —*adv.* **haugh•ti•ly** —*n.* **haugh•ti•ness**

ha•ven (hā´vən) *n.* 1. A harbor or port 2. Any place of shelter and safety

he•li•o•graph (hē´lē ō graf´) *n.* A device for signaling or sending messages by means of a movable mirror that reflects beams of light, especially sunlight

he•mo•glo•bin (hē´mə glō´bin) *or* (hĕ´mə glō´bin) *n.* A protein in red blood cells that carries oxygen from the lungs to the tissues of the body —*adj.* **he•mo•glo•bic, he•mo•glo•bin•ous**

her•mit (hûr´mĭt) *n.* A person who lives alone, especially one who lives in a wilderness

hi•a•tus (hī ā´təs) *n., pl.* **hi•a•tus•es** A break or interruption

hi•er•o•glyphs (hī´ər ə glĭfs) *n.* Ancient Egyptian writing

hom•age (hŏm´ĭj) *or* (ŏm´ĭj) *n.* 1. Respect: *to pay homage to one's ancestors* 2. Formal acknowledgment by a feudal vassal of loyalty to his lord

horde (hôrd) *or* (hōrd) *n.* 1. A large group; crowd 2. A tribe or troop of nomads 3. A pack of animals

hy•per•bo•le (hī pûr´bə lē) *n.* 1. An exaggeration, not meant to be taken literally, as *to wait forever*

hy•poth•e•sis (hī pŏth´ĭ sĭs) *n., pl.* **hy•poth•e•ses** (sēz) 1. A theory used to guide future testing or investigation 2. An assumption or guess

1. Pronunciation Guide:

ă	sat	ŏ	lot	ə	represents
ā	day	ō	so		a in alone
ä	calm	ōō	look		e in open
â	pare	ōō	root		i in easily
ĕ	let	ô	ball		o in gallop
ē	me	ŭ	cut		u in circus
ĭ	sit	û	purr		
ī	lie				

2. **Abbreviations:** *n.,* noun; *v.,* verb; *adj.,* adjective; *pl.,* plural

Directions: Use the dictionary and the guides on the left to answer questions 23–28.

23 How would you spell something that means an exaggerated statement?
 A hyprebole
 * B hyperbole
 C hyprebola
 D hyperbola

24 The *a* in *hiatus* sounds like the *a* in
 J homage.
 K heliograph.
 L haughty.
 * M haven.

25 How do the two pronunciations of *hemoglobin* differ?
 * A The *e* is pronounced differently.
 B The *i* is pronounced differently.
 C The *g* is pronounced differently.
 D The second *o* is pronounced differently.

26 What is the plural of *hypothesis*?
 J hypothesis
 K hypotheseses
 L hypothesises
 * M hypotheses

27 Which word fits best in this sentence?
 "The millionaire _____ demanded the best seat at the theater."
 A haughtiness
 * B haughtily
 C haughty
 D haughtibility

28 Which word fits best in the sentence?
 "The professor slowly read the _____ aloud."
 * J hieroglyphs
 K hemoglobin
 L hiatus
 M horde

Unit 9 Test Yourself: Maps, Diagrams, and Reference Materials

Directions: The Dewey decimal classification system arranges nonfiction library books in ten major categories according to subject. Use the categories below to answer questions 29–33.

000-099	General works (encyclopedias, magazines, newspapers)
100-199	Philosophy (psychology, ethics)
200-299	Religion (world religions, mythology)
300-399	Social sciences (customs, law, economics, government, education)
400-499	Languages (dictionaries, grammars)
500-599	Pure sciences (math, biology, chemistry, physics)
600-699	Applied sciences (medicines, business, engineering, farming, homemaking)
700-799	Arts and recreation (music, sports, painting, dance)
800-899	Literature (poetry, plays, essays)
900-999	History (biography, travel, geography)

29 Where would a book about bicycling through England be shelved?
 A 100–199
 B 300–399
 C 400–499
 *D 900–999

30 How would a book about England's monarchy be categorized?
 J General
 *K Social sciences
 L Pure sciences
 M Arts and recreation

31 Where would a book about medical breakthroughs of the nineteenth century be shelved?
 A 300–399
 B 500–599
 *C 600–699
 D 700–799

32 Where would the book *Extreme Sports: How Extreme Are They* be shelved?
 J 000–099
 K 300–399
 L 500–599
 *M 700–799

33 How would a book about famous trials be categorized?
 A Philosophy
 *B Social sciences
 C Languages
 D Literature

Directions: Questions 34–40 are about using library materials. Choose the best answer for each question.

34 Which of these would help you find out whether the word *democracy* comes from Greek or Latin?
 J An encyclopedia
 K A thesaurus
 L An almanac
 *M A dictionary

35 Which of these should you use to find pictures of clothing styles during American colonial times?
 A An atlas
 *B An encyclopedia
 C A dictionary
 D A glossary

Unit 9 Test Yourself: Maps, Diagrams, and Reference Materials

36 Which of these would most likely contain a story about the election of new leaders in a European country?
  * J *Newsweek*
    K *Sports Illustrated*
    L *Consumer Reports*
    M *National Geographic*

37 Where would you find a list of all of the cities in a particular state?
    A In a history book
    B In an encyclopedia
    C In a news magazine
  * D In an atlas

38 Which of these would you find in a thesaurus?
    J States and their capital cities
    K A list of famous sayings and quotations
  * L Words that mean the same as *flimsy*
    M A map of neighboring countries

39 How would you find out which books by Madeleine L'Engle your local library has?
  * A Search the catalog system for *L'Engle* as an author
    B Search the catalog system for *Madeleine* as an author
    C Look in the M section of the biographies
    D Look in the L section of the biographies

40 Under which label on a library shelf would you most likely find the book *Me: Stories of My Life* by Katharine Hepburn?
    J Drama
    K Biography
  * L Autobiography
    M Current Events

Directions: Before you use certain reference materials, you need to decide exactly which word or phrase to use to find the information you want. We call this word or phrase the *key term*. In questions 41–46, select the best key term.

41 Which key term should you use to find out how the Alhambra, a palace in the Spanish city of Granada, got an Arabic name instead of a Spanish one?
    A Spain
  * B Alhambra
    C Arabia
    D Palace

42 Lisbeth Zwerger illustrated a modern edition of *The Selfish Giant* by Oscar Wilde. Which key term should you use to find out which other books she has illustrated?
    J Wilde, Oscar
    K *The Selfish Giant*
  * L Zwerger, Lisbeth
    M Illustrators

43 Which key term should you use to find pictures of the characters in the comic-strip "Peanuts," created by Charles Schulz?
    A Peanuts
  * B Schulz, Charles
    C Comics
    D Characters

44 Which key term should you use to find a map showing which countries south of the equator have areas of rain forests?
  * J Rain forests
    K Southern countries
    L Equator
    M Maps

Say It's time to stop. You have finished the Test Yourself lesson. Check to see that you have completely filled in your answer circles with dark marks. Make sure that any marks for answers that you changed have been completely erased.

Go over the lesson with the students. Ask them whether they had enough time to finish the lesson. Did they remember to take their best guess when unsure of an answer? Did they refer to the reference sources to answer the questions?

Work through any questions that caused difficulty. If necessary, provide additional practice questions similar to the ones in this unit.

Have the students indicate completion of the lesson by entering their score for this activity on the progress chart at the beginning of the book.

 Test Yourself: Maps, Diagrams, and Reference Materials

45 Which key term should you use to find information on the blue wrasse, the ocean fish whose job it is to clean larger, more dangerous fish like the barracuda?
 A Barracuda
*B Blue wrasse
 C Ocean
 D Fish

46 Which key term should you use to find information about Abigail Powers Fillmore, the wife of United States President Millard Fillmore?
 J United States
 K President
 L Millard
*M Fillmore

Directions: Use the entries from the *Readers' Guide to Periodical Literature* to answer questions 47–51.

> Crabs
> Hermit crabs: moving from house to house as it grows. S. Bloomenthal. il *Wildlife Now* 48:16-18 Ag '92
> Blue crabs: The Thriving Life of the Chesapeake Bay. D. Adair. il *Beacon* 104:6-7 Jl '98
> Crab cakes: recipes your grandmother used to make. P.F. Cranston. il *Seashore Cook* 29: Je '95
> Crabber's Delight: the life of a commercial fisherman. [cover story; local news section; with editorial comment by R. Velasquez] il *Bayly Reporter* 101:4, 20-27+ Spr '97

47 If you were writing a report about what fishing for crab is like, which article would be most helpful?
 A The first
 B The second
 C The third
*D The fourth

48 In the first entry, what does the term *il* mean?
*J The material is accompanied by pictures.
 K The material is more than one page.
 L The material is available online.
 M The material is already checked out.

49 In the fourth entry, what is the phrase *Crabber's Delight*?
 A A summary of the article
*B The title of the article
 C A rating of the article
 D The subject of the article

50 In the fourth entry, who is R. Velasquez?
 J The author of the article
*K An editor at the newspaper
 L The article's illustrator
 M A local reporter

51 In the second entry, what is the word *Beacon*?
 A The title of the article
 B The subject of the article
*C The title of the magazine
 D The name of the author

Answer rows   45 Ⓐ ● Ⓒ Ⓓ   47 Ⓐ Ⓑ Ⓒ ●   49 Ⓐ ● Ⓒ Ⓓ   51 Ⓐ Ⓑ ● Ⓓ
              46 Ⓙ Ⓚ Ⓛ ●   48 ● Ⓚ Ⓛ Ⓜ   50 Ⓙ ● Ⓛ Ⓜ

85

Background

This unit contains three lessons that deal with science skills.

• **In Lessons 17a and 17b,** students answer questions about science. They work methodically and refer to a passage to answer questions. Students reread questions, consider every answer choice, and compare answer choices.

• **In the Test Yourself lesson,** the science skills and test-taking skills introduced in Lessons 17a and 17b are reinforced and presented in a format that gives students the experience of taking an achievement test. Techniques for managing time effectively when taking a standardized test are reinforced.

Instructional Objectives

Lesson 17a	**Science Skills**	Given a question about science, the student identifies which of four answer choices is correct.
Lesson 17b	**Science Skills**	
	Test Yourself	Given questions similar to those in Lessons 17a and 17b, the student utilizes science skills and test-taking strategies on achievement test formats.

Lesson 17a
Science Skills

Focus

Science Skills
- understanding scientific instruments, measurement, and processes
- understanding plant and animal behaviors and characteristics
- understanding properties of light
- using illustrations, charts, and graphs
- understanding sound
- recognizing states, properties, and composition of matter
- recalling characteristics of Earth and bodies in space
- understanding characteristics of bodies of water
- understanding gravity, inertia, and friction
- understanding life cycles and reproduction
- understanding electricity and circuits

Test-taking Skills
- working methodically
- referring to a passage to answer questions
- rereading a question

Directions: Read each question and the answer choices. Choose the best answer.

Sample A The time between seeing a lightning flash and hearing its thunder can be used to
- A identify the cloud that caused the lightning.
- B find out how much rain has fallen in the storm.
- *C determine how far away the lightning struck.
- D measure the power of the lightning bolt.

Sample B Which of these animals probably has the most babies at one time?
- *J A frog
- K A horse
- L A chicken
- M A whale

 **TIPS**
- For science items, it is especially important to read every word in the question and answer choices.
- Sometimes you have to read a passage to answer questions. Skim the passage, then read it again more carefully. Begin answering the questions only after reading the passage twice.

1 Which of these travels fastest?
- A Vibrations from an earthquake
- B Sound waves in water
- C Sound waves in air
- *D Light through space

2 Which of these animals feeds its babies with milk?
- *J Whale
- K Turtle
- L Shark
- M Alligator

GO

86   Answer rows   A ⓐⓑ●ⓓ   B ●ⓚⓛⓜ   1 ⓐⓑⓒ●   2 ●ⓚⓛⓜ

Samples A and B

Say Turn to Lesson 17a on page 86. In this lesson you will answer questions about science. Read the directions at the top of the page to yourself.

Allow time for the students to read the directions.

Say Look at Sample A and read the question. Which answer explains how you can use the time between seeing a lightning flash and hearing its thunder? *(pause)* Answer C is correct. It can help you *determine how far away the lightning struck.* Mark circle C for Sample A in the answer rows at the bottom of the page. Make sure the circle is completely filled in. Press your pencil firmly so that your mark comes out dark.

Check to see that the students have filled in the correct answer circle.

Say Move over to Sample B. Read the question and answer choices. What is the correct answer to the question? *(pause)* Answer J is correct because *a frog* has the most babies of the animals shown. Mark circle J for Sample B in the answer rows at the bottom of the page. Make sure the circle is completely filled in. Press your pencil firmly so that your mark comes out dark.

Check to see that the students have filled in the correct answer circle. Review the answers to the sample items, if necessary.

TIPS

Say Now let's look at the tips.

Have a volunteer read the tips aloud.

Say Remember to read the items carefully. Don't skip any words in the question or answer choices. Sometimes you will have to read a short passage as part of a science test. One or more items ask about information in the passage. You should skim the passage and then read it more carefully. After you understand the passage, begin answering the questions.

Practice

Say Let's do the Practice items now. Read the questions and answer choices carefully. Be sure to read the passage that relates to some items. When you come to the GO sign at the bottom of a page, continue working. Work until you come to the STOP sign at the bottom of page 91. Remember to make sure that your answer circles are completely filled in with dark marks. Completely erase any marks for answers that you change. Any questions? Start working now.

Allow time for the students to mark their answers.

 Unit 10 Lesson 17a **Science Skills**

Directions: Use the information below to answer questions 3–6.

A group of researchers wanted to learn when exercise was most effective. They designed a training schedule that was completed by two groups of twenty college students. One group trained at six o'clock in the morning and another group trained at six o'clock in the evening. A third group of twenty students did not train at all. The training schedule was six weeks long.

At the beginning of the study and each week during the study, the students ran a mile as fast as they could. The average time for each group for the first and last runs are shown below. The number of students in each group who completed the first and last runs are in parentheses below the average time.

	First Run	Last Run
No training	8:24 min. (20)	8:05 min. (17)
Morning training	8:22 min. (20)	7:21 min. (19)
Evening training	8:25 min. (20)	7:37 min. (20)

3 Which factor was changed in order to study its effect?
  A The length of the run
  B The type of exercise
  *C The time of exercise
  D The length of training

4 Why did the researchers have the participants run a mile before the training had started?
  J To see if anyone ran too fast for the study
  K To be sure everyone knew how to run
  L To make the training more effective
  *M To be able to identify and compare any changes

5 What can the researchers conclude about the improvement in the group with no training?
  *A Running a mile once a week improved the participants' running.
  B Training every day isn't necessary because people improve their running anyway.
  C The best way to train is to run a mile each week.
  D The group with no training must have been better runners from the beginning.

6 What can the researchers do to have more confidence in the results of the study?
  J Repeat the same study with the same participants.
  *K Repeat the same study with different participants.
  L Repeat the study, but have everyone run longer distances.
  M Repeat the study, but have everyone train in the morning.

GO →

Answer rows 3 Ⓐ Ⓑ ● Ⓓ   4 Ⓙ Ⓚ Ⓛ ●   5 ● Ⓑ Ⓒ Ⓓ   6 Ⓙ ● Ⓛ Ⓜ   87

Unit 10 Lesson 17a **Science Skills**   115

Unit 9 Lesson 17a **Science Skills**

7 When a plane flies high overhead, you see it long before you hear the engines. What causes this?
  A Planes always fly faster than the speed of sound.
 *B Light travels to the ground faster than sound does.
  C The sound has to travel up before it travels down.
  D Wind affects the sound so it doesn't travel in a straight line.

8 Which baby requires support from its parents for the longest time before it can live on its own?
  J A baby fish
  K A baby horse
  L A baby frog
 *M A baby human

9 If a person weighed 150 pounds on land, how much would they weigh if they stood on a scale in swimming pool that was 4 feet deep?
 *A Less than 150 pounds
  B Exactly 150 pounds
  C Exactly 154 pounds
  D Much more than 150 pounds

10 Which of these is caused by the same conditions that cause volcanoes?
  J Salt deposits in the desert
  K Canyons like the Grand Canyon
 *L Geysers like Old Faithful
  M Sand dunes on a beach

Lesson 17a **Science Skills**

Unit 10 Lesson 17a Science Skills

Directions: Use the information below to answer questions 11–15.

One winter day, Madeleine went to the beach with her parents. She noticed that the water in the ponds on the way to the beach was frozen. The salt water in the bay was not frozen. She tried this activity to understand more about what she saw.

Madeleine put eight ounces of water in two plastic containers. In one of the containers, she mixed one ounce of salt with the water. She put both containers in the freezer and checked them throughout the day to see which one froze solid first. She repeated the procedure two more times, once with sugar and once with rubbing alcohol. Her results are shown in the table below.

Experiment	Container 1	Container 2	First to Freeze
1	Only water	Water and salt	Container 1
2	Only water	Water and sugar	Container 1
3	Only water	Water and alcohol	Container 1

11 Which of these questions was Madeleine trying to answer?
- A Does the amount of water in a container affect how long it takes the water to freeze?
- B How much of a substance can be dissolved in water that is frozen?
- C Which substance can be added to water to make it freeze faster?
- *D Does dissolving a substance in water affect how long it takes the water to freeze?

12 What was varied in this study in order to study its effects?
- *J The substance dissolved in water
- K The temperature of the freezer
- L The amount of water in the container
- M The time it took for the water to freeze

Lesson 17a Science Skills

Unit 10 Lesson 17a **Science Skills**

13 Which of these conclusions can best be drawn from the results of the activity?
  A Dissolved solids affect the freezing point of water more than alcohol.
  B Dissolved salt affects the freezing point of water more than sugar.
 *C The freezing point of water is affected by dissolved substances.
  D When water is frozen, salt and sugar rise to the surface.

14 Madeleine noticed that the ocean near her home didn't freeze even when it got really cold. She knew that the salt solution in her activity froze, so she decided that something else was preventing the ocean from freezing. Which of these is the most likely reason?
  J Swimming fish warm the water.
 *K The waves and tide keep the water moving.
  L The sand mixes with water and absorbs heat from the sun.
  M Boats break up the ice.

15 Madeleine tried a different experiment. She used three containers of water and put salt in one, sugar in the second, and rubbing alcohol in the third. She put the containers in the freezer. Can she make a prediction, based the results of the first set of experiments?
  A Yes, she can predict that the solids will lower the freezing point of the water more than the alcohol.
  B Yes, she can predict that the alcohol will lower the freezing point of the water more than the solids.
  C Yes, she can predict that all three solutions will freeze at exactly the same time.
 *D No, she can't make a prediction based on the first set of experiments.

16 The sun's energy is the result of
  J burning carbon.
  K photosynthesis.
 *L a nuclear reaction.
  M expanding gases.

17 A microscope and a magnifying glass work because they can
 *A bend rays of light.
  B reflect rays of light.
  C absorb rays of light.
  D create rays of light.

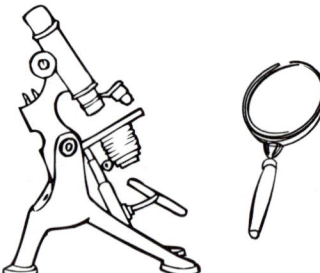

GO

Say It's time to stop. You have finished Lesson 17a.

Review the answers with the students. If any questions caused particular difficulty, work through each of the answer choices. Check to be sure that the students read the passages needed to answer some of the items.

Have the students indicate completion of the lesson by entering their score for this activity on the progress chart at the beginning of the book.

 Unit 10 Lesson 17a **Science Skills**

18 Which of these is something that a plant is least capable of doing?
 J Attracting insects
 K Making food
 ∗ L Moving from place to place
 M Adapting to warm climates

19 When objects from space reach Earth's atmosphere, the objects normally slow down. What force causes this?
 A Gravity
 ∗ B Friction
 C Magnetism
 D Heat

20 When ships sail out to sea, they seem to drop below the horizon. This is caused by
 J the magnetic field of Earth.
 K the reflection of light by the surface of the water.
 L the bending of light by gravity.
 ∗ M the curve of Earth's surface.

21 The scientist Gregor Mendel discovered the principles of genetics. In one of his experiments, he crossbred yellow and green peas. The first generation of peas was all yellow. The next generation was a mix of yellow and green peas. This led Mendel to conclude that
 ∗ A some traits are dominant and others are recessive.
 B each generation of peas would change colors.
 C the color of peas cannot be predicted.
 D the color trait was not passed from one generation to another.

22 When electricians cut a wire, they use a tool with a handle that doesn't conduct electricity well. The handle of the tool is probably made of
 ∗ J rubber.
 K copper.
 L iron.
 M silver.

Answer rows 18 ⓙⓚ●Ⓜ 19 Ⓐ●ⒸⒹ 20 ⒿⓀⓁ● 21 ●ⒷⒸⒹ 22 ●ⓀⓁⓂ   91

Lesson 17a **Science Skills**   119

Unit 10 Lesson 17b Science Skills

Focus

Science Skills
- understanding electricity and circuits
- recalling characteristics and functions of the human body
- understanding the history and language of science
- understanding scientific instruments, measurement, and processes
- using illustrations, charts, and graphs
- recognizing states, properties, and composition of matter
- recalling characteristics of Earth and bodies in space
- understanding the water cycle
- understanding plant and animal behaviors and characteristics
- understanding form and function
- recognizing chemical changes
- understanding weather, climate, and seasons

Test-taking Skills
- considering every answer choice
- comparing answer choices

Unit 10 Science — Lesson 17b Science Skills

Directions: Read each question and the answer choices. Choose the best answer.

Sample A Which of these is a good conductor of electricity?
- A Wood
- B Plastic
- C Stone
- *D Copper

Sample B A lightning rod on top of a structure protects it from lightning damage. How does a lightning rod work?
- J It reflects the current from the lightning back into the cloud.
- *K It directs the current from the lightning into the ground.
- L It absorbs the lightning, becomes hot, and then cools off.
- M It sends the current from the lightning into the building's electrical circuits.

TIPS
- Read the question and try to think of the answer yourself. Then look at the answer choices. If your answer matches one of the choices, it is probably correct.

1 What function do white blood cells perform?
- A They carry oxygen throughout the body.
- *B They attack organisms that have invaded the body.
- C They help digest food.
- D They add calcium to bones so people can grow taller.

2 The formula for table salt is NaCl. The formula for water is H_2O. What do these formulas tell you about a substance?
- J The electrical charge of each substance
- K The density of each substance
- L The source of each substance
- *M The elements in each substance

GO

92   Answer rows   A Ⓐ Ⓑ Ⓒ ●   B Ⓙ ● Ⓛ Ⓜ   1 Ⓐ ● Ⓒ Ⓓ   2 Ⓙ Ⓚ Ⓛ ●

Samples A and B

Say Turn to Lesson 17b on page 92. In this lesson you will answer more questions about science. Read the directions at the top of the page to yourself.

Allow time for the students to read the directions.

Say Look at Sample A and read the question. Which answer is a good conductor of electricity? *(pause)* Answer D, *copper*, is correct. Mark circle D for Sample A in the answer rows at the bottom of the page. Make sure the circle is completely filled in. Press your pencil firmly so that your mark comes out dark.

Check to see that the students have filled in the correct answer circle.

Say Move over to Sample B. Read the question and answer choices. What is the correct answer to the question? *(pause)* Answer K is correct. A lightning rod *directs* the *current from the lightning into the ground*. Mark circle K for Sample B in the answer rows at the bottom of the page. Make sure the circle is completely filled in. Press your pencil firmly so that your mark comes out dark.

Check to see that the students have filled in the correct answer circle. Review the answers to the sample items, if necessary.

120   Unit 10   Lesson 17b Science Skills

★TIPS

Say Now let's look at the tips.

Have a volunteer read the tips aloud.

Say Sometimes you can read a question and think of the answer. When this happens, compare the answer you thought of with the choices. If your answer matches one of the choices, that choice is probably correct.

Practice

Say Let's do the Practice items now. Read each question carefully. Look for key words In the question. When you come to the GO sign at the bottom of a page, continue working. Work until you come to the STOP sign at the bottom of page 97. Remember to make sure that your answer circles are completely filled in with dark marks. Completely erase any marks for answers that you change. Any questions? Start working now.

Allow time for the students to mark their answers.

 Lesson 17b **Science Skills**

Directions: Use the information below to answer questions 3–8.

  A farmer wanted to find the best time to pick apples for a local market. He picked apples at four times during harvest season. He picked the same number from each of his trees. He brought them to market and allowed people to taste the apples before they bought them. He also noted the color, measured how well the apples traveled to market, and asked customers what they thought about the texture of the apples. The farmer summarized the results of his study in the table below.

Time of Picking	Color	Taste	Condition	Texture
September 4	greenish	sour	very good	crunchy
September 11	pink	sour	very good	crisp
September 18	red	sweet	good	crisp
September 25	very red	sweet	good	mushy

3 What did the farmer vary in this study so he could learn its effect?
  A The trees from which the apples were picked
  B How the apples were brought to market
  C The way apples were picked
  *D The time of picking apples

4 Why did the farmer probably begin picking apples in September?
  J That is when most people go to the market.
  *K That is when the apples were becoming ripe.
  L That is when the weather is best for picking.
  M That is when the apples are most expensive.

5 Why were the apples picked on September 4 probably sour?
  *A They weren't ripe yet.
  B They were a poor variety.
  C They were damaged on the way to the market.
  D They were cheaper than the other apples.

Answer rows   3 Ⓐ Ⓑ Ⓒ ●   4 Ⓙ ● Ⓛ Ⓜ   5 ● Ⓑ Ⓒ Ⓓ

Unit 10 Lesson 17b **Science Skills**   121

Unit 10 Lesson 17b **Science Skills**

6 Why is the condition of the apples probably important to the farmer?
J It is easier to pick apples in good condition.
K It is easier to carry apples in good condition.
＊L Apples in good condition will sell better.
M Apples in good condition make better pies.

7 Why did the color of the apples change?
A They came from different seeds.
B They came from bigger trees.
C They were a different variety.
＊D They were getting riper.

8 Which group of apples was probably liked most by the customers at the market?
J September 4
K September 11
＊L September 18
M September 25

9 What does this Bohr model of the atom show that is correct?

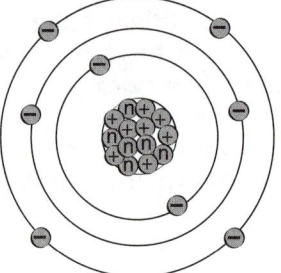

A Electrons in an atom always follow the same path.
B The electrons in an atom are very close to the nucleus.
＊C Atoms have electrons that move around a nucleus made of protons and neutrons.
D The nucleus of an atom is made of electrons.

10 Which of these has the least effect on Earth's landforms?
＊J Frost
K Wind
L Water
M Gravity

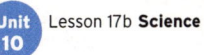

Unit 10 Lesson 17b **Science Skills**

11 When you plug an appliance into a wall socket, the electricity it uses is most likely
   A battery powered.
   B low voltage.
   C direct current.
∗ D alternating current.

12 When heat energy is transferred to water, which of these takes place?
   J Collection
   K Precipitation
∗ L Evaporation
   M Condensation

13 Which of these is known as a fact by scientists?
   A The presence of life on Mars
   B The cause of gravity
   C The skin color of dinosaurs
∗ D The preferred diet of gorillas

Directions: Use the following information to answer questions 14 and 15.

The remora is a small fish that has an oval sucking disk on the top of the head. The remora uses the disk to attach itself to larger fish such as sharks, swordfish, or even sea turtles. In effect, the remora is a hitchhiker that lets the larger fish carry it around without swimming itself. In addition, the remora feeds on scraps from the prey of the large fish.

14 The relationship between the remora and the larger animal can best be described as
∗ J one organism benefits from another.
   K one organism damages the other.
   L both organisms harm each other.
   M both organisms benefit each other.

15 The remora is often the same color as the fish to which it attaches. This is
   A caused by the larger fish.
∗ B a form of camouflage.
   C a result of eating the same food as the larger fish.
   D caused by the speed of the larger fish.

Answer rows 11 Ⓐ Ⓑ Ⓒ ● 12 Ⓙ Ⓚ ● Ⓜ 13 Ⓐ Ⓑ Ⓒ ● 14 ● Ⓚ Ⓛ Ⓜ 15 Ⓐ ● Ⓒ Ⓓ

Unit 10 Lesson 17b **Science Skills**

Directions: Use the information below to answer questions 16–19.

A school nurse wanted to see if students who washed their hands missed fewer days of school because of colds and the flu. She created this experiment to test the idea.

Twenty volunteers from each of four grades took part in the study. Five classes in each grade were used for a total of 100 students per grade. Ten of the students in each grade washed their hands in warm, soapy water for thirty seconds at three times: in the morning before school, after recess, and after lunch. The other ten students in each group did nothing. The hand washing was supervised by some high school students who were studying health.

The study lasted for the months of January and February. The nurse counted the number of days students in the groups missed school because of colds or the flu in January and February. The table below summarizes the results of the study.

Grade	Group	Number of Days Missed
5	With Hand Washing	15
	Without Hand Washing	326
6	With Hand Washing	19
	Without Hand Washing	355
7	With Hand Washing	12
	Without Hand Washing	302
8	With Hand Washing	23
	Without Hand Washing	398

16 Which factor was changed so its effects could be measured?
- J Number of classes
- K Number of students
- L Grade
- *M Hand washing

17 Why did the nurse include students in the study who did not wash their hands?
- A So the total number of volunteers in the study would be large.
- *B It's the only way to know if hand washing made a difference.
- C Many students wanted go participate but they didn't want to wash their hands.
- D There wasn't enough time to have all the students wash their hands.

18 What can the nurse conclude from the results of the study?
- *J Hand washing seems to reduce the number of days missed because of colds or flu.
- K Students who washed their hands liked school more than students who did not.
- L The cure for colds and the flu seems to be washing hands.
- M The more students wash their hands, the healthier they will be.

19 The nurse noticed another pattern in the information in the table. Which of these can also be concluded from the table?
- A Girls seemed to miss less school than boys.
- B The seventh-grade students washed their hands better than the other students.
- *C Students in different grades missed a different number of days of school.
- D When students washed their hands, they got better grades in school.

Say It's time to stop. You have finished Lesson 17b.

Review the answers with the students. If any questions caused particular difficulty, work through each of the answer choices. Ask volunteers to identify any questions that they could answer without looking at the choices.

Have the students indicate completion of the lesson by entering their score for this activity on the progress chart at the beginning of the book.

 Lesson 17b **Science Skills**

20 The human skull is hard in order to
  J balance the body.
  K strengthen the neck.
* L protect the brain.
  M be covered by hair.

21 Which of these is necessary in order for a fire to burn?
  A Hydrogen
* B Oxygen
  C Nitrogen
  D Chlorine

22 Cold air holds less moisture than warm air because
* J low temperatures cause moisture to condense.
  K high temperatures destroy moisture.
  L low temperatures create moisture.
  M high temperatures cause winds that dry air.

23 What happens during all chemical changes?
  A Matter is changed from one state to another.
  B One element is changed into another.
* C Atoms are rearranged to form new substances.
  D Atoms are created to form new elements.

24 Plate tectonics are most closely associated with
  J erosion.
* K earthquakes.
  L glaciers.
  M air pressure.

Answer rows 20 Ⓙ Ⓚ ● Ⓜ 21 Ⓐ ● Ⓒ Ⓓ 22 ● Ⓚ Ⓛ Ⓜ 23 Ⓐ Ⓑ ● Ⓓ 24 Ⓙ ● Ⓛ Ⓜ

Unit 10 Test Yourself: Science

Focus

Science Skills
- recognizing forms, sources, and principles of energy
- understanding life cycles and reproduction
- understanding sound
- understanding plant and animal behaviors and characteristics
- recognizing states, properties, and composition of matter
- recognizing chemical changes
- using illustrations, charts, and graphs
- understanding scientific instruments, measurement, and processes
- understanding the history and language of science
- recalling characteristics of Earth and bodies in space
- understanding diseases and their sources
- recalling characteristics and functions of the human body
- understanding weather, climate, and seasons
- understanding electricity and circuits
- understanding the water cycle

Test-taking Skills
- managing time effectively
- working methodically
- referring to a passage to answer questions
- rereading a question
- considering every answer choice
- comparing answer choices

This lesson simulates an actual test-taking experience. Therefore it is recommended that the directions be read verbatim and that the suggested procedures and time allowances be followed.

Unit 10 Test Yourself: Science

Directions: Read each question and the answer choices. Choose the best answer.

Sample A
Why is it important to insulate the roof of a house well in an area where the climate is cold?
A Wind is most likely to blow the roof off a house.
B Cold air comes in through the roof easily.
* C Heat rises from the house through the roof.
D Rain will keep the roof of the house cool.

Sample B
Which of these is a trait that is probably transmitted genetically from parents to children?
* J Eye color
K Favorite movies
L Number of friends
M Handwriting style

1. Sounds bounce off hard surfaces. As a result, many of the sounds around us
   A are absorbed by objects and we don't hear them at all.
   * B are a combination of the original sound plus echoes from nearby surfaces.
   C are only echoes of the original sound.
   D are unable to reach our ears because they have too far to travel.

2. What do plants give off that mammals need?
   J Nitrogen
   K Carbon dioxide
   * L Oxygen
   M Hydrogen

3. Hot air balloons rise because
   A gravity is as strong as lift so they move upward.
   B air currents carry them up.
   * C the air inside the balloons is less dense than the air outside.
   D the balloon and the basket it carries are less dense than the air.

4. Which of the following usually speeds up a chemical reaction?
   J Adding water to the reaction
   K Observing the reaction
   * L Raising the temperature
   M Separating the ingredients

98 Answer rows A Ⓐ Ⓑ ● Ⓓ   1 Ⓐ ● Ⓒ Ⓓ   3 Ⓐ Ⓑ ● Ⓓ
                B ● Ⓚ Ⓛ Ⓜ   2 Ⓙ Ⓚ ● Ⓜ   4 Ⓙ Ⓚ ● Ⓜ

Directions

Administration Time: approximately 50 minutes

Say Turn to the Test Yourself lesson on page 98.

Point out to the students that this Test Yourself lesson is timed like a real test, but that they will score it themselves to see how well they are doing. Remind the students to work quickly and not to spend too much time on any one item.

Say This lesson will check how well you learned the science skills you practiced in other lessons. Remember to make sure that the circles for your answer choices are completely filled in. Press your pencil firmly so that your marks come out dark. Completely erase any answers that you change. Do not write anything except your answer choices in your books.

Look at Sample A. Read the question and answer choices. Mark the circle for the answer you think is correct.

Allow time for the students to mark their answers.

Say The circle for answer C should have been marked. If you chose another answer, erase yours and fill in circle C now.

Check to see that the students have marked the correct answer circle.

Say Move over to Sample B. Read the question and answer choices. Mark the circle for the answer you think is correct.

Allow time for the students to mark their answers.

Say The circle for answer J should have been marked. If you chose another answer, erase yours and fill in circle J now.

Check to see that the students have marked the correct answer circle.

Say Now you will do more items. Do not spend too much time on any one question and pay attention to the directions. If you are not sure of an answer, take your best guess. Mark the circle for the answer you think might be right. When you come to the GO sign at the bottom of a page, continue working. Work until you come to the STOP sign at the bottom of page 107. When you have finished, you can check over your answers to this lesson. Then wait for the rest of the group to finish. Do you have any questions? You will have 45 minutes. Begin working now.

Allow 45 minutes.

Unit 10 Test Yourself: Science

Directions: Use the information below to answer questions 5–8.

Mr. Kelly likes to bake bread for his family. He noticed that how the bread dough rose depended on how he mixed in the yeast. He decided to test several different ways of using yeast to make dough. He called it the "bread test."

Mr. Kelly used exactly the same amounts of flour, yeast, water, sugar, oil, and salt to make three loaves of bread. The only thing that was different was how he included the yeast in the recipe.

In Recipe 1, he mixed all of the ingredients together at once. In Recipe 2, he activated the yeast by mixing it with the water and sugar. After fifteen minutes, he added the rest of the ingredients. In Recipe 3, he activated the yeast by mixing it with water, sugar, and a little flour. After fifteen minutes, he added the rest of the ingredients. All three bowls were covered with a damp cloth.

Two of the Kelly children helped with the bread test so that all three recipes were started at exactly the same time. The ingredients were mixed in the same kind of bowl. After thirty minutes and forty-five minutes, the height of the dough mix in each bowl was measured. The results of the bread test are shown in the table below.

	Height after 30 minutes	Height after 45 minutes
Recipe 1	3.2 inches	6.4 inches
Recipe 2	4.3 inches	6.1 inches
Recipe 3	5.1 inches	6.2 inches

5 In which of these questions was Mr. Kelly most interested?
  A How long does it take for dough to rise after yeast is added to it?
  B Why does adding yeast to dough make it rise?
  C Will adding yeast to dough cause it to rise?
  *D Does the way yeast is mixed into dough affect how the dough rises?

6 What was changed on purpose in the bread test to observe its effects?
  J How long the dough had to rise.
  *K How the yeast was added to the recipe.
  L How much of each ingredient was used.
  M The maximum amount each recipe was able to rise.

7 Which of these conclusions is supported by the information in the table?
  *A Bread rises faster if the yeast is activated.
  B Yeast needs flour to start working.
  C Adding flour slows down the action of yeast.
  D Sugar slows down the action of yeast.

8 Which of these has the greatest potential for affecting the results of the bread test?
  J The amount of moisture in the damp cloth
  K The size of the bowls
  *L How well the ingredients were mixed
  M The type of flour used

Answer rows 5 Ⓐ Ⓑ Ⓒ ●   6 Ⓙ ● Ⓛ Ⓜ   7 ● Ⓑ Ⓒ Ⓓ   8 Ⓙ Ⓚ ● Ⓜ

Unit 10 Test Yourself: Science

Directions: Use the information below to answer questions 9–12.

Wally learned from the NASA site on the Internet that sound travels at different speeds. He went to some other sites and found the speed of sounds in different materials. He summarized these speeds in the chart below.

Material	Speed in Feet per Second
Rubber	177
Air at 32 degrees	1,086
Air at 68 degrees	1,125
Cork	1,640
Water at 32 degrees	4,213
Water at 68 degrees	4,865
Oak	12,631
Steel	16,601

9 **Based on the information in the chart, when would sound travel fastest?**

A On a freezing cold winter night
B On a chilly fall day
C On a warm spring day
* D On a hot summer afternoon

10 **Sound travels faster through materials that are good conductors. Which of these would be the best conductor of sound?**

J A wooden board
* K A steel rod
L A frozen pond
M A cork floor

11 **To soundproof a room, it would be best to use**

* A rubber matting.
B wood paneling.
C steel foil.
D cork tiles.

12 **The information in the table suggests that the speed of sound in a material is related to**

J the usefulness of the material.
K the color of the material.
L the size of the material.
* M the density of the material.

GO

 Answer rows 9 Ⓐ Ⓑ Ⓒ ● 10 Ⓙ ● Ⓛ Ⓜ 11 ● Ⓑ Ⓒ Ⓓ 12 Ⓙ Ⓚ Ⓛ ●

Unit 10 — Test Yourself: Science

13 Because crickets are sensitive to changes in air temperature, the chirps of the male snowy tree cricket can be used to estimate the temperature. Count the number of chirps in 15 seconds and add 39 to calculate the temperature in degrees Fahrenheit. What can you figure out by using this formula?
* **A** Crickets chirp at faster as the temperature rises.
* **B** Crickets chirp at faster rates as the temperature falls.
* **C** Crickets chirp louder as the temperature rises.
* **D** Crickets chirp at a fairly consistent rate.

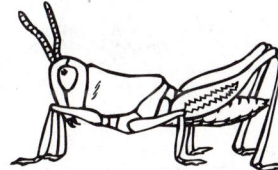

14 The male midwife toad carries the fertilized eggs on his back for at least a month. How is this different from most mammals?
* **J** Male mammals have nothing to do with the babies.
* **K** Female mammals carry fertilized eggs.
* **L** Most mammals lay eggs that are kept in nests.
* **M** The eggs of mammals are smaller than toad eggs.

15 Swimmers float in the ocean more easily than in a pond because
* **A** the viscosity of fresh water is greater than that of salt water.
* **B** the color of salt water is darker than that of fresh water.
* **C** the temperature of fresh water is lower than that of salt water.
* **D** the density of salt water is greater than that of fresh water.

16 A volcano that is quiet and has not erupted recently, but gives off volcanic gases is considered to be
* **J** extinct.
* **K** active.
* **L** dormant.
* **M** explosive.

17 About how fast does Earth rotate on its axis at the equator?
* **A** About the speed of light
* **B** About 1,000 miles an hour
* **C** About seven miles an hour
* **D** About the speed of a typical car

Answer rows   13 ● Ⓑ Ⓒ Ⓓ   14 Ⓙ ● Ⓛ Ⓜ   15 Ⓐ Ⓑ Ⓒ ●   16 Ⓙ Ⓚ ● Ⓜ   17 Ⓐ ● Ⓒ Ⓓ   101

Unit 10 Test Yourself: Science

Directions: Use the information below to answer questions 18–22.

Rosa had three spider plants. She put one on a windowsill in bright sunlight, one on the table in the middle of the room that had several windows, and one in a closet. She charted their growth and their appearance for several weeks.

At the end of that time, Rosa discovered that the plant on the table had grown the most and looked the healthiest. It had sprouted several babies, which are small offshoots. The plant in the closet had drooped and many of the leaves were brown and shriveled. No babies had grown on it. The plant in the window had yellowed, some of its leaves were brown and dry around the edges, and it had sprouted one small yellowish baby.

18 What was Rosa attempting to find out?
- J How fast spider plants grow
- K What conditions most affect spider plants' growth
- L How many babies spider plants can grow in three weeks time
- ✱ M What amount of sunlight is best for growing spider plants

19 To be sure her experiment was successful, Rosa needed to keep all these factors constant except
- A the amount of water each plant received.
- B the soil composition.
- ✱ C the amount of sunlight each plant received.
- D the original size of each plant.

GO

Unit 10 Test Yourself: Science

20 Based on her results, what conclusion can Rosa make about spider plants?
* J Spider plants grow best in indirect light.
K Spider plants do not need sunlight to grow well.
L Spider plants are difficult to grow well.
M Spider plants benefit from being kept in the dark.

21 All of the following factors might have influenced Rosa's results except
A how healthy each plant was when she started.
B how frequently she watered the plants.
* C what type of pot she used.
D whether babies were ready to sprout.

22 If Rosa decides to repeat this experiment, which of these would be least likely to help her achieve good results?
J Growing the plants from seeds
K Placing more than one plant in each location
* L Using a different kind of plant
M Measuring the amount of water she gives each plant.

23 Scientists often study the color of the light from a star. What does this information reveal?
* A The chemical elements that make up the star
B The distance the star is from Earth
C The star's position in the Milky Way
D The number of planets the star has

24 What time of day would an object's shadow be the longest?
* J In the late afternoon
K Around noontime
L In the late morning
M Just before sunrise

Unit 10 Test Yourself: Science

25 A virus that is transmitted from person to person can cause
 A broken bones.
 B sunburned skin.
 *C the flu.
 D poor eyesight.

26 Which of these is an accurate description of DNA?
 J The chemical in food that provides energy
 *K The substance that stores genetic information in an organism
 L The part of a plant that allows it to use the sun's energy
 M The part of an atom that is the heaviest

27 The digestive system involves primarily
 *A nutrients extracted from food.
 B oxygen and carbon dioxide from the atmosphere.
 C nerves that spread throughout the body.
 D muscles, bones, and joints.

28 A weather reporter will talk about high and low-pressure areas. What causes areas of low pressure in the atmosphere?
 J Lightning removes molecules of air from the atmosphere.
 K Plants absorb most of the carbon dioxide in the air.
 *L Increasing temperature causes the air to heat up and expand.
 M Earth's magnetic fields affect molecules in the atmosphere.

29 In the winter, you often generate static electricity when you walk across a carpet because of
 A low sunlight and cold temperatures.
 B steady winds in one direction.
 *C friction and low humidity.
 D snowflakes moving downward through the air.

Unit 10 Test Yourself: Science

Directions: Use the information below to answer questions 30–33.

Mona grew bean plants in special boxes that had lights of different colors. She thought that because bean plants were green, a blue light might be most effective in getting the plants to grow.

Mona planted several bean seeds in the same kind of soil in each box. She provided each plant with the same amount of water on the same schedule. Each box was lit by a different color light bulb: blue, red, yellow, and clear.

The heights of the plants in each box were measured at the end of each week. The average height of the plants in each box is shown in the table below.

	Red	Blue	Yellow	Clear
Week 1	15.8 cm	13.1 cm	16.3 cm	15.4 cm
Week 2	20.4 cm	17.0 cm	22.2 cm	23.1 cm
Week 3	27.4 cm	19.5 cm	32.0 cm	44.0 cm

30 What question was Mona's study designed to answer?
- J What color light is closest to the light the plant receives in nature?
- K Can bean plants be grown indoors?
- *L What color light is most effective for plant growth?
- M How fast do bean plants grow?

31 What factor did Mona deliberately change in this study?
- A The type of box in which the plants grew
- *B The color of the light in which the plants grew
- C Where and how she planted the seeds
- D The brand of light bulbs she used

32 What did Mona's final results show?
- J Blue and red light support plant growth equally.
- *K Clear light is the most effective for plant growth.
- L Red light is the least effective color for plant growth.
- M Yellow light makes plants grow slowly but live longer.

33 Suppose Mona had ended her experiment after the first week. Which color would she probably have identified as being the best for plant growth?
- A Clear
- *B Yellow
- C Red
- D Blue

Unit 10 Test Yourself: Science

34 What do plants need during photosynthesis to make their own food?
  J Sunlight, oxygen, and nitrogen
  *K Sunlight, water, and carbon dioxide
  L Oxygen, hydrogen, and starch
  M Nitrogen, sunlight, and carbon

35 In which type of climate would evaporation occur most quickly?
  A One with moist, dry air
  B One with damp, cool air
  C One with cold, dry air
  *D One with hot, dry air

36 What happens in a battery?
  J Electrical energy is drawn from the atmosphere.
  K Magnetic energy is changed to electrical energy.
  *L Chemical energy is changed to electrical energy.
  M Gravity is changed to a static electrical charge.

37 Which of these is a quick way to evaluate the density of an object?
  A See if it conducts heat.
  B Weigh it on a balance scale.
  C Drop it to the ground.
  *D Put it in water.

38 The center of our solar system is a
  J comet.
  K planet.
  *L star.
  M moon.

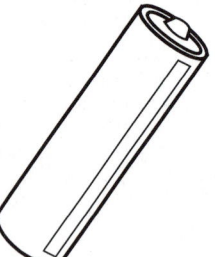

Say It's time to stop. You have finished the Test Yourself lesson. Check to see that you have completely filled in your answer circles with dark marks. Make sure that any marks for answers that you changed have been completely erased.

Go over the lesson with the students. Ask them if they had enough time to finish the lesson. Did they read the questions and answer choices carefully? Did they compare their answer with the other choices to be sure it was correct?

Work through any questions that caused difficulty. If necessary, provide additional practice questions similar to the ones in this unit.

Have the students indicate completion of the lesson by entering their score for this activity on the progress chart at the beginning of the book.

 Test Yourself: Science

Directions: Use the information below to answer questions 39–40.

Some animals reproduce rapidly, but only a few of their offspring survive to become adults. The following chart gives some examples.

Animal	Breeding Age	Number of Offspring
Elephant	30 years	1 every 4–6 years
Rabbit	8 months	10–30 every year
Crocodile	15 years	50 every year
Fruit Fly	10–14 days	Up to 900

39 Based on this information, which of these species is most likely to lose the most offspring?
   A The elephant
   B The rabbit
   C The crocodile
* D The fruit fly

40 What conclusion can you draw from the information in the table?
* J Larger animals take longer to reach breeding age than small animals.
   K Mammals always take longer to reach breeding age than non-mammals.
   L Rabbits are usually the dominant species in their habitat.
   M Crocodiles must feed on fruit flies in order to control the population.

41 When a volcano explodes, all of the following might be spewed out except
   A large rocks.
   B clouds of ash.
* C pieces of wood.
   D flows of lava.

42 Wood burning and metal rusting are similar because
   J both cause pollution.
   K both are physical changes.
   L both are forms of energy.
* M both involve oxygen.

43 Virginia removed a plastic cup of ice from the freezer. The ice was frozen solid, and it filled the cup completely. When the ice melts how much water will be formed?
   A The cup will still be filled completely.
* B The cup will be almost filled with water.
   C The cup will be filled and some water will spill out.
   D The cup will be half-filled.

To the Teacher:

The Test Practice unit provides the students with an opportunity to apply the reading, spelling, language, mathematics, science, study skills, and test-taking skills practiced in the lessons of this book. It is also a final practice activity to be used prior to administering the Iowa Tests of Basic Skills®. By following the step-by-step instructions on the subsequent pages, you will be able to simulate the structured atmosphere in which achievement tests are given. Take time to become familiar with the administrative procedures before the students take the tests.

Preparing for the Tests

1. Remove the Name and Answer Sheet from each student's book.
2. Put a "Testing—Do Not Disturb" sign on the classroom door to eliminate unnecessary interruptions.
3. Make sure the students are seated at comfortable distances from each other and that their desks are clear.
4. Provide each student sharpened pencils with erasers. Have an extra supply of pencils available. For the mathematics items, provide each student with scratch paper.
5. Distribute the students' books and answer sheets.
6. Instruct the students in filling out the identifying data on their Name and Answer Sheets. Instructions are given on the next page of this Teacher's Edition.
7. Encourage the students with a "pep talk."

Scheduling the Tests

Allow 10–15 minutes for the students to complete the identifying data on the Name and Answer Sheet before beginning Test 1.

Each test may be administered in a separate session, or you may follow the schedule below that indicates the recommended testing sessions.

Two sessions may be scheduled for the same day if a sufficient break in time is provided between sessions.

Recommended Session	Test	Administration Time (minutes)
1	1 Vocabulary	20
	2 Reading Comprehension	40
2	3 Spelling	25
	4 Capitalization	15
	5 Punctuation	15
3	6 Part 1 Usage	15
	6 Part 2 Expression	25
4	7 Part 1 Math Concepts	25
	7 Part 2 Math Estimation	15
5	8 Part 1 Math Problem Solving	20
	8 Part 2 Data Interpretation	15
	9 Math Computation	15
6	10 Maps and Diagrams	25
	11 Reference Materials	30
7	12 Science	45

Administering the Tests

1. Follow the time limit provided for each test by using a clock or a watch with a second hand to ensure accuracy.

2. Read the "Say" copy verbatim to the students and follow all the instructions given.

3. Make sure the students understand the directions for each test before proceeding.

4. Move about the classroom during testing to see that the directions are being followed. Make sure the students are working on the correct page and are marking their answers properly.

5. Without distracting the students, provide test-taking tips at your discretion. If you notice a student is unable to answer a question, encourage him or her to skip the question and go on to the next one. If students finish the test before time is called, suggest they go back to any skipped questions within that part of the test. However, do not provide help with the content of any question.

Name and Answer Sheet

To the Student:

Now that you have completed the lessons in this book, you are on the way to scoring high! The test in this part of your *Scoring High on the ITBS* will give you a chance to put the tips you have learned to work.

A few reminders…
- Be sure you understand all the directions before you begin each test. You may ask the teacher questions about the directions if you do not understand them.
- Work as quickly as you can during each test.
- When you change an answer, be sure to erase your first mark completely.
- You can guess at an answer or skip difficult items and go back to them later.
- Use the tips you have learned whenever you can.
- It is okay to be a little nervous.

Scoring High
on the
ITBS®

Book 8

Copyright © 2007 by SRA/McGraw-Hill

109

Preparing the Name and Answer Sheet

Proper marking of the grids on a machine-scorable answer sheet is necessary for the correct listing of students' test results. Use the directions below to give the students practice in completing the identifying data on an answer sheet.

Say You have to fill in some information on your Name and Answer Sheet before you begin the Test Practice section. I am going to tell you how to do this.

Make sure your Name and Answer Sheet is facing up and the heading STUDENT'S NAME is above the boxes with circles. In the boxes under the word LAST, print your last name. Start at the left and put one letter in each box. Print as many letters of your last name as will fit before the heavy rule. In the boxes under the word FIRST, print your first name. Put one letter in each box and print only as many letters of your first name as will fit before the heavy rule. If you have a middle name, print your middle initial in the box under MI.

Allow time for the students to print their names.

Say Look at the columns of letters under the boxes. In each column, fill in the space for the letter you printed in the box. Fill in only one space in each column. Fill in the empty space at the top of a column if there is no letter in the box.

Allow time for the students to fill in the spaces. Give help to individual students as it is needed.

138 Unit 11 Test Practice

Say Print the name of your school after the word SCHOOL.

Print your teacher's last name after the word TEACHER.

Fill in the space after the word FEMALE if you are a girl. Fill in the space after the word MALE if you are a boy.

Look at the heading BIRTH DATE. In the box under the word MONTH, print the first three letters of the month in which you were born. In the column of months under the box, fill in the space for the month you printed in the box.

In the box under the word DAY, print the one or two numerals of your birthdate. In the columns of numerals under the box, fill in the spaces for the numerals you printed in the box. If your birth date has just one numeral, fill in the space with a zero in it in the column on the left.

In the box under the word YEAR, print the last two numerals of your year of birth. In the columns of numerals under the box, fill in the spaces for the numerals you printed in the box.

Look at the heading GRADE. Fill in the space for the numeral that stands for your grade.

Check to see that the students have filled in all the identifying data correctly. Then have them identify the part of the Answer Sheet for each part of the Test Practice section.

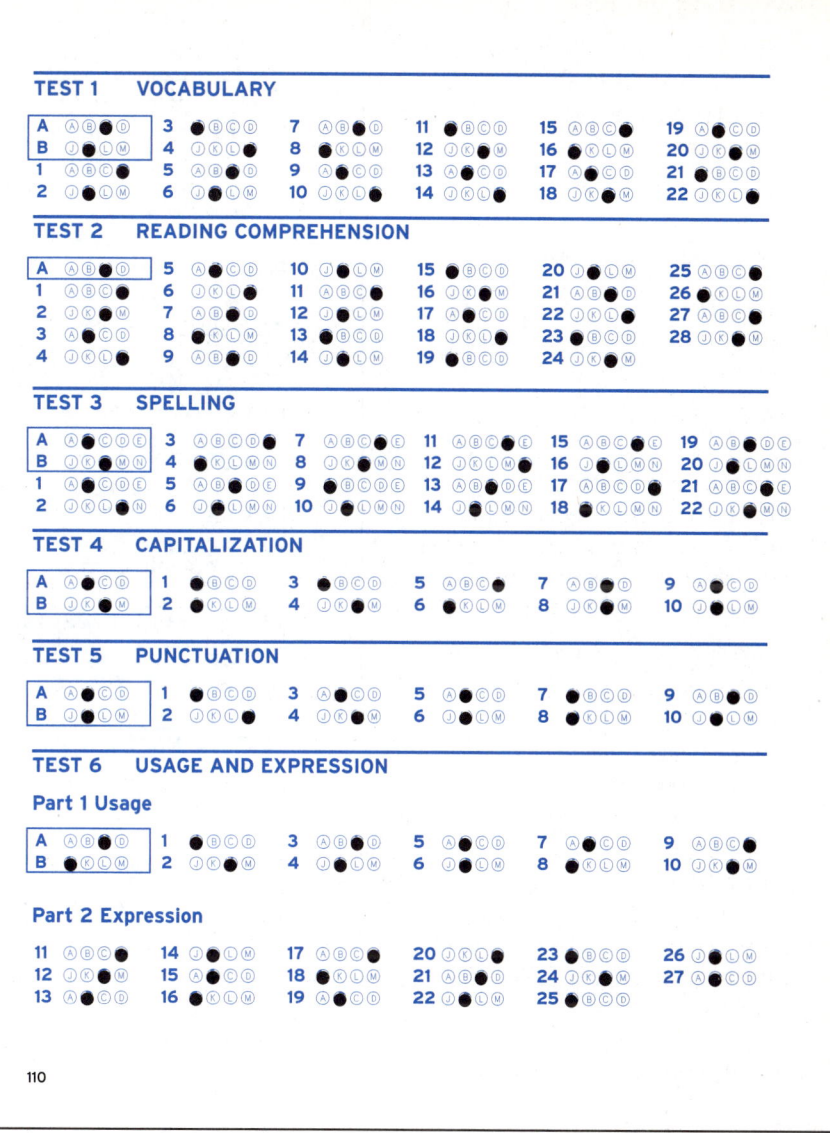

Unit 11 Test Practice 139

TEST 7 MATH CONCEPTS AND ESTIMATION

Part 1 Math Concepts

Part 2 Math Estimation

TEST 8 MATH PROBLEM SOLVING AND DATA INTERPRETATION

Part 1 Math Problem Solving

Part 2 Data Interpretation

TEST 9 MATH COMPUTATION

TEST 10 MAPS AND DIAGRAMS

TEST 11 REFERENCE MATERIALS

TEST 12 SCIENCE

A ⓐ ● ⓒ ⓓ	7 ● ⓑ ⓒ ⓓ	15 ● ⓑ ⓒ ⓓ	23 ⓐ ⓑ ⓒ ●	31 ⓐ ⓑ ● ⓓ	39 ⓐ ⓑ ⓒ ●
B ⓙ ⓚ ● ⓜ	8 ⓙ ● ⓛ ⓜ	16 ⓙ ⓚ ⓛ ●	24 ⓙ ⓚ ● ⓜ	32 ⓙ ⓚ ⓛ ●	40 ⓙ ⓚ ● ⓜ
1 ⓐ ● ⓒ ⓓ	9 ● ⓑ ⓒ ⓓ	17 ⓐ ⓑ ● ⓓ	25 ● ⓑ ⓒ ⓓ	33 ⓐ ⓑ ⓒ ●	41 ⓐ ● ⓒ ⓓ
2 ● ⓚ ⓛ ⓜ	10 ⓙ ⓚ ⓛ ●	18 ⓙ ● ⓛ ⓜ	26 ⓙ ● ⓛ ⓜ	34 ⓙ ⓚ ⓛ ●	42 ● ⓚ ⓛ ⓜ
3 ⓐ ⓑ ● ⓓ	11 ⓐ ⓑ ● ⓓ	19 ⓐ ● ⓒ ⓓ	27 ⓐ ⓑ ● ⓓ	35 ● ⓑ ⓒ ⓓ	43 ⓐ ● ⓒ ⓓ
4 ⓙ ⓚ ⓛ ●	12 ⓙ ⓚ ● ⓜ	20 ⓙ ⓚ ● ⓜ	28 ⓙ ⓚ ● ⓜ	36 ⓙ ⓚ ● ⓜ	44 ● ⓚ ⓛ ⓜ
5 ⓐ ⓑ ⓒ ●	13 ⓐ ⓑ ● ⓓ	21 ⓐ ⓑ ● ⓓ	29 ● ⓑ ⓒ ⓓ	37 ⓐ ⓑ ● ⓓ	
6 ⓙ ● ⓛ ⓜ	14 ⓙ ⓚ ⓛ ●	22 ● ⓚ ⓛ ⓜ	30 ⓙ ● ⓛ ⓜ	38 ⓙ ● ⓛ ⓜ	

Unit 11 Test 1 Vocabulary

Administration Time: 20 minutes

Say Turn to the Test Practice section of your book on page 113. This is Test 1, Vocabulary.

Check to see that the students have found page 113.

Say Look at your answer sheet. Find the part of the answer sheet called Test 1, Vocabulary. All your answers for this test should be marked on your answer sheet, not in your book.

Check to see that the students have found the correct part of the answer sheet.

Say This test will check how well you know vocabulary words. Remember to make sure that the circles for your answer choices are completely filled in. Press your pencil firmly so that your marks come out dark. Completely erase any marks for answers that you change.

Look at Sample A. Read the phrase and fill in the circle for the answer that means the same as the underlined word. Mark your answer in the row for Sample A on the answer sheet.

Allow time for the students to read the item and mark their answers.

Say You should have filled in answer circle C because a beacon is a *guiding light*. If you did not fill in answer C, erase your answer and fill in answer C now.

Check to see that the students have filled in the correct answer circle.

Say Do Sample B now. Read the phrase and fill in the circle for the answer that means the same as the underlined word. Mark your answer in the row for Sample B on the answer sheet.

Allow time for the students to read the item and mark their answers.

Unit 11 Test Practice
Test 1 Vocabulary

Directions: Read the phrase and the answer choices. Choose the answer that means the same as the underlined word.

Sample A Follow the beacon
A computer map
B written directions
* C guiding light
D narrow trail

Sample B The sprawling city
J historic
* K spread out
L quiet
M storm-damaged

1. A perplexing situation
   A funny
   B legal
   C relaxing
   * D confusing

2. Arrive at the settlement
   J place where ships land
   * K area where people live
   L harbor
   M store

3. The market was bustling.
   * A filled with activity
   B empty
   C just opening
   D expensive

4. Slight pain
   J lasting
   K agonizing
   L sharp
   * M little

5. To bore a hole
   A look into
   B fill with water
   * C drill
   D fix

6. To pardon someone
   J contact
   * K forgive
   L like
   M obey

7. To shear the wool
   A weave
   B dye
   * C cut
   D spin

8. A famous composer
   * J songwriter
   K architect
   L doctor
   M ballet dancer

9. A brilliant scientist
   A unknown
   * B very smart
   C military
   D no longer living

10. A good apprentice
    J customer
    K friend
    L captain
    * M helper

GO

Say You should have filled in answer circle K because *sprawling* means about the same as *spread out* in this phrase. If you did not fill in answer K, erase your answer and fill in answer K now.

Check to see that the students have filled in the correct answer circle.

Say Now you will answer more questions. Read each item. Fill in the space for your answers on the answer sheet. Be sure the number of the answer row matches the item you are doing. Work by yourself. When you come to the GO sign at the bottom of the page, turn to the next page and continue working. Work until you come to the STOP sign at the bottom of page 114. When you have finished, you can check over your answers to this test. Then wait for the rest of the group to finish. Do you have any questions?

Answer any questions that the students have.

Say Start working now. You have 15 minutes.

Allow 15 minutes.

Say It's time to stop. You have completed Test 1. Check to see that you have completely filled in your answer circles with dark marks. Make sure that any marks for answers that you changed have been completely erased. Now you may close your books.

Review the items with the students. Have them indicate completion of the lesson by entering their score for this activity on the progress chart at the beginning of the book. Then collect the students' books and answer sheets if this is the end of the testing session.

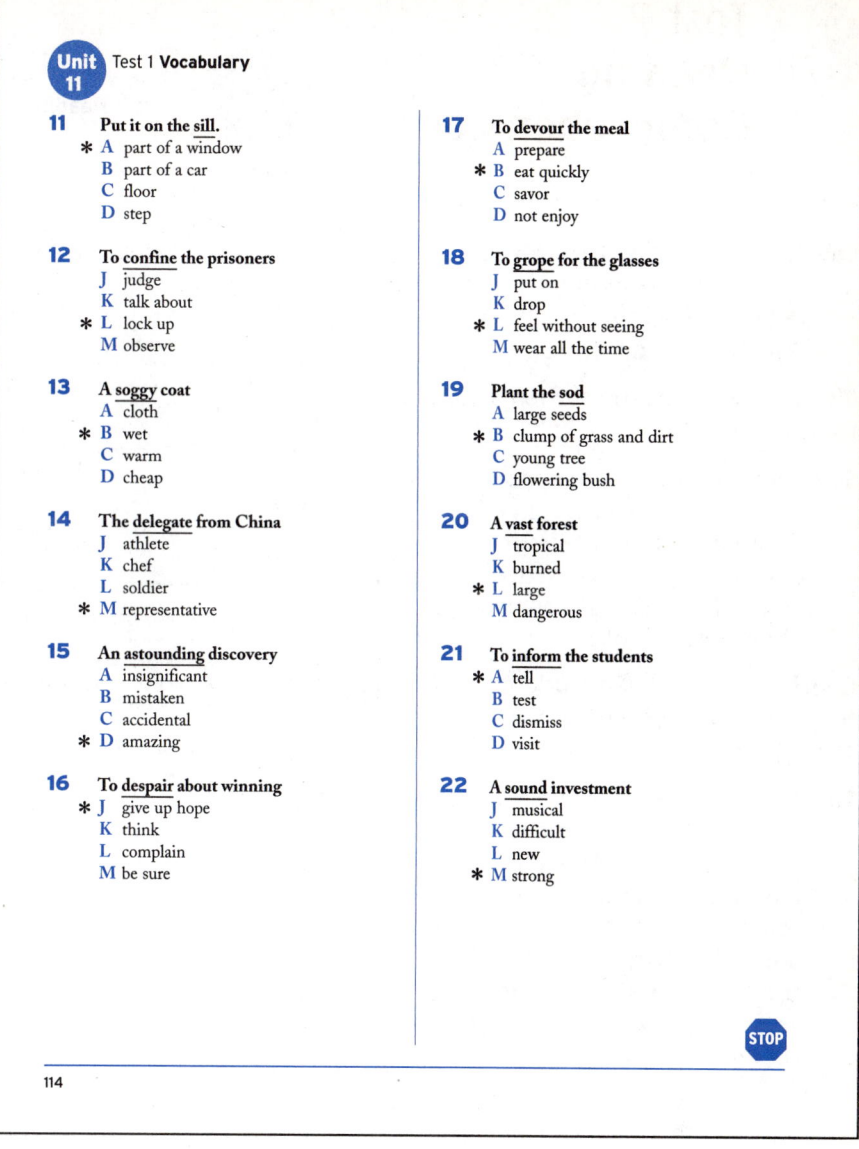

Unit 11 — Test 1 Vocabulary

11 Put it on the <u>sill</u>.
* A part of a window
  B part of a car
  C floor
  D step

12 To <u>confine</u> the prisoners
  J judge
  K talk about
* L lock up
  M observe

13 A <u>soggy</u> coat
  A cloth
* B wet
  C warm
  D cheap

14 The <u>delegate</u> from China
  J athlete
  K chef
  L soldier
* M representative

15 An <u>astounding</u> discovery
  A insignificant
  B mistaken
  C accidental
* D amazing

16 To <u>despair</u> about winning
* J give up hope
  K think
  L complain
  M be sure

17 To <u>devour</u> the meal
  A prepare
* B eat quickly
  C savor
  D not enjoy

18 To <u>grope</u> for the glasses
  J put on
  K drop
* L feel without seeing
  M wear all the time

19 Plant the <u>sod</u>
  A large seeds
* B clump of grass and dirt
  C young tree
  D flowering bush

20 A <u>vast</u> forest
  J tropical
  K burned
* L large
  M dangerous

21 To <u>inform</u> the students
* A tell
  B test
  C dismiss
  D visit

22 A <u>sound</u> investment
  J musical
  K difficult
  L new
* M strong

Unit 11 Test 2 Reading Comprehension

Administration Time: 40 minutes

Say Turn to the Test Practice section of your book on page 115. This is Test 2, Reading Comprehension.

Check to see that the students have found page 115.

Say Look at your answer sheet. Find the part called Test 2, Reading Comprehension. All your answers for this test should be marked on your answer sheet, not in your book.

Check to see that the students have found the correct part of the answer sheet.

Say This test will check your reading comprehension. Remember to make sure that the circles for your answer choices are completely filled in. Press your pencil firmly so that your marks come out dark. Completely erase any marks for answers that you change.

Look at Sample A. Read the passage to yourself. Then read the question beside the passage. On your answer sheet, find the answer circles for Sample A. Mark the circle for the answer you think is right.

Allow time for the students to read the item and mark their answers.

Say You should have filled in answer circle C. You can infer that *people tried to imitate birds* when they built ornithopters. If you did not fill in answer C, erase your answer and fill in answer C now.

Check to see that the students have filled in the correct answer circle.

Unit 11 Test Practice
Test 2 Reading Comprehension

Directions: Read the passage and the answer choices. Choose the best answer.

Sample A
The first attempts at human flight were made with a strange-looking device called an ornithopter. This odd aircraft uses the flapping movement of a pair of wings. You can buy a miniature ornithopter at a toy or hobby store, but no ornithopter large enough to carry a human has been invented yet.

Ornithopters were probably invented before planes because
A planes were expensive.
B people were smaller.
∗ C people tried to imitate birds.
D planes required fuel.

Battle Cry
Ant soldiers marching single-track,
They have one mind, they won't turn back.
Their goal, my kitchen countertop.
But cleaning up will make them stop.

1 In the future, the narrator will probably
A learn how to understand ants.
B buy a different kind of cleaner.
C find out what foods ants don't like.
∗ D have a cleaner countertop.

2 How does the narrator regard the ants?
J As proud
K As clever
∗ L As a nuisance
M As unimportant

3 What do the words *one mind* refer to?
A The ants' tiny heads
∗ B The ants' determination
C The ants' leader
D The ants' cleverness

4 Why does the narrator describe the ants as soldiers?
J They look just like a type of ant called an army ant.
K They make the sound of marching soldiers.
L They look like they're wearing uniforms.
∗ M They have invaded the kitchen countertop.

Say Now you will answer more questions. Read the passages and the questions that follow them. Fill in the space for your answers on the answer sheet. Be sure the number of the answer row matches the item you are doing. Work by yourself. When you come to the GO sign at the bottom of a page, turn to the next page and continue working. Work until you come to the STOP sign at the bottom of page 120. When you have finished, you can check over your answers to this test. Then wait for the rest of the group to finish. Do you have any questions?

Answer any questions that the students have.

Say Start working now. You have 35 minutes.

Allow 35 minutes.

 Unit 11 Test 2 **Reading Comprehension**

The writer of this story observed an unusual animal in its native habitat.

1   I watch the tiny burrow's entrance carefully through my binoculars. There it is again. I can see the movement of a small animal emerging warily from the hole. Finally, the creature steps out into the daylight where the sun shines down on its beautiful gray and brown fur.

2   I've been on the prairies of Montana for two days, staking out pygmy rabbits. The species has grown increasingly rare because it feeds heavily on sagebrush.

3   Unfortunately for the pygmy rabbit and other prairie animals, the habitat of the sagebrush is being increasingly destroyed by overgrazing cattle, wildfires, and human settlements. Without its primary food source, the pygmy rabbit population has been shrinking.

4   Focusing my binoculars, I notice how carefully the pygmy rabbit moves as it leaves its burrow, constantly pausing and sniffing. There are coyotes and owls to be wary of, and if the rabbit realizes I am here, it will instantly vanish. Watching it hop into some of the prairie's tall grass, I mentally review what I know of this graceful little animal.

5   Biologists have learned that the pygmy rabbit is the smallest rabbit in North America, and it is the only rabbit that digs its own burrow. The rabbit can grow up to eleven inches long and usually weighs less than a pound. Because the pygmy rabbit is so shy, gathering useful data on the animal is extremely difficult.

6   I am most interested in the arrangement of the pygmy rabbits' burrows and the relationship between the male and female rabbits. The information that I gather here in the prairie will be used to help the zoo where I work begin a pygmy rabbit–breeding program. No pygmy rabbits have ever bred in captivity before, so it is important that I learn as much about them as possible. If our work is successful, we hope to breed the rabbits at the zoo and reintroduce them into the wild.

7   Although the rabbits are small in size, they should not be few in number. Their presence on the prairie shows that the environment is in balance, and that balance is good not just for rabbits, but also for humans and other living things. Right now, however, I need my binoculars again; there's another rabbit!

5 Why is the narrator spending time on the Montana prairies?
    A   To capture male and female pygmy rabbits
* B   To study pygmy rabbits
    C   To write a story about a pygmy rabbit
    D   To learn about the enemies of the pygmy rabbit

6 Why is sagebrush important for the pygmy rabbit?
    J   It is all that is left in the prairie for the rabbit to eat.
    K   The rabbit builds nests in the sagebrush.
    L   Sagebrush is taking over the prairie and crowding out the tiny rabbit.
* M   Sagebrush provides food and cover for the rabbit.

116

Unit 11 Test 2 **Reading Comprehension**

7 In paragraph 6, what does the narrator mean by saying the zoo hopes to "reintroduce" the rabbits into the wild?
  A It plans to create a prairie-like habitat for the rabbits.
  B It wants to see if zoo-bred rabbits and wild rabbits will get along.
  *C It plans to return the rabbits to their natural habitat.
  D It wants to observe the communication patterns of wild rabbits.

8 According to paragraphs 4 and 5, which of these best describes the pygmy rabbit?
  *J Cautious
  K Lively
  L Sleek
  M Social

9 In paragraph 1, what does *warily* mean?
  A Eagerly
  B Sleepily
  *C Timidly
  D Hungrily

10 In paragraph 7, what is meant by saying that the rabbits "should not be few in number"?
  J The rabbits were not always this small.
  *K The rabbits' population should not be small.
  L The rabbits are not easy to keep track of.
  M The rabbits' habitat should not be ignored.

11 What does the narrator emphasize about the rabbits?
  A Their method for finding burrows
  B Their intelligence and sensitivity
  C Their ability to survive against all odds
  *D Their beauty and elusiveness

12 How does the narrator hope to help the pygmy rabbits?
  J By moving to Montana permanently
  *K By learning as much about them as possible
  L By adopting them as domestic pets
  M By fighting for the protection of sagebrush

13 When did the narrator supposedly write this article?
  *A While observing the rabbits
  B After returning to the zoo
  C Before going to Montana
  D During time off in the evening

117

146 Unit 11 **Test Practice**

Unit 11 Test 2 Reading Comprehension

Few people recognize the name of this building, but everyone has probably seen it in a movie.

> There is a famous skyscraper in New York City known as the Chrysler Building. You have probably seen this 1,046-foot-tall building in a movie, a television show, or an advertisement. Directors love to include it in their work. The skyscraper's elegant pointed tower and automobile-like decorations are an example of a design style called Art Deco.
>
> Art Deco designs emerged between 1920 and 1940. They often featured a bold use of colors and distinctive shapes and forms. The designs were usually simple, symmetrical, and repetitive. One type of Art Deco, called the streamlined style, uses the curves and sweeping lines of automobiles, planes, blimps, and steamships. The Chrysler Building is a great example of this style because not only did an automobile company build the skyscraper, it also used car designs on the building itself.
>
> The Chrysler Building has eagle gargoyles—the heads of imaginary creatures—coming out of the corners of its sixty-first floor. The gargoyles look like the hood ornaments that are found on some automobiles. Thirty floors below are giant winged radiator caps! Set into the building's base are various abstract features of automobiles. The Chrysler Building's memorable Art Deco designs have made it one of the world's most stunning skyscrapers. It will no doubt reach for the sky in style for decades to come.

14 Why is the Chrysler Building recognizable to many people?
- J Because it has eagle gargoyles
- *K Because it is a favorite of movie directors
- L Because it was built between 1920 and 1940
- M Because it is New York's tallest skyscraper

15 The streamlined style seems to have been most influenced by
- *A modes of transportation.
- B wild animals and plants.
- C the desire to reach the sky.
- D famous Hollywood directors.

16 Which of these might describe an Art Deco design?
- J Realistic flower patterns
- K Plenty of curls and twists
- *L Long curved lines
- M Short, square, and boxy

17 This passage is most likely taken from
- A a history of Chrysler automobiles.
- *B an article about buildings in New York.
- C a brochure for an art gallery show.
- D an English literature book.

Unit 11 Test 2 Reading Comprehension

In this passage, the writer explains the background of perhaps the most famous speech in American history.

1 The Battle of Gettysburg marked the beginning of the end of the bloody Civil War, which would take more American lives than any other war. Though a triumph for the North and for the freedom of all American people, the battle was bittersweet, with almost 50,000 lives lost in seven days.

2 A man named David Wills was asked by the governor of Pennsylvania to think about what to do with the battlefield after the struggle ended. Because of the number of men killed, Wills suggested a cemetery at the site of the battle. When his plan was approved, arrangements were made to dedicate the cemetery.

3 Abraham Lincoln, the president whose Gettysburg Address has captured more interest than the cemetery itself, was not the primary speaker at the event. In fact, though he was invited, few expected that he would attend. His son had been sick around the time of the dedication. Lincoln, however, recognized the significance the battle would have in American history and gladly agreed to speak.

4 Many myths surround Lincoln's preparations for the address. It is said that he wrote it on an envelope on the way to Gettysburg the day before the dedication. Though there is little evidence hinting at when he wrote the speech and how much he prepared for the address, accounts of friends and colleagues suggest he wrestled with how to adequately express the significance of the dedication and the battle's place in history.

5 Lincoln stayed with David Wills in his home the night before the event, as did many of the dignitaries attending the dedication. After dinner the night before the dedication, Lincoln excused himself to work on his speech. At eleven o'clock at night, Lincoln left his room to read the address to Secretary of State William Seward. At midnight, he went back to his room to finish the speech.

6 The town of Gettysburg overflowed with people coming to the celebration and memorial. As the ceremony began, the key speaker, Edward Everett, known for his public-speaking skills, took the stage. He spoke for almost two hours. Lincoln spoke last at the event, and for only two minutes. In this short period of time, he offered a simple yet profound summary of the significance of the lives lost at Gettysburg and the freedom those lives paid to protect.

7 Lincoln's last words offered a challenge to those listening and to the generations that followed:

8 "It is for us, the living, rather, to be dedicated, here, to the unfinished work that they have thus far so nobly carried on. It is rather for us to be here dedicated to the great task remaining before us; that from these honored dead we take increased devotion to that cause for which they here gave the last full measure of devotion; that we here highly resolve that these dead shall not have died in vain; that the nation shall, under God, have a new birth of freedom, and that the government of the people, by the people, for the people, shall not perish from the earth."

18 What is the effect of introducing the Battle of Gettysburg in paragraph 1?
- J It explains why Lincoln waited till the last minute to write his address.
- K It sets the stage for Lincoln's refusal to speak at the dedication.
- L It introduces the idea of freedom.
- *M It explains the importance of the battle in American history.

19 Why was Lincoln not expected to attend the dedication?
- *A His son was sick.
- B He opposed the battle.
- C He was busy with presidential affairs.
- D His train was late.

Say It's time to stop. You have completed Test 2. Check to see that you have completely filled in your answer circles with dark marks. Make sure that any marks for answers that you changed have been completely erased. Now you may close your books.

Review the items with the students. Have them indicate completion of the lesson by entering their score for this activity on the progress chart at the beginning of the book. Then collect the students' books and answer sheets if this is the end of the testing session.

 Unit 11 Test 2 **Reading Comprehension**

20 What was the purpose of Lincoln's speech?
  J To persuade the audience to join the war effort
*K To express the significance of the battle to American freedom
  L To describe the events of the battle
  M To honor the politicians who participated in the dedication

21 In paragraph 4, what do accounts from Lincoln's friends suggest about his preparation for the speech?
  A He had trouble writing speeches to the public.
  B He was too busy to write the speech ahead of time.
*C He thought about what to say for a long time.
  D He had his speech written weeks before the dedication.

22 In paragraph 8, what does the phrase "last full measure of devotion" mean?
  J Lincoln could not measure how much devotion the men had.
  K Lincoln was fully devoted to the cause of freedom.
  L The devotion of the audience was measured by their appearance at the dedication.
*M The men who died gave their lives because they were devoted to the cause of freedom.

23 Which event marked the turning point of the Civil War?
*A The Battle of Gettysburg
  B The Gettysburg Address
  C The dedication of the cemetery
  D Edward Everett's speech

24 Which of these best characterizes paragraph 6?
  J Fast-paced action
  K Strong character development
*L Detailed description
  M Persuasive debate

25 Why was the Battle of Gettysburg called "bittersweet"?
  A The battlefield was difficult for David Wills to care for.
  B Many people came together to help the wounded in battle.
  C The South gained a significant victory over the North.
*D Many Americans died in the battle that would help end the war.

26 Why did Lincoln say that the living had unfinished work to carry on?
*J Americans were responsible for upholding the freedom for which the soldiers died.
  K Many events remained for the dedication of the cemetery.
  L The war was still going on.
  M The people who organized the dedication created a memorial that would never be finished.

27 How does the author portray Lincoln in paragraph 5?
  A As interested in social status
  B As witty and humorous
  C As happy and easygoing
*D As concerned about his speech

28 This passage describes the
  J Battle of Gettysburg.
  K Civil War.
*L Gettysburg Address.
  M Emancipation Proclamation.

Unit 11 Test 3 Spelling

Administration Time: 25 minutes

Say Turn to Test 3 on page 121.

Check to see that the students have found page 121.

Say Look at your answer sheet. Find the part called Test 3, Spelling. All your answers for this test should be marked on your answer sheet, not in your book.

Check to see that the students have found the correct part of the answer sheet.

Say This test will check how well you can find misspelled words. Remember to make sure that the circles for your answer choices are completely filled in. Press your pencil firmly so that your marks come out dark. Completely erase any marks for answers that you change.

Look at the words for Sample A. Find the word that has a spelling mistake. If none of the words has a mistake, choose the last answer, No mistakes. Mark the circle for your answer.

Allow time for the students to mark their answers.

Say Answer circle B, f-o-u-n-t-e-n, should have been marked because it is a misspelling of the word f-o-u-n-t-a-i-n. If you chose another answer, erase yours and fill in answer circle B now.

Check to see that the students have filled in the correct answer circle.

Say Look at Sample B. Find the word that has a spelling mistake. If none of the words has a mistake, choose the last answer, No mistakes. Mark the circle for your answer.

Allow time for the students to mark their answers.

Say Answer circle L, t-h-u-n-d-e-r-e-r-i-n-g, should have been marked because it is a misspelling of the word t-h-u-n-d-e-r-i-n-g. If you chose another answer, erase yours and fill in answer circle L now.

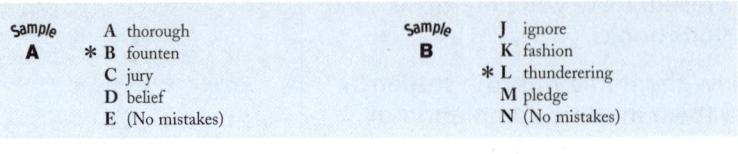

Directions: Fill in the space for any word that has a spelling mistake. If there is no mistake, fill in the last answer space.

Sample A		Sample B	
A	thorough	J	ignore
*B	founten	K	fashion
C	jury	*L	thunderering
D	belief	M	pledge
E	(No mistakes)	N	(No mistakes)

1		5	
A	attendance	A	gasoline
*B	permishon	B	accomplish
C	minute	*C	cabture
D	helpless	D	innocent
E	(No mistakes)	E	(No mistakes)

2		6	
J	manual	J	fuel
K	defense	*K	cliking
L	altitude	L	replace
*M	scintist	M	imitation
N	(No mistakes)	N	(No mistakes)

3		7	
A	scrapbook	A	wrench
B	touchdown	B	damage
C	snowplow	C	mansion
D	bloodstream	*D	acer
*E	(No mistakes)	E	(No mistakes)

4		8	
*J	boomming	J	rotten
K	demonstrate	K	depth
L	resemble	*L	observeable
M	identify	M	harsh
N	(No mistakes)	N	(No mistakes)

Check to see that the students have filled in the correct answer circle.

Say Now you will do more spelling items. Look for a word that has a spelling mistake. If none of the words has a mistake, choose the last answer. Work by yourself. When you come to the GO sign at the bottom of the page, turn to the next page and continue working. Work until you come to the STOP sign at the bottom of page 122. When you have finished, you can check over your answers to this test. Then wait for the rest of the group to finish. Any questions?

Answer any questions that the students have.

Say Start working now. You will have 20 minutes.

Allow 20 minutes.

Say It's time to stop. You have completed Test 3. Check to see that you have completely filled in your answer circles with dark marks. Make sure that any marks for answers that you changed have been completely erased. Now you may close your books.

Review the items with the students. Have them indicate completion of the lesson by entering their score for this activity on the progress chart at the beginning of the book. Then collect the students' books and answer sheets if this is the end of the testing session.

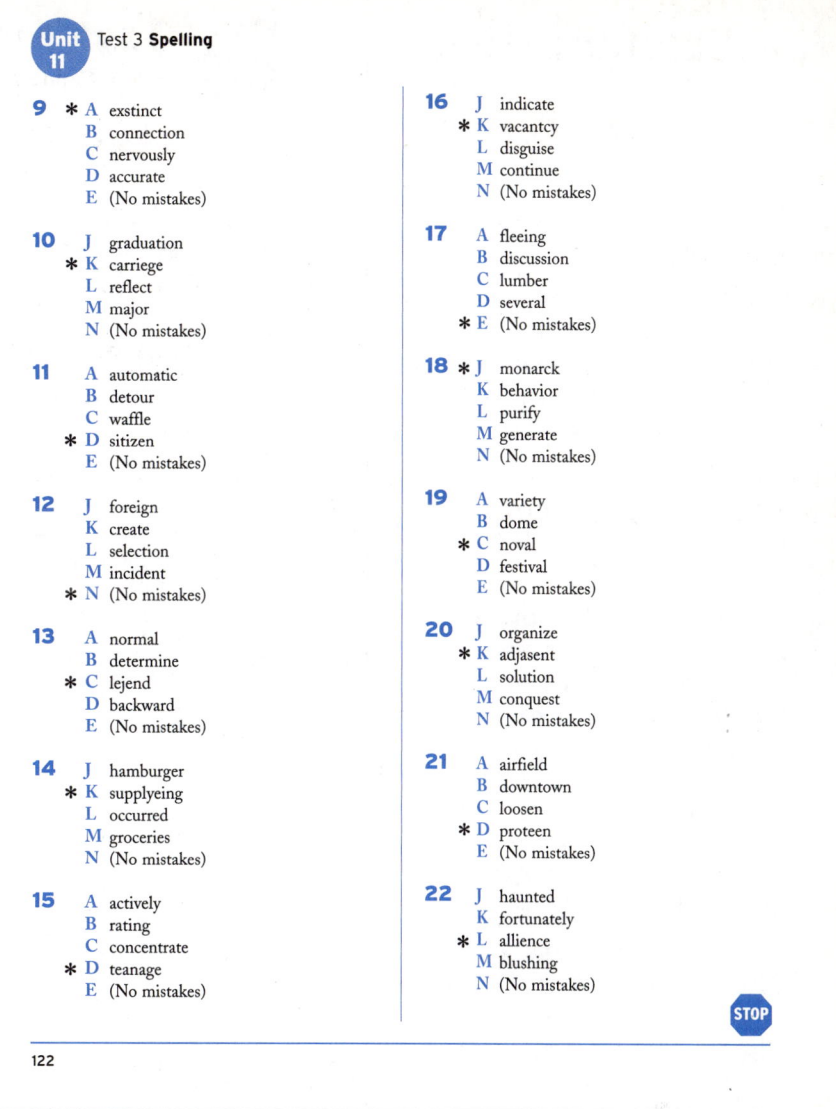

Unit 11 Test 3 **Spelling**

9 *A exstinct
   B connection
   C nervously
   D accurate
   E (No mistakes)

10 J graduation
   *K carriege
   L reflect
   M major
   N (No mistakes)

11 A automatic
   B detour
   C waffle
   *D sitizen
   E (No mistakes)

12 J foreign
   K create
   L selection
   M incident
   *N (No mistakes)

13 A normal
   B determine
   *C lejend
   D backward
   E (No mistakes)

14 J hamburger
   *K supplyeing
   L occurred
   M groceries
   N (No mistakes)

15 A actively
   B rating
   C concentrate
   *D teanage
   E (No mistakes)

16 J indicate
   *K vacantcy
   L disguise
   M continue
   N (No mistakes)

17 A fleeing
   B discussion
   C lumber
   D several
   *E (No mistakes)

18 *J monarck
   K behavior
   L purify
   M generate
   N (No mistakes)

19 A variety
   B dome
   *C noval
   D festival
   E (No mistakes)

20 J organize
   *K adjasent
   L solution
   M conquest
   N (No mistakes)

21 A airfield
   B downtown
   C loosen
   *D proteen
   E (No mistakes)

22 J haunted
   K fortunately
   *L allience
   M blushing
   N (No mistakes)

STOP

122

Unit 11 Test 4 Capitalization

Administration Time: 15 minutes

Say Turn to Test 4 on page 123.

Check to see that the students have found page 123.

Say Look at your answer sheet. Find the part called Test 4, Capitalization. All your answers for this test should be marked on your answer sheet, not in your book.

Check to see that the students have found the correct part of the answer sheet.

Say This test will check how well you can find capitalization mistakes. Remember to make sure that the circles for your answer choices are completely filled in. Press your pencil firmly so that your marks come out dark. Completely erase any marks for answers that you change.

Look at Sample A. Read the answer choices. Find the answer that has a capitalization mistake. If there is no mistake, choose the last answer. Mark the circle for your answer on the answer sheet.

Unit 11 Test Practice
Test 4 Capitalization

Directions: Fill in the space for the answer that has a mistake in capitalization. Fill in the last answer space if there is no mistake.

Sample A
- A After Mom told me some stories
- *B about aunt Margaret, I was even
- C more excited to meet her in person.
- D (No mistakes)

Sample B
- J When Jonathon Allred was elected
- K governor, his wife began a much-needed
- *L restoration of the state Capitol.
- M (No mistakes)

1.
   - *A On august 19, an African and
   - B Caribbean dance class will be
   - C held at Stokes Community Center.
   - D (No mistakes)

2.
   - *J The roaring twenties, also
   - K referred to as the Jazz Age, was
   - L a colorful period in U.S. history.
   - M (No mistakes)

3.
   - *A The peace corps is an
   - B overseas volunteer program
   - C of the U.S. government.
   - D (No mistakes)

4.
   - J Two of the brightest stars in
   - K the sky are found in the constellation
   - *L orion, also known as the Hunter.
   - M (No mistakes)

5.
   - A Hundreds celebrate their Italian
   - B heritage at the Portland, Oregon,
   - C Festa Italiana in July each summer.
   - *D (No mistakes)

6.
   - *J 444 Sky way Boulevard
   - K Colorado Springs, CO 80905
   - L January 12, 2001
   - M (No mistakes)

7.
   - A Personnel Department
   - B Wheelchair Sports, U.S.A.
   - *C dear sir or madam:
   - D (No mistakes)

8.
   - J As president of the student body
   - K at Yampa Middle School, I am writing
   - *L to ask if you ever make Presentations.
   - M (No mistakes)

9.
   - A We plan to host a sporting event
   - *B for disabled students. we would
   - C appreciate some advice on the topic.
   - D (No mistakes)

10.
    - J Thank you for your kind consideration.
    - *K respectfully,
    - L Valerie Vasquez
    - M (No mistakes)

Allow time for the students to mark their answers.

Say Answer circle B should have been marked because the word *Aunt* should be capitalized in this context. If you chose another answer, erase yours and fill in answer circle B now.

Check to see that the students have filled in the correct answer circle.

Say Look at Sample B. Find the answer that has a capitalization mistake. If there is no mistake, choose the last answer. Mark the circle for your answer.

Allow time for the students to mark their answers.

Say Answer circle L should have been marked because the word *capitol* should not be capitalized. If you chose another answer, erase yours and fill in answer circle L now.

Check to see that the students have filled in the correct answer circle.

Say Now you will do more items. Look for an answer that has a capitalization mistake. If none of the answers has a mistake, choose the last answer. Work until you come to the STOP sign at the bottom of the page. When you have finished, you can check over your answers to this test. Then wait for the rest of the group to finish. Any questions?

Answer any questions that the students have.

Say Start working now. You will have 10 minutes.

Allow 10 minutes.

Say It's time to stop. You have completed Test 4. Check to see that you have completely filled in your answer circles with dark marks. Make sure that any marks for answers that you changed have been completely erased. Now you may close your books.

Review the items with the students. Have them indicate completion of the lesson by entering their score for this activity on the progress chart at the beginning of the book. Then collect the students' books and answer sheets if this is the end of the testing session.

Test Practice
Test 4 Capitalization

Directions: Fill in the space for the answer that has a mistake in capitalization. Fill in the last answer space if there is no mistake.

Sample A
- A After Mom told me some stories
- *B about aunt Margaret, I was even
- C more excited to meet her in person.
- D (No mistakes)

Sample B
- J When Jonathon Allred was elected
- K governor, his wife began a much-needed
- *L restoration of the state Capitol.
- M (No mistakes)

1
- *A On august 19, an African and
- B Caribbean dance class will be
- C held at Stokes Community Center.
- D (No mistakes)

2
- *J The roaring twenties, also
- K referred to as the Jazz Age, was
- L a colorful period in U.S. history.
- M (No mistakes)

3
- *A The peace corps is an
- B overseas volunteer program
- C of the U.S. government.
- D (No mistakes)

4
- J Two of the brightest stars in
- K the sky are found in the constellation
- *L orion, also known as the Hunter.
- M (No mistakes)

5
- A Hundreds celebrate their Italian
- B heritage at the Portland, Oregon,
- C Festa Italiana in July each summer.
- *D (No mistakes)

6
- *J 444 Sky way Boulevard
- K Colorado Springs, CO 80905
- L January 12, 2001
- M (No mistakes)

7
- A Personnel Department
- B Wheelchair Sports, U.S.A.
- *C dear sir or madam:
- D (No mistakes)

8
- J As president of the student body
- K at Yampa Middle School, I am writing
- *L to ask if you ever make Presentations.
- M (No mistakes)

9
- A We plan to host a sporting event
- *B for disabled students. we would
- C appreciate some advice on the topic.
- D (No mistakes)

10
- J Thank you for your kind consideration.
- *K respectfully,
- L Valerie Vasquez
- M (No mistakes)

Test 5 Punctuation

Administration Time: 15 minutes

Say Turn to Test 5 on page 124.

Check to see that the students have found page 124.

Say Look at your answer sheet. Find the part called Test 5, Punctuation. All your answers for this test should be marked on your answer sheet, not in your book.

Check to see that the students have found the correct part of the answer sheet.

Say This test will check how well you can find punctuation mistakes. Remember to make sure that the circles for your answer choices are completely filled in. Press your pencil firmly so that your marks come out dark. Completely erase any marks for answers that you change.

Look at Sample A. Read the answer choices. Find the answer that has a punctuation mistake. If there is no mistake, choose the last answer. Mark the circle for your answer on the answer sheet.

Allow time for the students to mark their answers.

Say Answer circle B should have been marked because the word *parent's* does not need an apostrophe. If you chose another answer, erase yours and fill in answer circle B now.

Check to see that the students have filled in the correct answer circle.

Say Look at Sample B. Find the answer that has a punctuation mistake. If there is no mistake, choose the last answer. Mark the circle for your answer.

Allow time for the students to mark their answers.

Say Answer circle K should have been marked because a comma is needed after the word *water*. If you chose another answer, erase yours and fill in answer circle K now.

Test Practice
Test 5 Punctuation

Directions: Fill in the space for the answer that has a mistake in punctuation. Fill in the last answer space if there is no mistake.

Sample A
- A As part of the surprise party for
- *B their parent's, the children invited
- C friends, family, and neighbors.
- D (No mistakes)

Sample B
- J To strain the plankton from
- *K the ocean water the blue whale
- L uses a series of plates called baleen.
- M (No mistakes)

1.
- *A "Want some juice" asked
- B Trey. The refrigerator, which was
- C stuffed full, held a dozen flavors.
- D (No mistakes)

2.
- J Mary Fisk, a schoolteacher,
- K writes books in her spare time.
- L Most of them are about history.
- *M (No mistakes)

3.
- A We picked strawberries in
- *B June put them into freezer bags
- C and enjoyed them all year long.
- D (No mistakes)

4.
- J Christopher surprised everyone
- K at the pizza party when he said,
- *L I've never liked pizza very much.
- M (No mistakes)

5.
- A Henry checked the weather
- *B forecast and found it would be cold
- C but that didn't bother him at all.
- D (No mistakes)

6.
- J 112 Millplain Road
- *K Vancouver WA 98682
- L April 23, 2001
- M (No mistakes)

7.
- *A Michael M Richardson
- B Dark Horse Comics
- C Portland, OR 97222
- D (No mistakes)

8.
- *J Dear Mr. Richardson;
- K Thank you for your recent talk on comics
- L at the Evergreen Middle School Art Fair.
- M (No mistakes)

9.
- A Would you believe that after your visit, a
- B group of inspired students began publishing
- *C a comic about life in a middle school.
- D (No mistakes)

10.
- J I'm enclosing a copy of our first issue.
- *K Sincerely
- L Omar Twomey
- M (No mistakes)

124

Check to see that the students have filled in the correct answer circle.

Say Now you will do more items. Look for an answer that has a punctuation mistake. If none of the answers has a mistake, choose the last answer. Work until you come to the STOP sign at the bottom of the page. When you have finished, you can check over your answers to this test. Then wait for the rest of the group to finish. Any questions?

Answer any questions that the students have.

Say Start working now. You will have 10 minutes.

Allow 10 minutes.

Say It's time to stop. You have completed Test 5. Check to see that you have completely filled in your answer circles with dark marks. Make sure that any marks for answers that you changed have been completely erased. Now you may close your books.

Review the items with the students. Have them indicate completion of the lesson by entering their score for this activity on the progress chart at the beginning of the book. Then collect the students' books and answer sheets if this is the end of the testing session.

Unit 11

Test Practice
Test 5 **Punctuation**

Directions: Fill in the space for the answer that has a mistake in punctuation. Fill in the last answer space if there is no mistake.

| Sample A | A As part of the surprise party for
∗ B their parent's, the children invited
C friends, family, and neighbors.
D (No mistakes) | Sample B | J To strain the plankton from
∗ K the ocean water the blue whale
L uses a series of plates called baleen.
M (No mistakes) |

1 ∗ A "Want some juice" asked
    B Trey. The refrigerator, which was
    C stuffed full, held a dozen flavors.
    D (No mistakes)

2   J Mary Fisk, a schoolteacher,
    K writes books in her spare time.
    L Most of them are about history.
∗ M (No mistakes)

3   A We picked strawberries in
∗ B June put them into freezer bags
    C and enjoyed them all year long.
    D (No mistakes)

4   J Christopher surprised everyone
    K at the pizza party when he said,
∗ L I've never liked pizza very much.
    M (No mistakes)

5   A Henry checked the weather
∗ B forecast and found it would be cold
    C but that didn't bother him at all.
    D (No mistakes)

6   J 112 Millplain Road
∗ K Vancouver WA 98682
    L April 23, 2001
    M (No mistakes)

7 ∗ A Michael M Richardson
    B Dark Horse Comics
    C Portland, OR 97222
    D (No mistakes)

8 ∗ J Dear Mr. Richardson;
    K Thank you for your recent talk on comics
    L at the Evergreen Middle School Art Fair.
    M (No mistakes)

9   A Would you believe that after your visit, a
    B group of inspired students began publishing
∗ C a comic about life in a middle school.
    D (No mistakes)

10   J I'm enclosing a copy of our first issue.
∗ K   Sincerely
    L   Omar Twomey
    M (No mistakes)

Unit 11 Test 6 Part 1 Usage

Administration Time: 15 minutes

Say Turn to Test 6, Part 1 on page 125.

Check to see that the students have found page 125.

Say Look at your answer sheet. Find the part called Test 6, Part 1, Usage. All your answers for this test should be marked on your answer sheet, not in your book.

Check to see that the students have found the correct part of the answer sheet.

Say This test will check how well you can find mistakes in English usage and expression. Remember to make sure that the circles for your answer choices are completely filled in. Press your pencil firmly so that your marks come out dark. Completely erase any marks for answers that you change.

Look at Sample A. Read the answer choices. Find the answer that has a mistake in usage. If there is no mistake, choose the last answer. Mark the circle for your answer on the answer sheet.

Allow time for the students to mark their answers.

Say Answer circle C should have been marked because the words *have rode* should be *ride*. If you chose another answer, erase yours and fill in answer circle C now.

Check to see that the students have filled in the correct answer circle.

Say Look at Sample B. Find the answer that has a usage mistake. If there is no mistake, choose the last answer, No mistake. Mark the circle for your answer.

Allow time for the students to mark their answers.

Say You should have marked answer circle J because the word *flied* should be *flown*. If you chose another answer, erase yours and fill in answer circle J now.

Unit 11 Test Practice
Test 6 Part 1 Usage

Directions: Fill in the space for the answer that has a mistake in usage or expression. Fill in the last answer space if there is no mistake.

Sample A
A In 1970, a woman named Diane
B Crump became the first female jockey
*C to have rode in the Kentucky Derby.
D (No mistake)

Sample B
*J "I've never flied in anything but
K a jet before," said Amy, as she eagerly
L climbed aboard the small biplane.
M (No mistakes)

1. *A Classes of students competes in
   B Rio Middle School's annual poetry
   C reading contest during the fall.
   D (No mistakes)

2. J Modern scientists constantly strive
   K to learn more about Mars. It often
   *L posed more questions than answers.
   M (No mistakes)

3. A Tom was a city boy who moved
   B to a farm. He thought one chicken
   *C was a rooster until it lain an egg.
   D (No mistakes)

4. J "Welcome," said the hostess,
   *K greeting her guests warm. "I'm so
   L glad you were able to come tonight."
   M (No mistakes)

5. A Before Dad got in the car, he gave
   *B each of us a hug and blowing kisses
   C as he backed down the driveway.
   D (No mistakes)

6. J When the speech began, Georgine
   *K couldn't barely hear what was being said.
   L She had to close her eyes and listen hard.
   M (No mistakes)

7. A Because he often gets into trouble
   *B for having spoke too soon, Tim now
   C tries to count to five before responding.
   D (No mistakes)

8. *J I might could check to see if the
   K fruit stand is hiring any summer help.
   L It seems like a decent place to work.
   M (No mistakes)

9. A Janice helped move a fig tree from
   B her yard to a neighbor's. She thought
   C the fig tree would do better there.
   *D (No mistakes)

10. J It is said that in order to
    K enjoy a harvest, the farmer
    *L must first sown the seeds.
    M (No mistakes)

Check to see that the students have filled in the correct answer circle.

Say Now you will do more items. Look for an answer that has a mistake in usage. If none of the answers has a mistake, choose the last answer. Work until you come to the STOP sign at the bottom of the page. When you have finished, you can check over your answers to this test. Then wait for the rest of the group to finish. Do you have any questions?

Answer any questions that the students have.

Say Start working now. You will have 10 minutes.

Allow 10 minutes.

Say It's time to stop. You have completed Test 6, Part 1. Check to see that you have completely filled in your answer circles with dark marks. Make sure that any marks for answers that you changed have been completely erased. Now you may close your books.

Review the items with the students. Have them indicate completion of the lesson by entering their score for this activity on the progress chart at the beginning of the book. Then collect the students' books and answer sheets if this is the end of the testing session.

 Unit 11

Test Practice
Test 6 Part 1 **Usage**

Directions: Fill in the space for the answer that has a mistake in usage or expression. Fill in the last answer space if there is no mistake.

| Sample A | A In 1970, a woman named Diane
B Crump became the first female jockey
∗ C to have rode in the Kentucky Derby.
D (No mistake) | Sample B | ∗ J "I've never flied in anything but
K a jet before," said Amy, as she eagerly
L climbed aboard the small biplane.
M (No mistakes) |

1 ∗ A Classes of students competes in
    B Rio Middle School's annual poetry
    C reading contest during the fall.
    D (No mistakes)

2   J Modern scientists constantly strive
    K to learn more about Mars. It often
  ∗ L posed more questions than answers.
    M (No mistakes)

3   A Tom was a city boy who moved
    B to a farm. He thought one chicken
  ∗ C was a rooster until it lain an egg.
    D (No mistakes)

4   J "Welcome," said the hostess,
  ∗ K greeting her guests warm. "I'm so
    L glad you were able to come tonight."
    M (No mistakes)

5   A Before Dad got in the car, he gave
  ∗ B each of us a hug and blowing kisses
    C as he backed down the driveway.
    D (No mistakes)

6   J When the speech began, Georgine
  ∗ K couldn't barely hear what was being said.
    L She had to close her eyes and listen hard.
    M (No mistakes)

7   A Because he often gets into trouble
  ∗ B for having spoke too soon, Tim now
    C tries to count to five before responding.
    D (No mistakes)

8 ∗ J I might could check to see if the
    K fruit stand is hiring any summer help.
    L It seems like a decent place to work.
    M (No mistakes)

9   A Janice helped move a fig tree from
    B her yard to a neighbor's. She thought
    C the fig tree would do better there.
  ∗ D (No mistakes)

10   J It is said that in order to
    K enjoy a harvest, the farmer
  ∗ L must first sown the seeds.
    M (No mistakes)

Unit 11 Test 6 Part 2 Expression

Administration Time: 25 minutes

Say Turn to Test 6, Part 2 on page 126.

Check to see that the students have found page 126.

Say Look at your answer sheet. Find the part called Test 6, Part 2, Expression. All your answers for this test should be marked on your answer sheet, not in your book.

Check to see that the students have found the correct part of the answer sheet.

Say This test will check how well you know English expression. Remember to make sure that the circles for your answer choices are completely filled in. Press your pencil firmly so that your marks come out dark. Completely erase any marks for answers that you change. Read the directions for each section. Mark the space for the answer you think is correct. Work by yourself. When you come to the GO sign at the bottom of a page, continue working. Work until you come to the STOP sign at the bottom of page 128. When you have finished, you can check over your answers to this test. Then wait for the rest of the group to finish. Do you have any questions?

Answer any questions that the students have.

Say Start working now. You will have 20 minutes.

Allow 20 minutes.

Unit 11 Test Practice
Test 6 Part 2 Expression

Directions: Use this paragraph to answer questions 11–16.

> [1]Ur, which dates back further than 3000 B.C., <u>noteworthy for several reasons is</u>. [2]Its compact homes were built right next to each other, <u>so</u> no space between. [3]The city resembled a huge network of children's building blocks stacked together. [4]Other cities in the Middle East are also very old. [5]The doors to these structures were always set in the roof. [6]What is perhaps most interesting, Ur was originally built without any streets.

11 Choose the best opening sentence to add to this paragraph.
  A What made Ur such a remarkable city were the ancient customs.
  B Urban planning in 3000 B.C. left a lot to be desired.
  C It is interesting to compare today's cities with the cities of old.
  *D One of the first cities in the world was a place named Ur.

12 Which sentence should be left out of this paragraph?
  J 2
  K 3
  *L 4
  M 5

13 Where is the best place for sentence 6?
  A Where it is now
  *B Between sentences 1 and 2
  C Between sentences 3 and 4
  D Between sentences 4 and 5

14 What is the best way to write the underlined part of sentence 1?
  J for several reasons noteworthy is.
  *K is noteworthy for several reasons.
  L for several reasons is noteworthy.
  M (No change)

15 What is the best way to write the underlined part of sentence 2?
  A and
  *B with
  C still
  D (No change)

16 Choose the best sentence to add to the end of this paragraph.
  *J Inhabitants had to climb ladders to enter or leave their homes.
  K Some Native American dwellings featured rooftop entrances.
  L If Ur were still around today, where would people keep their cars?
  M Digs at Ur have yielded facts about the people who lived there.

Test 6 Part 2 **Expression**

Directions: In questions 17–21, choose the best way to express the idea.

17
- A For a young girl, she was much older until people mistook her.
- B She was much older until people mistook her for a young girl.
- C People mistook her, for she was a young girl until she was much older.
- *D Until she was much older, people mistook her for a young girl.

18
- *J The principal's speech at graduation was repetitive.
- K The principal's speech at graduation, it was repetitive.
- L At graduation, it was repetitive, the principal's speech went on and on.
- M The principal's speech was repetitive, saying things over at graduation.

19
- A Chuck handing it back to the waiter, signed his name on it before.
- *B Chuck signed his name on the bill before handing it back to the waiter.
- C Chuck signed his name on it to the waiter before handing it back.
- D Before handing it back to the waiter, Chuck he signed his name on the bill.

20
- J We saw a play last week about Shakespeare's life at camp.
- K About Shakespeare's life last week at camp we saw a play.
- L We saw a play about Shakespeare's life at camp last week.
- *M Last week at camp we saw a play about Shakespeare's life.

21 Which of these would be most appropriate in a letter requesting a band's demo recording?
- A Could you send a demo recording of your band? I am in charge of picking out a band for the dance, but it's next week, so send it as soon as possible. I've also got to know how much you charge.
- B It's a hard job selecting a band for a school dance, and I'm pretty sure we've got somebody lined up, but just in case, could you send me a copy of your demo recording?
- *C As a member of the dance committee, I am writing to request a copy of your band's demo recording. I understand that most bands send these free of charge. If this is not the case, please let me know.
- D What kind of music does your band play? I am curious to find out, so could you please send me a demo or something? If I don't hear from you within the next week, don't bother sending anything.

127

Say It's time to stop. You have completed Test 6, Part 2. Check to see that you have completely filled in your answer circles with dark marks. Make sure that any marks for answers that you changed have been completely erased. Now you may close your books.

Review the items with the students. Have them indicate completion of the lesson by entering their score for this activity on the progress chart at the beginning of the book. Then collect the students' books and answer sheets if this is the end of the testing session.

 Test 6 Part 2 Expression

Directions: For questions 22–26, choose the best way to write the underlined part of the sentence.

22 Wendell loved reading, but he enjoyed mystery and **an adventure** books best.
J adventurous   *K adventure   L being adventurous   M (No change)

23 The cake tasted strange because we **should substitute** salt for sugar.
*A had substituted   B will have substituted   C did substitute   D (No change)

24 Mom always likes to scour the sink before **to leave**.
J will be leaving   K left   *L leaving   M (No change)

25 Jaquie had very little time **learning** the new language.
*A to learn   B still learning   C for to learn   D (No change)

26 Debbie traveled and studied in Oxford as well as **Belize**.
J studied Belize.   *K in Belize.   L Belize too.   M (No change)

27 Which of these would be most persuasive in a letter to a school principal?

A A large number of students have been complaining about how Wilson Junior High is so unattractive. Although benches may not be the best solution, it's what a group of us would like to try. With benches added to the courtyard, people may enjoy sitting there more?

C It's hard to sit down and enjoy your surroundings in a place without benches. It's also surprising that in all the years Wilson Junior High has been here, no one has even considered putting in a few benches for the students to sit on. Our class would like to change that.

*B The students at Wilson Junior High would like to improve the central courtyard here. By raising money for the purchase and installation of benches, we hope to strengthen involvement and pride in our school. Attached is a list of students dedicated to this proposal.

D While visiting another junior high recently, we were surprised to find that the school had an attractive courtyard area where students sat and enjoyed lingering between classes. It was such a nice area that students had trouble leaving it. We think that's a great concept.

Unit 11 Test 7 Part 1 Math Concepts

Administration Time: 25 minutes

Distribute scratch paper to the students.

Say Turn to Test 7, Part 1 on page 129.

Check to see that the students have found page 129.

Say Look at your answer sheet. Find the part called Test 7, Part 1, Math Concepts. If you need to, you may work on scratch paper, but be sure to mark all your answers for this test on your answer sheet.

Check to see that the students have found the correct part of the answer sheet.

Say This test will check how well you understand and solve mathematics problems. Remember to make sure that the circles for your answer choices are completely filled in. Press your pencil firmly so that your marks come out dark. Completely erase any marks for answers that you change.

Look at Sample A. Read the problem and the four answer choices. Then solve the problem. On your answer sheet, find the answer circles for Sample A. Mark the circle for the answer to the problem.

Allow time for the students to mark their answers.

Say Answer circle C should have been filled in because 18 is the solution to the expression. If you chose another answer, erase yours and fill in circle C now.

Check to see that the students have filled in the correct answer circle.

Say Now do Sample B. Solve the problem and mark the circle for the answer you find.

Allow time for the students to mark their answers.

Say Answer circle K should have been filled in. If you chose another answer, erase yours and fill in circle K now.

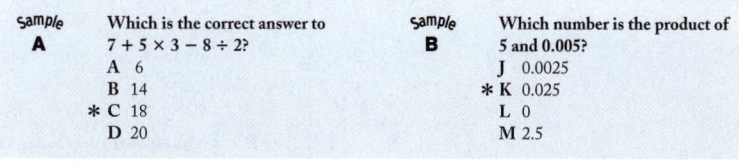

Directions: Read each mathematics problem. Choose the best answer.

Sample A Which is the correct answer to $7 + 5 \times 3 - 8 \div 2$?
A 6
B 14
∗ C 18
D 20

Sample B Which number is the product of 5 and 0.005?
J 0.0025
∗ K 0.025
L 0
M 2.5

1 92, 79, 89, and 90 were the scores for 4 basketball games. The average (mean) of these 4 scores is about
A 80.
∗ B 90.
C 95.
D 350.

2 In what order should you place the numbers 2, 4, 6, and 8 into the boxes below so that the smallest possible answer will be formed?

□ − □ + □ − □ = ?

∗ J 8, 6, 2, 4
K 8, 2, 6, 4
L 6, 4, 8, 2
M 4, 2, 8, 6

3 Which is a right angle?

4 Which of the following is not the same as $\frac{4}{10}$?
J $\frac{2}{5}$
∗ K $4\frac{1}{10}$
L $\frac{8}{20}$
M $\frac{24}{60}$

5 The area of a rectangular room is 40 square feet. What are the length and width of the room?
A 4 ft by 8 ft
∗ B 5 ft by 8 ft
C 4 ft by 12 ft
D 20 ft by 20 ft

6 Which set of numbers shows the greatest variability?
J 10, 12, 18, 22
K 31, 38, 45, 52
L 19, 30, 40, 45
∗ M 8, 19, 27, 64

Check to see that the students have filled in the correct answer circle.

Say Now you will solve more mathematics problems. Work by yourself. Remember that you may use scratch paper to solve the problems. When you come to the GO sign at the bottom of a page, turn to the next page and continue working. Work until you come to the STOP sign at the bottom of page 131. When you have finished, you can check over your answers to this test. Then wait for the rest of the group to finish. Any questions?

Answer any questions that the students have.

Say Start working now. You will have 20 minutes.

Allow 20 minutes.

Unit 11 Test Practice 161

Unit 11 Test 7 Part 1 **Math Concepts**

7 What is the ratio of the number of triangles to the number of squares?

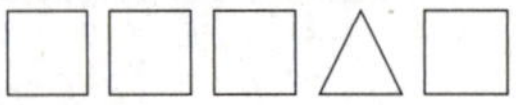

□ □ □ △ □

* **A** 1 to 4
  B 4 to 1
  C 1 to 5
  D 4 to 5

8 Mrs. Schnell wants to buy 4 bottles of juice. Each bottle weighs 1 pound 9 ounces. How much would 4 bottles weigh?

  J 4 pounds 9 ounces
* **K** 6 pounds 4 ounces
  L 7 pounds
  M 8 pounds 4 ounces

9 What should replace the □ in the number sentence $\frac{2}{5} \times \frac{3}{7} = \frac{(2 \times 3)}{\square}$?

  A 1×1
  B 5×1
  C $5 + 7$
* **D** 5×7

10 What number is expressed by $(4 \times 10^3) + (7 \times 10^2) + (9 \times 10) + (6 \times 1)$?

  J 479.6
* **K** 4,796
  L 104,796
  M 479,600

11 Which of the following figures shows parallel line segments?

  A (90° angle)   **C** (45° angle)

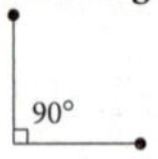

* **B** (parallel segments)   **D** (100° angle)

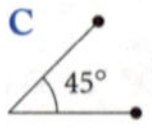

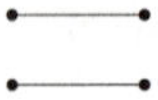

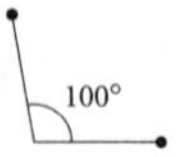

12 Which of the following statements about $-\frac{1}{3}$ is true?

* **J** It is greater than $-\frac{1}{2}$.
  K It is greater than $+\frac{1}{4}$.
  L 3 times $-\frac{1}{3}$ is greater than $-\frac{1}{3}$.
  M $-\frac{1}{4}$ times $-\frac{1}{3}$ is less than $-\frac{1}{3}$.

13 Which is the value of m if $\frac{15}{(m+3)} = 3$?

* **A** 2
  B 5
  C 6
  D 15

14 Which of the following is another name for $4\frac{1}{5}$?

  J $\frac{5}{5}$
  K $\frac{6}{5}$
  L $\frac{20}{5}$
* **M** $\frac{21}{5}$

GO

Say It's time to stop. You have completed Test 7, Part 1. Check to see that you have completely filled in your answer circles with dark marks. Make sure that any marks for answers that you changed have been completely erased. Now you may close your books.

Review the items with the students. Have them indicate completion of the lesson by entering their score for this activity on the progress chart at the beginning of the book. Then collect the students' books and answer sheets if this is the end of the testing session.

 Test 7 Part 1 **Math Concepts**

15 The distance of a bike race was measured by rounding up or down to the nearest kilometer. The largest difference between the measurement and the actual distance would be
  A 1 meter.
✶ B 500 meters ($\frac{1}{2}$ kilometer).
  C 1 kilometer.
  D 2 kilometers.

16 What fraction of the figure is shaded?

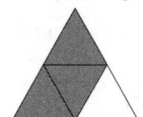

✶ J $\frac{3}{4}$
  K $\frac{1}{4}$
  L $\frac{1}{2}$
  M $\frac{2}{3}$

17 In the equation $6x + 3 = 33$, what is the value of x?
  A 4
✶ B 5
  C 6
  D 7.5

18 The length of time needed to bake bread is best measured by
✶ J minutes.
  K days.
  L months.
  M years.

Unit 11 Test 7 Part 2 Math Estimation

Administration Time: 15 minutes

Distribute scratch paper to the students.

Say Turn to Test 7, Part 2 on page 132.

Check to see that the students have found page 132.

Say Look at your answer sheet. Find the part called Test 7, Part 2, Math Estimation. If you need to, you may work on scratch paper, but be sure to mark all your answers for this test on your answer sheet.

Check to see that the students have found the correct part of the answer sheet.

Say This test will check how well you understand and solve estimation problems. Remember to make sure that the circles for your answer choices are completely filled in. Press your pencil firmly so that your marks come out dark. Completely erase any marks for answers that you change.

Look at Sample A. Read the problem and the four answer choices. Then solve the problem. On your answer sheet, find the answer circles for Sample A. Mark the circle for the answer to the problem.

Allow time for the students to mark their answers.

Say Answer circle B should have been filled in because *$20* is the closest estimate of the solution. If you chose another answer, erase yours and fill in circle B now.

Check to see that the students have filled in the correct answer circle.

Say Now do Sample B. Solve the problem and mark the circle for the answer you think is best.

Allow time for the students to mark their answers.

Test Practice
Test 7 Part 2 Math Estimation

Directions: Read each mathematics problem. Choose the answer that is the best estimate of the exact answer.

Sample A The closest estimate of 60% of $33.03 is ____.
- A $10
- *B $20
- C $30
- D $40

Sample B The closest estimate of 213 × 983 is ____.
- J 200
- K 2,000
- L 20,000
- *M 200,000

19 MARSHAL'S SCHOOL SUPPLIES
Paper	$2.90/package
Ruler	$0.85
Crayons	$1.39
Glue	$3.99

The cost of the 4 items above is ____.
- A less than $9.00
- B more than $10.00
- *C between $9.00 and $9.50
- D between $9.50 and $10.00

20 The closest estimate of 4,719 + 8,093 + 24,901 is ____.
- J 400
- K 4,000
- *L 40,000
- M 400,000

21 The closest estimate of the number of square tiles that will fit into the rectangular box is ____.
- A 2
- *B 3
- C 4
- D 5

(Box 17" tall; Tiles $4\frac{5}{9}$" tall)

22 The closest estimate of $17\frac{2}{6} + 5\frac{7}{9} + 9\frac{1}{4} + 3\frac{2}{3}$ is ____.
- J 34
- *K 36
- L 37
- M 38

23 Five people split the cost of a cake. The cake costs $14.50. The closest estimate of each person's share is ____.
- A $2.50
- *B $3.00
- C $3.50
- D $4.00

24 The closest estimate of 34,129 − 5,976 is ____.
- J 27,000
- *K 28,000
- L 29,000
- M 30,000

STOP

132

Say Answer circle M should have been filled in because the closest estimate to the solution is *200,000*. If you chose another answer, erase yours and fill in circle M now.

Check to see that the students have filled in the correct answer circle.

Say Now you will solve more estimation problems. Work by yourself. Remember that you may use scratch paper to solve the problems. Work until you come to the STOP sign at the bottom of the page. When you have finished, you can check over your answers to this test. Then wait for the rest of the group to finish. Any questions?

Answer any questions that the students have.

Say Start working now. You will have 10 minutes.

Allow 10 minutes.

Say It's time to stop. You have completed Test 7, Part 2. Check to see that you have completely filled in your answer circles with dark marks. Make sure that any marks for answers that you changed have been completely erased. Now you may close your books.

Review the items with the students. Have them indicate completion of the lesson by entering their score for this activity on the progress chart at the beginning of the book. Then collect the students' books and answer sheets if this is the end of the testing session.

Test Practice
Test 7 Part 2 **Math Estimation**

Directions: Read each mathematics problem. Choose the answer that is the best estimate of the exact answer.

Sample A The closest estimate of 60% of $33.03 is ____.
  A $10
 *B $20
  C $30
  D $40

Sample B The closest estimate of 213 × 983 is ____.
  J 200
  K 2,000
  L 20,000
 *M 200,000

19
MARSHAL'S SCHOOL SUPPLIES
Paper $2.90/package
Ruler $0.85
Crayons $1.39
Glue $3.99

The cost of the 4 items above is ____.
  A less than $9.00
  B more than $10.00
 *C between $9.00 and $9.50
  D between $9.50 and $10.00

20 The closest estimate of 4,719 + 8,093 + 24,901 is ____.
  J 400
  K 4,000
 *L 40,000
  M 400,000

21 The closest estimate of the number of square tiles that will fit into the rectangular box is ____.
  A 2
 *B 3
  C 4
  D 5

(Box 17" tall; Tiles $4\frac{5}{9}$" tall)

22 The closest estimate of $17\frac{2}{6} + 5\frac{7}{9} + 9\frac{1}{4} + 3\frac{2}{3}$ is ____.
  J 34
 *K 36
  L 37
  M 38

23 Five people split the cost of a cake. The cake costs $14.50. The closest estimate of each person's share is ____.
  A $2.50
 *B $3.00
  C $3.50
  D $4.00

24 The closest estimate of 34,129 − 5,976 is ____.
  J 27,000
 *K 28,000
  L 29,000
  M 30,000

Unit 11 Test 8 Part 1 Math Problem Solving

Administration Time: 20 minutes

Distribute scratch paper to the students.

Say Turn to Test 8, Part 1 on page 133.

Check to see that the students have found page 133.

Say Look at your answer sheet. Find the part called Test 8, Part 1, Math Problem Solving. If you need to, you may work on scratch paper, but be sure to mark all your answers for this test on your answer sheet.

Check to see that the students have found the correct part of the answer sheet.

Say This test will check how well you understand and solve word problems. Remember to make sure that the circles for your answer choices are completely filled in. Press your pencil firmly so that your marks come out dark. Completely erase any marks for answers that you change.

Look at Sample A. Read the problem and the four answer choices. Then solve the problem using the information in the chart from Peter's Pet Store. On your answer sheet, find the answer circles for Sample A. Mark the circle for the answer to the problem.

Allow time for the students to mark their answers.

Say Answer circle B should have been filled in because the estimate *is higher than the actual price*. If you chose another answer, erase yours and fill in circle B now.

Check to see that the students have filled in the correct answer circle.

Unit 11 Test Practice
Test 8 Part 1 Math Problem Solving

Directions: Read each mathematics problem. Choose the best answer.

Sample A Elizabeth and Emma decided to wash dogs for a fundraiser. They needed 6 bottles of dog shampoo, which they bought from Peter's Pet Store. They estimated the total cost by rounding the price to the nearest half dollar. Which statement about their estimate is true?

A Their estimate is $18.
* B Their estimate is higher than the actual price.
C Their estimate is lower than the actual price.
D Their estimate is $20.

Directions: Use the information below to answer questions 1–7. Do not allow for sales tax.

Peter's Pet Store	
Rabbit cage	$42.95
Rabbit feed	$12.55
Dog leash	$2.98
Dog chew toys	$6.75
Dog shampoo	$3.80
Cat scratching post	$25.50
Cat water and food dish	$4.90
Case of cat food	$12.00
Fish tank	$39.95
Fish net	$4.50

1 Doug bought a rabbit cage. He gave the clerk $45. How much change should he receive?
* A $2.05
B $2.95
C $3.05
D Not given

2 Mrs. Cass bought 2 dog leashes. She had $10. How much did the 2 dog leashes cost?
J $4.04
K $6.96
L $7.02
* M Not given

3 Loraine spent $46.65 for a fish tank, fish net, and a new goldfish. How much did the goldfish cost?
* A $2.20
B $2.25
C $6.70
D Not given

4 Separate water and food bowls for cats cost $2.55 each. How much did Jonas save by buying the combined water and food bowl?
* J $0.20
K $2.35
L $5.10
M Not given

Say Now you will solve more mathematics problems. Remember that you may use scratch paper to solve the problems. When you come to the GO sign at the bottom of the page, turn the page and continue working. Work until you come to the STOP sign at the bottom of page 134. When you have finished, you can check over your answers to this test. Then wait for the rest of the group to finish. Any questions?

Answer any questions that the students have.

Say Start working now. You will have 15 minutes.

Allow 15 minutes.

Say It's time to stop. You have completed Test 8, Part 1. Check to see that you have completely filled in your answer circles with dark marks. Make sure that any marks for answers that you changed have been completely erased. Now you may close your books.

Review the items with the students. Have them indicate completion of the lesson by entering their score for this activity on the progress chart at the beginning of the book. Then collect the students' books and answer sheets if this is the end of the testing session.

 Test 8 Part 1 **Math Problem Solving**

5 It costs $0.95 to buy a single can of cat food. How much money is saved by buying a case of cat food that has 16 cans in it instead of buying the cans separately?
* A $3.20
  B $11.05
  C $15.20
  D Not given

6 Caroline wanted to buy 2 packages of dog chew toys and 3 bags of rabbit feed. Caroline had $50. Did she have enough money?
* J No, she did not have enough money.
  K Yes, and she had $1.15 left over.
  L Yes, and she had $11.40 left over.
  M Yes, she had exactly the right amount.

7 Mrs. O'Brien bought some cat food by the case. Which of the following is <u>not</u> necessary to figure out how much she spent in all on cat food?
  A The number of cases she bought
  B The amount of food in each can
* C The number of cans in a case
  D The cost of each can in a case

Unit 11 **Test Practice**

Test 8 Part 2 Data Interpretation

Unit 11

Administration Time: 15 minutes

Distribute scratch paper to the students.

Say Turn to Test 8, Part 2 on page 135.

Check to see that the students have found page 135.

Say Look at your answer sheet. Find the part called Test 8, Part 2, Data Interpretation. If you need to, you may work on scratch paper, but be sure to mark all your answers for this test on your answer sheet.

Check to see that the students have found the correct part of the answer sheet.

Say This test will check how well you understand and solve problems involving a chart. Remember to make sure that the circles for your answer choices are completely filled in. Press your pencil firmly so that your marks come out dark. Completely erase any marks for answers that you change. Remember that you may use scratch paper to solve the problems. Work until you come to the STOP sign at the bottom of the page When you have finished, you can check over your answers to this test. Then wait for the rest of the group to finish. Any questions?

Answer any questions that the students have.

Say Start working now. You will have 10 minutes.

Allow 10 minutes.

Say It's time to stop. You have completed Test 8, Part 2. Check to see that you have completely filled in your answer circles with dark marks. Make sure that any marks for answers that you changed have been completely erased. Now you may close your books.

Test 8 Part 2 Data Interpretation

Directions: Use the table below to answer questions 8–11.

Number of CDs and Tapes Sold by Company

Company	CDs	Tapes	Total Sold	Percentage of Total
George's Grooves	875,948	89,832	965,780	8.8
The Burnside Beat	352,347	159,348	511,695	4.7
Fremont's Funk	1,135,923	923,773	2,059,696	18.7
Prekker Music	483,438	347,578	831,016	7.6
Century Records	1,937,473	1,038,392	2,975,865	27.0
More Than Music	733,037	493,028	1,226,065	11.1
Listening Pleasure	890,847	190,395	1,081,242	9.9
Hero's Harmonies	1,048,729	291,938	1,340,667	12.2
TOTAL	7,457,742	3,534,284	10,992,026	100.0

8 About how many tapes did Fremont's Funk sell?
- J 19
- *K 900,000
- L 1,000,000
- M 3,500,000

9 Which of the following statements about the relationship between More Than Music's and Hero's Harmonies' CD and tape sales is true?
- A More Than Music sold more CDs and tapes.
- B More Than Music sold more CDs.
- *C More Than Music sold more tapes.
- D More Than Music sold a larger percentage of the total.

10 At George's Grooves, about how many CDs were sold for each tape sold?
- J 8
- *K 10
- L 80
- M 100

11 Which statement can be supported with information given in this table?
- A The store that sold the fewest total CDs and tapes also sold the fewest tapes.
- B The total number of tapes sold is less than one third the total number of CDs sold.
- *C The total CDs and tapes sold by Fremont's Funk and Hero's Harmonies is greater than the total number of CDs and tapes sold by Century Records.
- D Century Records sold more CDs and tapes total than the companies with the next two largest total numbers of CDs and tapes sold.

STOP

135

Review the items with the students. Have them indicate completion of the lesson by entering their score for this activity on the progress chart at the beginning of the book. Then collect the students' books and answer sheets if this is the end of the testing session.

Test 9 Math Computation

Administration Time: 15 minutes

Distribute scratch paper to the students.

Say Turn to Test 9 on page 136.

Check to see that the students have found page 136.

Say Look at your answer sheet. Find the part called Test 9, Math Computation. If you need to, you may work on scratch paper, but be sure to mark all your answers for this test on your answer sheet.

Check to see that the students have found the correct part of the answer sheet.

Say This test will check how well you can solve computation problems. Remember to make sure that the circles for your answer choices are completely filled in. Press your pencil firmly so that your marks come out dark. Completely erase any marks for answers that you change.

Look at Sample A. Read the problem and the four answer choices. Then solve the problem. On your answer sheet, find the answer circles for Sample A. Mark the circle for the answer to the problem. If the correct answer is not given, choose answer D.

Allow time for the students to mark their answers.

Say Answer circle C should have been filled in. If you chose another answer, erase yours and fill in circle C now.

Check to see that the students have filled in the correct answer circle.

Say Now do Sample B. Solve the problem and mark the circle for the answer you find. Mark the circle for the answer you think is best.

Allow time for the students to mark their answers.

Test Practice
Test 9 Math Computation

Directions: Solve each problem. Choose the answer you think is correct. If the correct answer is not given, fill in the space for the last answer, N.

| Sample A | $0.3 \overline{)0.27}$ | A 0.009
B 0.09
*C 0.9
D N | Sample B | $700 - 22$ | J 688
K 778
L 722
*M N |

1. $\frac{3}{5} + \frac{1}{2} + \frac{2}{4} =$
   A $\frac{6}{11}$
   *B $1\frac{3}{5}$
   C $1\frac{3}{4}$
   D N

2. $4{,}195 - 3{,}732$
   *J 463
   K 1,463
   L 7,927
   M N

3. $14.3 \times 0.22 =$
   *A 3.146
   B 3.164
   C 31.46
   D N

4. $2\frac{1}{6} + 1\frac{5}{6}$
   J 3
   *K 4
   L 5
   M N

5. $\frac{2}{5} + \frac{1}{5} + \frac{7}{5} + \frac{1}{5} =$
   A $1\frac{3}{5}$
   B $\frac{14}{5}$
   C 2
   *D N

6. $0.276 - 0.132 =$
   J 0.142
   *K 0.144
   L 0.398
   M N

7. $40 \overline{)900}$
   A 22 r10
   B 22 r30
   C 23
   *D N

8. $0.942 - 0.379$
   J 0.536
   K 0.537
   *L 0.563
   M N

9. $\frac{3}{5} \div 9 =$
   *A $\frac{1}{15}$
   B $\frac{5}{9}$
   C $\frac{3}{5}$
   D N

10. $4\frac{1}{4} + 4\frac{3}{8}$
    J $8\frac{1}{3}$
    K $8\frac{1}{2}$
    *L $8\frac{5}{8}$
    M N

Say Answer circle M should have been filled in because the solution to the problem, *678*, is not one of the answer choices. If you chose another answer, erase yours and fill in circle M now.

Check to see that the students have filled in the correct answer circle.

Say Now you will solve more computation problems. Remember that you may use scratch paper to solve the problems. Work until you come to the STOP sign at the bottom of the page. When you have finished, you can check over your answers to this test. Then wait for the rest of the group to finish. Any questions?

Answer any questions that the students have.

Say Start working now. You will have 10 minutes.

Allow 10 minutes.

Say It's time to stop. You have completed Test 9. Check to see that you have completely filled in your answer circles with dark marks. Make sure that any marks for answers that you changed have been completely erased. Now you may close your books.

Review the items with the students. Have them indicate completion of the lesson by entering their score for this activity on the progress chart at the beginning of the book. Then collect the students' books and answer sheets if this is the end of the testing session.

Test Practice
Test 9 Math Computation

Directions: Solve each problem. Choose the answer you think is correct. If the correct answer is not given, fill in the space for the last answer, N.

| Sample A | $0.3\overline{)0.27}$ | A 0.009
B 0.09
∗ C 0.9
D N | Sample B | $700 - 22$ | J 688
K 778
L 722
∗ M N |

1. $\frac{3}{5} + \frac{1}{2} + \frac{2}{4} =$
   A $\frac{6}{11}$
   ∗ B $1\frac{3}{5}$
   C $1\frac{3}{4}$
   D N

2. $4{,}195 - 3{,}732$
   ∗ J 463
   K 1,463
   L 7,927
   M N

3. $14.3 \times 0.22 =$
   ∗ A 3.146
   B 3.164
   C 31.46
   D N

4. $2\frac{1}{6} + 1\frac{5}{6}$
   J 3
   ∗ K 4
   L 5
   M N

5. $\frac{2}{5} + \frac{1}{5} + \frac{7}{5} + \frac{1}{5} =$
   A $1\frac{3}{5}$
   B $\frac{14}{5}$
   C 2
   ∗ D N

6. $0.276 - 0.132 =$
   J 0.142
   ∗ K 0.144
   L 0.398
   M N

7. $40\overline{)900}$
   A 22 r10
   B 22 r30
   C 23
   ∗ D N

8. $0.942 - 0.379$
   J 0.536
   K 0.537
   ∗ L 0.563
   M N

9. $\frac{3}{5} \div 9 =$
   ∗ A $\frac{1}{15}$
   B $\frac{5}{9}$
   C $\frac{3}{5}$
   D N

10. $4\frac{1}{4} + 4\frac{3}{8}$
    J $8\frac{1}{3}$
    K $8\frac{1}{2}$
    ∗ L $8\frac{5}{8}$
    M N

136

Unit 11 Test 10 Maps and Diagrams

Administration Time: 25 minutes

Say Turn to Test 10 on page 137.

Check to see that the students have found page 137.

Say Look at your answer sheet. Find the part called Test 10, Maps and Diagrams. Mark all your answers for this test on your answer sheet.

Check to see that the students have found the correct part of the answer sheet.

Say This test will check how well you can use maps and diagrams. Remember to make sure that the circles for your answer choices are completely filled in. Press your pencil firmly so that your marks come out dark. Completely erase any marks for answers that you change.

Look at the map and read the question for Sample A. On your answer sheet, find the answer circles for Sample A. Mark the circle for the answer to the question.

Allow time for the students to mark their answers.

Say Answer circle B should have been filled in because *Togada* shares a border with every other country on the map. If you chose another answer, erase yours and fill in circle B now.

Check to see that the students have filled in the correct answer circle.

Say Now you will answer more questions. Mark your answers on the answer sheet. When you come to a GO sign, continue working. Work until you come to the STOP sign at the bottom of page 139. When you have finished, you can check over your answers to this test. Then wait for the rest of the group to finish. Any questions?

Answer any questions that the students have.

Directions: Read each question. Choose the best answer.

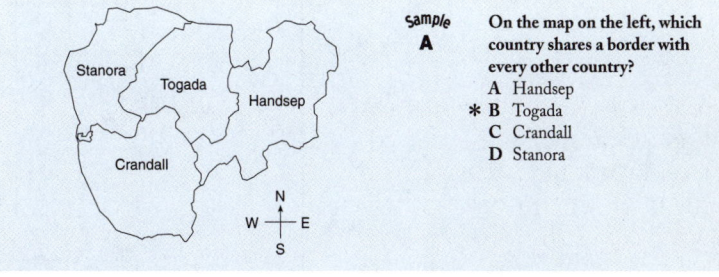

Sample A On the map on the left, which country shares a border with every other country?
A Handsep
* B Togada
C Crandall
D Stanora

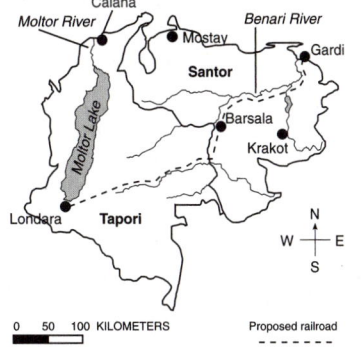

Directions: This map shows the imaginary countries of Tapori and Santor surrounded by an ocean. Use the map to answer questions 1–3.

1 About how wide is Tapori?
A 100 kilometers
B 150 kilometers
* C 250 kilometers
D 500 kilometers

2 Which of these is an accurate statement about the proposed railroad?
* J It crosses the border between the countries south of Barsala.
K It crosses Moltor Lake at about the middle.
L It links Gardi and Mostay.
M It serves only the west side of the country.

3 Which city in Tapori is near the mouth of a river near the ocean?
A Gardi
B Mostay
C Londara
* D Calana

Say Start working now. You will have 20 minutes.

Allow 20 minutes.

Unit 11 — Test 10 Maps and Diagrams

Sheet Designs	Ⓐ Flowered	Ⓑ Striped	Ⓒ Polka Dot	Ⓓ Geometric			
Brand and Design	Price Range	Fabric	Threads per inch	Customer Rating	Sizes			

Brand and Design	Price Range	Fabric	Threads per inch	Customer Rating	Twin	Double	Queen	King
Deluxe Ⓐ	$$	Cotton	250	***		✓		
Deluxe Ⓑ	$	Blend	100	*	✓	✓	✓	✓
Deluxe Ⓒ	$$	Cotton	180	**	✓		✓	✓
Deluxe Ⓓ	$$	Linen	200	***			✓	✓
Hathaway Ⓑ	$$$	Linen	250	**	✓	✓	✓	✓
Hathaway Ⓒ	$$$	Silk	200	**		✓	✓	✓
Mrs. B's Ⓐ	$	Cotton	150	*	✓	✓		
Mrs. B's Ⓑ	$	Blend	100	*		✓	✓	
Mrs. B's Ⓒ	$$	Cotton	100	**		✓	✓	✓
Generé Ⓑ	$	Blend	175	***	✓	✓		
Generé Ⓒ	$	Blend	150	*		✓		
Generé Ⓓ	$	Blend	100	**	✓	✓	✓	✓

Prices: $ = under $50 $$$ = over $100
Rating: * = lowest   *** = highest

Directions: This chart was made to help customers at a department store compare different kinds of sheets. Use the chart to answer questions 4–10.

4 Of the sheets that are made of cotton, which are the least expensive?
J Deluxe A
K Deluxe C
* L Mrs. B's A
M Mrs. B's C

5 If you had a maximum of $50 to spend on twin sheets, which sheets could you buy?
* A Generé B
B Mrs. B's C
C Hathaway B
D Deluxe D

6 What makes Hathaway sheets different from all of the other sheets?
J They are made of linen.
K They have more threads per inch.
L They have a higher customer rating.
* M They cost more than $100.

7 How do the Deluxe B and Generé D sheets differ?
A In their price range
B In their fabric type
* C In their customer rating
D In their threads per inch

8 Which of these seems to contribute most to the price of sheets?
* J The fabric
K The threads per inch
L The customer rating
M The sizes

9 Which brand offers the most designs and sizes of sheets?
A Deluxe
B Hathaway
C Mrs. B's
* D Generé

10 How is this chart organized?
J By size
* K By brand
L By price range
M By design

GO

138

Say It's time to stop. You have completed Test 10. Check to see that you have completely filled in your answer circles with dark marks. Make sure that any marks for answers that you changed have been completely erased. Now you may close your books.

Review the items with the students. Have them indicate completion of the lesson by entering their score for this activity on the progress chart at the beginning of the book. Then collect the students' books and answer sheets if this is the end of the testing session.

 Unit 11 Test 10 **Maps and Diagrams**

Directions: The top map is part of a road map. The bottom map is a city map of Sumter. Use these maps to answer questions 11–16.

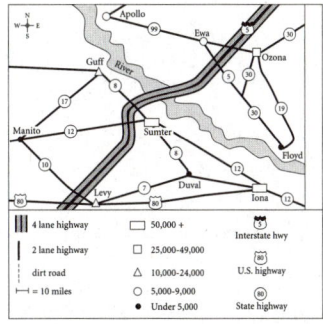

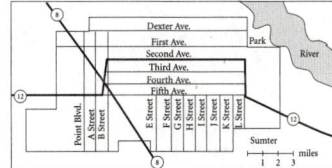

11 Where would a sign that said "30 miles to Sumter" and "30 miles to Iona" be posted?
   A Guff
   B Manito
   C Levy
 * **D** Duval

12 Which town has the fewest people living in it?
   J Ozona
   K Ewa
 * **L** Floyd
   M Levy

13 Lori is driving from Iona to Sumter on Highway 12. If she turns north onto one of these streets, which one will lead her directly to Dexter Avenue?
   A First Avenue
   B L Street
   C E Street
 * **D** B Street

14 Hector used to drive from Manito to Sumter for trumpet lessons, but now he gets his lessons in Guff. How many miles shorter is this new trip, one way?
   J 1 mile
   K 5 miles
 * **L** 10 miles
   M 20 miles

15 Jake lives on the corner of G Street and Fifth Avenue in Sumter. He wants to go to Guff. About how many miles does he have to go to get on Highway 8?
 * **A** 4 miles
   B 12½ miles
   C 20 miles
   D 50 miles

16 Mrs. Ricka drives into Sumter going east on Highway 12. She wants to get on Highway 8 going south. Where should she make a right-hand turn?
   J Second Avenue
   K Third Avenue
 * **L** Fourth Avenue
   M Fifth Avenue

Unit 11 Test 11 Reference Materials

Administration Time: 30 minutes

Say Turn to Test 11 on page 140.

Check to see that the students have found page 140.

Say Look at your answer sheet. Find the part called Test 11, Reference Materials. Mark all your answers for this test on your answer sheet.

Check to see that the students have found the correct part of the answer sheet.

Say This test will check how well you understand reference materials. Remember to make sure that the circles for your answer choices are completely filled in. Press your pencil firmly so that your marks come out dark. Completely erase any marks for answers that you change.

Look at the entry from a dictionary and read the question for Sample A. On your answer sheet, find the answer circles for Sample A. Mark the circle for the answer to the question.

Allow time for the students to mark their answers.

Say Answer circle D should have been filled in because *a seamstress* would be most likely to use the word *grosgrain*. If you chose another answer, erase yours and fill in circle D now.

Check to see that the students have filled in the correct answer circle.

Say Now you will answer more questions. There are different kinds of questions in this test, so be sure to read the directions for each part carefully. Mark your answers on the answer sheet. When you come to a GO sign, continue working. Work until you come to the STOP sign at the bottom of page 143. When you have finished, you can check over your answers to this test. Then wait for the rest of the group to finish. Any questions?

Answer any questions that the students have.

Say Start working now. You will have 25 minutes.

Allow 25 minutes.

Test Practice
Test 11 Reference Materials

Directions: Read each question. Choose the best answer.

Sample A
gros•grain (grō′ grān′) *n.* A heavy corded ribbon or cloth of silk or rayon.

Based on the definition on the left, you would be most likely to use the word *grosgrain* if you were
A a butcher.
B a sailor.
C a candle maker.
* D a seamstress.

Directions: Use this dictionary and the guides to answer questions 1–8.

sen•tient (sĕn′ shənt, -shē ənt) *adj.* Having the power of perception by the senses; conscious
se•pi•a (sē′ pē ə) *n.* A brown pigment used with brush and pen
se•quen•tial (sĭ kwĕn′ shəl) *adj.*
1. Characterized by a regular sequence of parts
2. Following; subsequent
se•ques•ter (sĭ kwĕs′ tər) *v.* To remove or withdraw into solitude or retirement
se•ri•al (sîr′ ē əl) *n.* Anything published in short installments
ser•pen•tine (sûr′ pən tēn′, -tĭn′) *adj.*
1. Resembling a serpent, in form or movement
2. Shrewd or cunning
sex•ton (sĕk′ stən) *n.* An official of a church charged with taking care of the building and its people
sham (shăm) *n.* Something that is not what it purports to be; an imitation
sha•man (shä′ mən, shā′-) *n.* A person who acts as intermediary between the natural and supernatural worlds to cure illnesses and predict the future
sheath (shēth) *n.* 1. A case for a blade of a sword 2. A close-fitting dress, skirt, or coat

shop•worn (shŏp′ wôrn′, -wōrn′) *adj.* Worn or marred, as goods handled and exposed in a store
sil•ver•ing (sĭl′ vər ĭng) *n.* The act or process of coating with silver or a substance resembling silver

1. **Pronunciation Guide:**

ă	sat	ŏ	lot	ə	represents
ā	day	ō	so		a in alone
ä	calm	ŏŏ	look		e in open
â	pare	ōō	root		i in easily
ĕ	let	ô	ball		o in gallop
ē	me	ŭ	cut		u in circus
ĭ	sit	û	purr		
ī	lie				

2. **Abbreviations:** *n.,* noun; *v.,* verb; *adj.,* adjective; *pl.,* plural

1 How would you spell the word that means something that is published in short segments?
A sereal
* B serial
C seriel
D seriale

140

Test 11 **Reference Materials**

2 The *i* in *sentient* sounds like the *i* in
J bisect.
K basic.
L believe.
* M beautiful.

3 How do the two pronunciations of *shaman* differ?
A The *sh* is pronounced differently.
* B The first *a* is pronounced differently.
C The second *a* is pronounced differently.
D The accent is on different syllables.

4 What is the plural of *sheath*?
* J sheaths
K sheathes
L sheathers
M sheathies

5 Which word fits best in this sentence? "The lizard's graceful departure created a _____ pattern across the sand."
A sentient
B shopworn
* C serpentine
D sequential

6 Which word fits best in this sentence? "The artist's clever use of _____ gave her pieces a dark, aged look."
J sham
* K sepia
L sexton
M silvering

7 Which word fits best in this sentence? "The sick man sought out the help of a Native American _____."
* A shaman
B sheath
C sexton
D sentient

8 In which sentence is the word *sequential* used correctly?
J The tour group found the strange green moss to be almost sequential.
K The hotel manager tried to impress us with his sequential attitude.
* L I put the books in sequential order using the numbers on their spines.
M It is sequential whether we meet at the train station or the park.

Unit 11 — Test 11 Reference Materials

Directions: This is an index from a book called *History of Art for Young People*. Use the index to answer questions 9–14.

> **Baroque art**, 250–281; in Flanders: painting, 259–262, 264; in France: 274–281; architecture, 278–280; painting, 275–278; sculpture, 281; in Germany: architecture, 282, 284; painting, 285; in Holland: painting, 264–273
> **Cézanne, Paul**, 342–343; *Fruit Bowl, Glass, and Apples*, 343, 346, 360; *Mont Sainte-Victoire Seen from Bibemus Quarry*, 343, 367, 357
> **Classicism**, 116, 207; in Baroque art, 253, 274–275, 278, 279; in Byzantine art, 100; in Carolingian art, 107, 110; in Gothic art, 141, 142, 144–145, 147, 148–150
> **Egyptian art**, 22-31, 59, 92–93; architecture, 28–29, 40; sculpture, 30
> **Florence, Italy,** 132, 153, 177, 209; "Gates of Paradise" bronze doors, 189; Cathedral, 139
> **Gogh, Vincent van**, 344–346, 350, 352, 357, 360; *Self-Portrait*, 346, 361; *Wheat Field and Cypress Trees*, 345, 359
> **Greek art**, 46–66, 100; architecture, 53–54; painting, 47–50, 68; sculpture, 57–61, 63
> **Leonardo da Vinci**, 193, 207–211, 217, 219, 223, 231, 249, 276; *Adoration of the Magi*, 207–208; *Last Supper*, 208–209; *Mona Lisa*, 209, 211.
> **Michelangelo Buonarroti**, 9, 66, 207; *Creation of Adam*, 214; *David*, 212; *Last Judgment*, 214; *Night*, 215
> **Picasso, Pablo**, 352, 354, 365–367; Blue Period of, 352, 356, 365; *Bull's Head*, 8; *Mother and Child*, 369; *Old Guitarist*, 352; *Three Dancers*, 371; *Three Musicians*, 369

9 Which page would contain an example of a painting by Vincent van Gogh?
* A 345
  B 347
  C 348
  D 349

10 Which page would be most likely to have examples of Baroque art from Germany?
  J 250
  K 265
  L 270
* M 285

11 Which page would explain what Spanish painter Pablo Picasso's Blue Period was?
  A 350
  B 351
  C 354
* D 365

12 Which pages would you read if you were gathering information about the buildings in ancient Egypt?
  J 22–25
* K 28–29
  L 30–41
  M 92–93

13 Which page would show a painting of a woman by Leonardo da Vinci?
  A 190
  B 193
  C 207
* D 211

14 Which page would show examples of sculpture from Greece?
  J 30
  K 53
* L 59
  M 281

Say It's time to stop. You have completed Test 11. Check to see that you have completely filled in your answer circles with dark marks. Make sure that any marks for answers that you changed have been completely erased. Now you may close your books.

Review the items with the students. Have them indicate completion of the lesson by entering their score for this activity on the progress chart at the beginning of the book.

Discuss the tests with the students. Ask whether they felt comfortable during the tests, or if they were nervous. Were they able to finish all the questions in each test? Which tips that they learned were most helpful? Did they have any other problems that kept them from doing their best?

After the tests have been scored, go over any questions that caused difficulty. If necessary, review the skills that will help the students score their highest.

 Unit 11 Test 11 **Reference Materials**

Directions: Before you use certain reference materials, you need to decide exactly which word or phrase to use to find the information you want. We call this word or phrase the *key term*. In questions 15–18, select the best key term.

15 Which key term should you use to find information about Margaret Thatcher, the former prime minister of England?
A England
B Prime Minister
* C Thatcher, Margaret
D Minister

16 Which key term should you use to find information on President Kennedy's promotion of NASA's space programs during what is now called the Apollo era?
J President Kennedy
K NASA
L Space programs
* M Apollo

17 Norman Rockwell, whose work first appeared in *Boy's Life*, became a popular cover artist for a magazine called *The Saturday Evening Post*. Which key term should you use to find out other places his art appeared?
* A Rockwell, Norman
B *The Saturday Evening Post*
C Cover artists
D *Boy's Life*

18 Which key term should you use to find pictures of fashionable French ladies' hats during the 1700s?
J 1700s
K Fashion
L France
* M Hats

Directions: Use the entries from the *Reader's Guide to Periodical Literature* to answer questions 19–21.

> Spiders
> Why I like jumping spiders. M. Moffett. *International Wildlife* May 15 '95
> A new spin on spider silk: scientists are trying to copy the itsy-bitsy spider's superstrong fiber. [nature column] *Time for Kids* Oct '97
> Along came a spider. A. Acerrano. *Sports Afield* Feb '95
> Don't get bugged. R. Frishman. [disease prevention][summer safety guide] *Ladies Home Journal* Jul '98

19 If you were writing a report about spider safety, which article would be most helpful?
A The first
B The second
C The third
* D The fourth

20 In the second entry, what does the information in brackets reveal?
* J The article is part of a regular feature.
K The article is a cover story.
L The article includes photographs.
M The article is a book review.

21 In the first entry, who is M. Moffett?
A The name of the publisher
B The name of the photographer
C The person who discovered jumping spiders
* D The person who wrote the article

143

Unit 11 Test Practice

Test 12
Science

Administration Time: 45 minutes

Say Turn to Test 12 on page 144.

Check to see that the students have found page 144.

Say Look at your answer sheet. Find the part called Test 12, Science. Mark all your answers for this test on your answer sheet.

Check to see that the students have found the correct part of the answer sheet.

Say This test will check how well you understand science. Remember to make sure that the circles for your answer choices are completely filled in. Press your pencil firmly so that your marks come out dark. Completely erase any marks for answers that you change.

Read Sample A to yourself. Think about the question and look at the answer choices. On your answer sheet, find the answer circles for Sample A. Mark the circle for your answer.

Allow time for the students to mark their answers.

Say Answer circle B should have been filled in because a squid is most like *an octopus*. If you chose another answer, erase yours and fill in circle B now.

Check to see that the students have filled in the correct answer circle.

Say Now do Sample B. Read the question and decide which answer is correct. Mark the circle for the answer you think is best.

Allow time for the students to mark their answers.

Say Answer circle L should have been filled in because it is a fact that *light can travel through a vacuum*. If you chose another answer, erase yours and fill in circle L now.

Check to see that the students have filled in the correct answer circle.

Test Practice
Test 12 Science

Directions: Read each question and the answer choices. Choose the best answer.

Sample A A squid is most like
- A a seal.
- * B an octopus.
- C a whale.
- D an alligator.

Sample B Which of these is a proven fact?
- J Asteroids are part of a destroyed planet.
- K The universe is 13.6 billion years old.
- * L Light can travel through a vacuum.
- M Life once existed on Venus.

1 Which of these is true about light?
- A Sound and light travel at the same speed.
- * B Light rays can bend.
- C Dull surfaces reflect light better than shiny surfaces.
- D The sun's light doesn't affect Earth's temperature.

2 Which of these is a difference between plant and animal cells?
- * J Only plant cells have a rigid cell wall.
- K All animal cells are much larger than plants cells.
- L Only plant cells have a nucleus and cytoplasm.
- M All animal cells contain chlorophyll.

3 What is the purpose of adding oil to a car's engine?
- A To increase the mass of the engine so it can pull larger loads
- B To increase the temperature and pressure of the engine
- * C To reduce friction and allow the engine to run more smoothly
- D To protect the engine from insect damage

4 When you drop a ball, what always happens?
- J It absorbs magnetic energy from Earth.
- K It rises higher on each consecutive bounce.
- L It bounces between six and ten times.
- * M It bounces to a lower height than the height from which it was dropped.

GO

Say Now you will answer more questions. Mark your answers on the answer sheet. When you come to a GO sign, continue working. Work until you come to the STOP sign at the bottom of page 153. When you have finished, you can check over your answers to this test. Then wait for the rest of the group to finish. Any questions?

Answer any questions that the students have.

Say Start working now. You will have 40 minutes.

Allow 40 minutes.

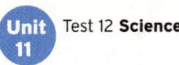 Test 12 **Science**

Directions: Use the information below to answer questions 5–8.

The Stenocara beetle lives in the desert of southwest Africa. The only water in this area comes from a morning fog several times a month. This fog disappears so quickly that it will not stick to most surfaces.

The back of Stenocara has ridges and waxy furrows that cause the fog to form droplets that run down into its mouth. Scientists are studying the beetle's back so they can find ways to capture the fog as a water source for this arid area.

5   **The water that runs down the beetle's back is a result of**
     A   respiration.
     B   evaporation.
     C   reproduction.
*   D   condensation.

6   **The design of the beetle's back is most similar to which of these landforms?**
     J   Desert plateau
*   K   Mountains and valleys
     L   Streams and oceans
     M   Underwater caves

7   **The beetle's unique way of collecting water is**
*   A   a good example of adaptation.
     B   a type of metamorphosis.
     C   an unusual form of digestion.
     D   an attempt to modify the environment.

8   **What phenomenon in nature does the beetle's water-collecting action most resemble?**
     J   A river running into the mouth of an ocean to create a larger water source
*   K   Moist air condensing on vegetation in mountain valleys
     L   Flash flood waters rushing down the side of a mountain and flowing into the sea
     M   The heat of Earth's core pushing magma into an exploding volcano

Unit 11 Test 12 **Science**

9 In order for electrical current to move through a wire, it needs to
* **A** be part of a complete circuit.
B have an insulator.
C be covered with non-flammable material.
D be connected to a ground wire.

10 All of the following are important components of the blood except
J white blood cells.
K plasma.
L red blood cells.
* **M** hydrogen.

11 The gene for blue eyes is recessive in dogs, and the gene for brown eyes is dominant. What does it mean if two brown-eyed dogs have a blue-eyed puppy?
A One of the dogs had a recessive gene for blue eyes.
B The puppy's genes were somehow changed.
* **C** Both dogs had a recessive gene for blue eyes.
D One of the dogs had a dominant gene for blue eyes.

12 All of the following can help reduce the possibility of electrical shocks except
J using plastic-coated wires.
K wearing rubber gloves when connecting wires.
L turning off the main breaker when working on electrical repairs.
* **M** using water as insulation for ground wires.

13 Which of these is true about white blood cells?
A White blood cells are found in just a small number of humans.
B White blood cells are identical to red blood cells except for their color.
* **C** White blood cells protect the body by fighting infection.
D White blood cells are made by disease organisms.

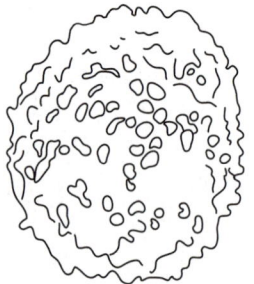

GO

146

180 Unit 11 **Test Practice**

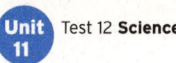 Test 12 **Science**

Directions: Use the information below to answer questions 14–18.

Based on her own experiences, Callie hypothesized that the light level affects a person's ability to read. She created this experiment to test the hypothesis.

Callie set up a chart with large letters at the end of a hallway and lit the area with different intensities of light. The measure of light intensity was the lux. The higher the lux number, the brighter the light.

Callie asked twelve people to read the chart with varying light intensities equal to 9 lux, 27 lux, 81 lux, 243 lux, and 759 lux. The people all stood ten feet from the chart. She counted how many letters were read correctly and recorded that information in the table below.

Brightness	Total Number of Letters Read Correctly
19 lux	57
27 lux	63
81 lux	70
243 lux	97
759 lux	167

14 What factor did Callie change on purpose in this experiment?
- J The number of people who read the chart
- K The number of letters on the chart
- L The placement of the chart
- ✱ M The brightness of the lighting

15 What conclusion can Callie draw from her results?
- ✱ A People can read letters better in brighter light.
- B Some letters are harder to read than others.
- C People read equally well in bright or dim light.
- D Reading letters is easier than reading words.

Test 12 **Science**

16 Which factor is <u>most</u> likely to have affected Callie's results?
   J Whether her subjects were girls or boys
   K The time of day the study was conducted
   L The number of subjects she used
* M How well the subjects could see

17 Some people couldn't read the chart in any of the lighting. What should Callie do about these subjects?
   A Let them practice reading the letters
   B Repeat the study and change the letters
* C Ignore their results
   D Ask them to read the chart again

18 If Callie repeats her experiment, which of these would probably allow her to draw additional conclusions?
   J Increase the number of subjects
   K Use only people she knows
   L Change the reading distance from ten to eleven feet
* M Compare the abilities of older and younger subjects

19 In order for sound to be transmitted
   A friction must have created it.
* B matter must be present.
   C magnetism must be involved.
   D light must be shining.

20 What is the role of a vulture in its ecosystem?
   J It is a decomposer.
   K It is a predator.
   L It is a parasite.
* M It is a scavenger.

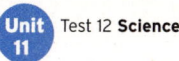 Test 12 **Science**

Directions: Use the information below to answer questions 21–25.

While they were baking one morning, Rasheed's mother explained that in warm water, yeast breaks down sugar into ethyl alcohol and carbon dioxide, causing it to bubble. It is this carbon dioxide that causes bread to rise.

Later that day, Rasheed experimented by putting a tablespoon of yeast and a tablespoon of sugar into a soda bottle half-filled with warm water. He put his thumb over the opening of the bottle and shook it well to mix the ingredients. Then he covered the opening of the bottle with a balloon.

Over the next few hours, the balloon inflated. When Rasheed tied the balloon, it felt heavier than a regular balloon, and this gave him an idea. He used a pump to blow up another balloon to the same size. He placed them on a balance and observed that it tilted toward the balloon filled with the carbon dioxide.

21 What caused the balloon to inflate?
- A Water from the bottle
- *B Carbon dioxide gas created by the yeast
- C Fumes from the ethyl alcohol created by the yeast
- D Air from the bottle

22 The breaking down of sugar by yeast is an example of a
- *J chemical reaction.
- K physical reaction.
- L gravitational reaction.
- M condensation reaction.

149

Unit 11 Test 12 **Science**

23 Yeast generating carbon dioxide is most like
   A cows making milk.
   B sheep growing wool.
   C mammals breathing oxygen.
 * D plants generating oxygen.

24 Why did the first balloon feel heavier than usual?
   J That balloon was larger than usual, so it contained more air.
 * K Carbon dioxide must be heavier than air.
   L The yeast had moved into the balloon.
   M It was filled with liquid instead of gas.

25 Why did Rasheed use a pump instead of just blowing up the second balloon?
 * A A person's breath contains more carbon dioxide than regular air.
   B He must have been tired from doing the experiment.
   C The pump was able to fill the air with pure air.
   D If he had blown up the balloon, he could not have filled it to the right size.

26 Sunlight falling on a solar cell knocks electrons out of their orbits around the atoms. These electrons
   J gather other free electrons to form new atoms.
 * K move through the cell as an electrical current.
   L change themselves into solids.
   M provide insulation against the sun's heat.

27 Jorge noticed that when he placed flowers in a vase full of water, the straight stems looked bent. This is because
   A streaks on glass cause objects to look crooked.
   B some objects absorb less light than other objects.
 * C light rays bend as they pass through water and glass.
   D water density puts pressure on less dense objects so they bend.

28 Which of these is an example of matter?
   J Heat
   K Light
 * L Steam
   M Magnetism

GO

150

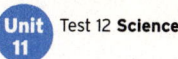 Test 12 **Science**

29 Where would erosion most likely occur?
* A In steep, rainy areas
 B In thickly forested areas
 C In damp, marshy areas
 D In grassy meadowlands

30 Electricity will travel best through
 J air.
* K copper.
 L water.
 M oil.

31 Why do car windows fog up in the winter?
 A The inside of the glass is expanding faster than the outside.
 B The cold air is causing a physical change to the surface of the glass.
* C Moisture in the air inside the car is condensing on the windows.
 D Carbon dioxide is appearing on the surface of the windows.

32 At places where Earth's tectonics plates collide
 J gravity pulls the edges down and forms valleys.
 K the tops of mountains are flattened.
* L molten rock often flows from volcanoes.
 M icebergs are broken loose from glaciers.

33 Sounds waves will travel through all of the following except
 A a solid object like a board.
 B a liquid like water.
 C a gas like the atmosphere.
* D a vacuum such as in space.

Unit 11 Test 12 **Science**

Directions: Use the information below to answer questions 34–35.

Adin performed a magic trick for a friend. He had her look at a coin in the bottom of a cup, then step back so she couldn't see the coin. When Adin poured water into the cup, his friend could see the coin without changing her position.

34 What made Adin's trick work?
- J Light passed through the cup.
- K The coin dissolved in water.
- *L The light was bent by the water.
- M The water reflected the light.

35 Which of these is caused by the same phenomenon that happened during Adin's trick?
- *A Sunlight being concentrated by a magnifying glass
- B Repeated reflections caused by two mirrors that are close together
- C A beam of light shining on a dark wall
- D Being able to see lightning before hearing it

36 What is an ecosystem?
- J A family of animals or plants that can survive in only one place on Earth
- K A region of Earth that is not owned by any government or individual
- *L The interaction of plants and animals with each other and the environment
- M An area defined by the weather that occurs there in each season

37 Which of these is true about outer space?
- A Comets are bright because they burn up as a result of friction in space.
- B Sounds are louder in space because of the lack of atmosphere.
- *C The force of gravity increases as you move closer to an object with mass.
- D Light moves more slowly in space than in the atmosphere.

38 A botanist found that being tall is a dominant trait (T) in a given plant and being short (t) is recessive. To develop a tall variety of the plant, the botanist would get positive results with all of the following pairs except
- J TT and Tt.
- *K tt and tt.
- L Tt and Tt.
- M TT and TT.

GO

Say It's time to stop. You have completed Test 12. Check to see that you have completely filled in your answer circles with dark marks. Make sure that any marks for answers that you changed have been completely erased. Now you may close your books.

Review the items with the students. Have them indicate completion of the lesson by entering their score for this activity on the progress chart at the beginning of the book.

Discuss the tests with the students. Ask if they felt comfortable during the tests, or if they were nervous. Were they able to finish all the questions in each test? Which tips that they learned were most helpful? Did they have any other problems that kept them from doing their best?

Go over any questions that caused difficulty. If necessary, review the skills that will help the students score their highest.

 Test 12 **Science**

39 Which of these is the most common way that mountains are formed?
 A The distortion of Earth's core
 B The collapse of a volcano
 C The pressure of meteor collisions
*D The collision of tectonic plates

40 Which of the following is the correct composition of water?
 J 1 hydrogen and 2 oxygen atoms
 K 1 oxygen and 2 helium atoms
*L 1 oxygen and 2 hydrogen atoms
 M 1 hydrogen and 1 oxygen atom

41 Battery-powered cars produce less air pollution than gas-powered cars. One environmental hazard associated with battery-powered cars is that
 A electric engines are heavier than gas engines.
 B cars running on electricity waste more energy.
*C batteries contain toxic substances that are hard to dispose of.
 D static electricity caused by battery-powered cars increases lightning risk.

42 Fuses are the weakest links in an electrical circuit. They burn out if the current is too strong. Is this beneficial? Why or why not?
*J Yes. When the fuse melts and breaks the circuit, excess current cannot cause a fire.
 K No. When fuses burn out, the electric current leaks out and is wasted.
 L Yes. Once fuses burn out, only weaker current can flow through the wires.
 M No. When fuses burn out, people turn on more electric appliances and increase usage.

43 Which of the following helps keep the human body cool?
 A Respiration
*B Perspiration
 C Condensation
 D Exhalation

44 Which of these has the least effect on weather?
 J Wind speed
 K Air pressure
*L Time of sunrise
 M Humidity

153

Test Practice 187